EMANCIPATION, REVOLUTION, AND OPPRESSION:

A True Story of Perserverance and Hope

by Massoum Montakhab, DSc, Ph.D.

Edited by

Dr. Alexandra Bakarich

PITTSBURGH, PENNSYLVANIA 15222

ISBN: 978-0-8059-8768-3
Printed in the United States of America

First Printing

For more information or to order additional books,
please contact:
RoseDog Books
701 Smithfield Street
Third Floor
Pittsburgh, Pennsylvania 15222
U.S.A.
1-800-834-1803
www.rosedogbookstore.com

Dedicated to:

my daughters

Minoo, Nikou, Nikrou

my grand children

saparak, Shayma, Adib, Hessam

and my great grand children

Cameron, Kevin

Keon, Kayhon, Mateen

Alexander

My special thanks goes to two of my great grand sons Kevin and Keon for their computer help in the last review of the manuscript.

Acknowledgments

Many colleagues and friends, including my daughter Nikou, have repeatedly asked me to write about my life. To be honest, I was absolutely skeptical and reluctant to do so. Destiny has offered me a lot of grace and grief in my personal and professional life that I'm sure everyone in this world has to deal with. But I simply didn't want to remember the hardships that I had faced and specifically the wounds from which I greatly suffered during the past thirty years of my life.

One day, Mr. Victor Manier who is a chemical engineer, author and my colleague at MDS in the capacity of general contractor, came to my office to ask a question. We started talking about our areas of interest. He asked me why I hadn't started writing my memoirs and emphasized that my next generation should know about me. Based on my reluctance I said, "I may do it someday." Victor repeated my words. "Someday… Someday will be too late. Even tomorrow …" The next day he came with a pamphlet that explained about the writing business.

A week later a woman came to visit me carrying a spiral booklet that was a sample of her work. She told me that she could accept a story recorded as a taped interview, which would result in something similar to her sample book. I looked through the spiral booklet then I mentioned a few stories about my up and down life. She said that it would be a very attractive subject and advised me to hire a ghostwriter. Although I was still reluctant and indifferent - I had no desire to write and no strength to think about the past - the thought never left my mind. I cannot clearly explain what triggered my senses and why

I was encouraged to make a nest for all of the children of my family spread around the world due to the compulsory migration of their ancestors because of the last revolution in Iran. At last, I decided to start writing a very simple story that my children and their children could understand so they can better visualize their ancestor's history.

Now I sincerely thank God for giving me a healthy brain which has kept my memory intact, a strong hand to be able to write almost seven hundred pages of cursive writing and above all, the ability to endure almost two years of constant thinking and writing this memoir. I must admit that I am not computer savvy and I cannot type well. Nor was it possible for me to dictate without keeping a daily journal and explaining the events in a chronological order. It was best to think, write and rewrite events as I remembered them, just to get it over with.

I appreciate the ability and patience of Ms. Christina Cook for reading my handwritten notes, typing them and sending them to Dr. Lex Bakarich who constantly reviewed, edited, and questioned me about missing parts in the manuscript. My heartfelt appreciation goes to my daughter Nikou, my long-time active and sincere colleague, for her accepted comments and continuous efforts in organizing the chapters. Thanks go to Victor for his inspiration and encouragement that made me finally get started. Finally, my heart goes to the late Dr. Zahra Parandoosh, our friend, colleague and next-door neighbor of MDS for her sincere efforts in trying to introduce a publishing company to me and also to her daughter Sasha for typing some pages of this manuscript.

Contents

❧

Foreword

I first met "Dr. M" when she and her daughter Nikou came to my house to discuss my assistance with an NIH contract submission. They saw the copper and brass treasures that my family had brought back from our four-year stay in Iran and we found a subject of mutual interest. Thus was started a business relationship, but more importantly a friendship that has blossomed and grown. Today I think of Dr. M as my second mother. As she and I would reminisce about my time in Iran and she told me some of her life events, I encouraged her to begin to write her life story as I was writing that of my parents. I explained that we needed to write them now while events were still fresh in our minds. To better understand us, the younger generations need to know about our trials and hardships as well as the celebrations of our lives. We have seen so many changes during our lifetime; future generations need to know what our day-to-day lives were like. I hope this book will help Dr. M's grandchildren and great-grandchildren and great-great-grandchildren to appreciate her even more than ever.

As I read through Dr. M's stories as she prepared this memoir, I told her that the breadth of her abilities and her many accomplishments never ceased to amaze me! She has such a strong desire even now to be working - not just busy but effectively working toward a specific goal. Today at age 86, while she may be not be actively participating on a study she is always in the office during the week and contributes to the administration of the company. On the weekend she may be found altering a blouse or dress for a special occasion or working out in the garden. And, of course, there will be a shopping spree or two thrown in somewhere during that time period. More power to her!

With much love,
Lex Bakarich
2-15-07

CHAPTER I

The Story of My Life

I came into this world during a period of semi-revolution, which started long before I was born. From a historical point of view, the country of Iran suffered from serious turmoil resulting from the fall of the Ghajar Dynasty and the rise of the Pahlavi Dynasty due in part to the interference of the two Super Powers - the Russian Government and the British Empire - and the influence of the clergy and religious authority. This is written in detail in many history books so it is not for me to explain further.

What I describe here are those things and events that I saw, witnessed and understood from a young age, written as best possible as they truly happened without exaggeration. The memories come from the information center of my brain, which houses the most unforgettable events and surroundings of my life. I believe in the course of one's life many things happen daily but the things that remain in the center of collective memories are the focal points that won't ever be forgotten unless the mind is trapped in the net of amnesia or Alzheimer's disease.

At the present time as I write these memoirs, I am grateful that God gave me the ability and the power to explain everything that I witnessed in my lifetime. It is difficult to describe all the hardships and the sufferings of the past that are still so vivid, especially of those who are no longer with us or who suffered from something that was unpleasant for them. I can see the moments of happiness and sadness so clearly, minute by minute, from the start to the end, and my perspective on life has been forever changed. Sometimes I don't believe my eyes; I keep asking myself, "Am I the same person who suffered that much and tried to pass those barriers and yet stood like steel?"

My wording will be simple and understandable and I promise that the content of these memoirs is only what I clearly remember and have not fabricated.

I was born, grew up, married, raised my children and lived for 37 consecutive years in the city of Tehran, Iran. Then I was absent for almost 8 years for further education. I returned to Tehran, where I lived with dignity and worked hard. I experienced a great deal of success and gained much fame. After 14 years, and as a result of the Islamic fanatic revolution, I left my Motherland forever on May 13, 1980. I started a new life all over again, with new hardships. I knew that hardship would always be a part of life, but at what time in my life? At such a young age? Middle age? Or a rather mature age? Would it happen before a full power life or after all the success and fame that makes a big difference?

My Father, Ebrahim Montakhab –Ol-Ayaleh

My father was a very handsome well-known businessman, always well dressed in the most modern fashion of the day. He was very young looking so no one realized just how old he was, including my mother. With his outstanding figure she believed him to be no more than 50 when he was actually 70 years old. Unfortunately I have no photograph of my father.

In those days, according to the family stories, no one asked the age of a well-known man. My 29-year-old mother never checked and didn't realize the age difference between her and the man she was going to marry was 41 rather than 21 years. She just assumed. Birth certificates were created for the first time during the Pahlavi reign not the Ghajar Dynasty. Before that, when a child was born, the oldest member of the family, if he was able to write, would write the name of the child, the religion, the sex, and the date and time of birth on the last page of the Koran. At that time when my father wanted to marry my mother, who was supposed to find the Koran and tell my mother his age?

So I was conceived from the sperm of a 75-year-old man in the womb of a 34 year old woman and born without any birth defects. According to my grandmother who was a very soft-spoken sweet person, I stepped into this world at 5 am on a very cold and snowy day. That day was Iranian *Noruz* (New Year), the first day of spring. Customarily on that day all the younger generation was obliged to visit the oldest member of the family and show their great respect. All the children, grandchildren and great grandchildren (if there were any) would come to visit, kiss the ancient's hand and offer congratulations on the New Year. In return the ancient kissed their face, especially on the forehead, and gave each of them a gold or silver coin, depending on their relationship. But in general everyone in the house had a share of some equal gift or money from the head of the household. This custom is still common among Iranians living anywhere in the world. Therefore Noruz was a very exciting day, especially for someone like my parents who had a newborn baby.

In those days the husband never attended the delivery like today. On that busy day, my grandmother handed me into my father's arms 8 hours after my birth. They wanted me to have time to wake up, open my eyes and see my mother then my father's face before I became acquainted with my half-sisters and -brothers. The delay also gave time for prayer to get rid of evil eyes from the bedroom. At that first meeting I know I was unable to see clearly but as grandmother always explained to me, by the time I was 2-3 months old I could recognize my father very well.

Father was a very strong man in his decisions, very honest in his business, very kind to his family and very well respected among his relatives and friends. He was very healthy until he was 92 when he started to suffer from asthma because of the construction and expansion of the street by our house. He died at the age of 94 after a short period of suffering.

It was not uncommon in those days for there to be a huge gap in ages between parents and children compared with today's relationship of parents and children. A child was never allowed to ask any questions about their parents' education and background, especially if the father was a great figure in the family and difficult to get close to. Whatever I learned about my father's past I heard from my mother that she heard from my father in passing. I never had a chance to ask my half-sisters or -brothers any questions about my parents because I was younger than their own children. By the time I was old enough to be curious and ask, they were so old that I didn't want to bother them and ask questions about their past. Besides it was **not** proper to do so.

Whatever I learned about Father's education I gleaned from the copies of his hand-written letters, the style and the way he defended, criticized, and reminded the person referred to in the letters. I believe that he was well educated, but it was an informal education; no degrees or certificates existed in the education system in those days and men were free to learn as much as they wished. In spite of the fact that my father first married at age 16, as he always mentioned he used to spend every Friday studying the subjects that he was the most interested in even after my younger sister was born. He was an active learner at least until he was 85.

My father was a very successful businessman but after the Russian Revolution when first their money was devalued and the Russian *mannot* was changed to the ruble, he lost a great deal and was almost bankrupted. We had three big chests full of Russian *mannot* in the basement. According to my father that money was ready to be sent to Moscow when Revolutionaries captured his Russian counterpart. The wheat that had been ready to ship to Iran had been embargoed and the chests of *mannot* became worthless. According to my mother, wheat and bread formed the main food for both middle and especially the lower class people; Iranians had to face strong bread rationing due to a severe wheat shortage, resulting in a great many deaths from hunger.

My three half-brothers were well educated but none of my nieces and nephews knew the extent of their education. They were involved in our father's business. My four half-sisters and three sisters-in-law were limited in their education because of the restrictive rule of education for women. They were all able to read the Koran and religious guidelines but I have no idea whether or not any of them was able to write.

My father used to wake up very early in the morning to pray, even before the dawn, so my mother and nannies had to wake up for their prayers as well. Breakfast was fresh-baked bread, butter, cheese, honey or jam of some kind and tea. My father had his own breakfast tray that included yogurt, fruit of the season, particularly cucumber in spring and early summer, then watermelon and cantaloupe or other summer fruits like apricots, peaches and plums. But from fall to the end of winter he would have at least two home-grown sweet or sour pomegranates (depending on his health status, he could or could not have the sour ones). He was allergic to eggs although he loved them and refused to give in to the resultant sickness - at least a twelve-hour stream of saliva secretion so he could not eat, talk or drink. He had to sit upright and keep a container under his mouth to collect sometimes more than a liter of saliva. My father used to smoke water pipes so much that he would be considered a chain smoker; my mother did also but not as much as my father. He retired at age 87 but he continued to be busy with people who came to our house, went to his own private room and consulted with him. A young boy was hired to be at his service all the time because women were not allowed to go close when he had a guest.

At lunchtime, Father came to the west side of the house and ate with us. We usually ate some kind of rice for lunch. He then slept for at least two hours before starting his afternoon prayers. We usually had some type of stewed meat for dinner unless guests came to the house and lunch and dinner had to be reversed. Lunch was served at noon and dinner one or two hours after sunset (except during the month of Ramadan when eating times were different from the other 11 months of the year).

Father had his own bedroom away from everyone else in the house, including my mother. She was only allowed in his room upon his request. My father usually spent time with us either after his breakfast or in the afternoon when his prayers were over if we didn't have any guests at home. It was not common for a man to spend much of his time with the family, playing with the children, especially with girls. If a father was concerned about his children, it was about his sons not his daughters.

My Mother

My mother, Sakineh Khanoom Zand, was a lovely, tall, good-looking woman with brown eyes, brown hair and an olive complexion. She was a very religious Muslim, always calm, quiet and kind, with a great deal of patience. All my half-brothers and -sisters and their families loved her and treated her as their own mother with high respect. As my grandmother told me the story of my mother's life she said my grandfather (her husband) wouldn't let his two daughters learn anything except how to read the Koran. In those days there were no schools in existence for girls and girls were not allowed to learn to write. They had to learn to read the Koran and a few simple religious books in their house with the help of their father. Therefore my mother couldn't write or sign her name. She had a gold ring on her finger with her name engraved on the heart-shaped flat area of the ring; she used it as a signature stamp. As my sister and I grew up we both forced her to at least learn to write her name in case she needed to sign any important papers. She tried and learned but it was temporary; any time she had to go to the escrow office we had to teach her again.

My mother, passport photo, 1943

My mother was a great lady but she was old-fashioned, naive and stubborn. Whenever I criticized her about my arranged marriage and asked her how she could ignore my hunger strike, my tears and my great sadness during the middle of my state exams and why she ignored all the advice of my father's family and especially my brother who asked her repeatedly to stop the arranged marriage, she referred to my father's advanced age and the fact that I was so active, so fascinated by modern life and pro-reform that she believed I would become uncontrollable and disobedient to her.

Despite all her attempts to prevent my education, I still eventually accomplished everything I wanted to. It may have been later than expected and I may have taken the long way around or entered from the back door but I finally did it, no matter how hard, how rocky, how rough the road was. And so today I forgive my mother and always ask God to bless her soul. She didn't know any other, better way of life.

My Grandmother

My maternal grandmother Mariam Khanoom was a wonderful woman who was very good looking. She had green eyes, light brown hair, a light skin complexion and was tall and thin. She could write, read any books and could translate the Koran from Arabic to Farsi. She said her own father taught her on a regular basis every day. He taught her the alphabet and its combinations (spelling) but never wanted her to learn to write. He also taught her the Koran and how to translate it. Her mother died suddenly so she took care of her father (who never married again) and a younger sister. She had constant contact with her father who continued her education; her knowledge was great and she was quite well educated for a woman in those days.

Grandmother married at age 13, which was very late in those days for a girl like her. She said her first child was born at age 14 and every year thereafter she delivered another child. A few days prior to her next delivery her living child was usually found dead. When I asked her why, what was the cause, she said that no one knew except God. I assume she was almost constantly pregnant for 15 or 16 consecutive years; out of 15 children she ended up with two live girls, my mother and my aunt. Mother was eight years older than my aunt.

I always asked Grandmother how she learned to write and why she didn't teach her two daughters to write. Finally she told me that while she was in her father's room, she would sneakily keep her eyes on his hands and tried to imitate the way he wrote and used her knowledge of the alphabet and combinations. I asked again and again about my mother and her response was that her husband was against her two daughters learning to write. A good wife had to obey her husband; so she didn't ask or oppose her husband's ideas about her two daughters' writing or their education. My grandfather believed that if his daughters were to learn to write, they might learn how to write love letters and find boyfriends.

My grandmother was a very quiet lady. She always told her grandchildren stories about animal behaviors and tried to teach us to understand and recognize good from bad behavior at an early age. I clearly remember those nights when my sister, my two cousins and I would sit around her and we kept asking her for one more story. She never refused our demands and kept telling childhood stories, in particular the story of Maktab and Mullah Baji because it was very funny to her.

Grandmother always tried to keep us busy and taught me and my sister the art of doll making and kite-making to my cousins. She encouraged the use of imagination and taught us in a manner similar to that of cartoons on TV today. We had to repeat the story of the cat and the white mouse. She played the cat and we were the mice. She tried to catch us and we tried to escape until all of us got tired; she believed if a child was stimulated and encouraged at a very early age the child would be more full of life and joy later on.

As I got older I kept asking my grandmother about my mother's life when she was my age. I asked why mother couldn't write and if grandmother punished her by placing a pencil between her fingers and pressing it hard until she cried and so she would forget about writing (as had been my fate). Usually there was a lot of laughing instead of answering my questions.

Grandmother had enough education to be a teacher for the Palace and to teach the farmers' girls. As one member of the Ghajar Dynasty had a harem, he always picked a girl from each farm that he visited. The girl was sent to my grandmother to teach her the Koran and to make her ready to cope with hundreds of other girls in the same situation (in the harem). These girls were very lucky if they were with the Shah as his wife for one or two times and then remained in the harem untouched for the rest of their lives.

My grandmother was very wise and knowledgeable. She had an understanding of the usefulness of plants and fruits. I remember the way she made hand cream - it was a hand treatment as well as a cream. She mixed many different summer and fall fruits, added beeswax and goat fat and let it boil until concentrated, then made small bars used after we wash our hands to prevent broken skin. And she made special face soap from regular soap which was soaked in water for more than 20 days. Then it was removed from the water and mixed with well-ground almonds and a bit of almond oil to make the bar of soap. I never left her alone while she was making either type of soap. She used a Turkish coffee cup as a mold and made twenty bars at a time. My duty was to collect the bars when they were cool. However, when she was busy grinding some formula to make tablets for coughs or constipation, I escaped from the kitchen and left her alone.

Grandmother was very strong and a self-made person. Although she was religious she was very broad-minded and modest. She died of pneumonia at age 80+ when I was thirteen years old, God bless her soul. I learned a lot from her and I will never forget her kindness and her beautiful face.

My Grandfather

I never had a chance to see any of my grandfathers, either paternal or maternal. My father lost his father when he was a child and my mother lost hers long before I was born. My grandmother advised me not to ask my parents about their fathers because it was not proper for a child to keep asking the parents about their lost parents. It was my grandmother who told me what little I know about her own father and her husband (my grandfather). Most of what she told me had to do with their opinions of girls learning to read and write.

Our Home

In town, most houses were surrounded by tall walls because of the religious belief that no one should see even the shadow of a woman without cover inside their house. However, on the farms, no walls were made; first because of the size of the farms and second because no such restriction was required because of the farm clothing. Women farmers were always covered enough in their work clothes and no modern dress was used at all on the farms.

As I remember, our house was good sized with a large pond full of goldfish and a wide path around the pond. There were four 15 x 15 foot planter gardens surrounded by evergreen hedges and numerous fruit trees, like sweet and sour pomegranate, quince, plum, peaches and apricots. In addition, there were maples and willow trees and various colors of roses, which made a very beautiful and unforgettable view.

The pond and its two side gardens (east and west) were separated by two large paths. The south path was almost nine feet wide; the north path was more than 25 feet wide. In the summer, the north path was covered with a big Persian carpet in the late afternoon and the sleeping tent was erected by sunset. My sister and I used to sleep inside it. The tent was made of sheer fabric and was 12 feet square and nine feet tall. It looked like a room with sheer walls and ceiling. On a clear night we could see the beautiful sky and the blinking shiny stars, especially at the beginning and end of the month when there was no moon. The carpet and the tent were folded and moved to the basement every morning and brought back by one of the nannies in the afternoon.

I grew up in this house until I was 15. I vividly remember when I was 5 or 6 years old how the sky was clear and it was so pleasant when my mother or grandmother told me stories and I watched the movement of the blinking stars, which disappeared in less than a blink of an eye. It was fascinating to sleep in the open air, especially when we would wake up early in the morning before sunrise and feel the natural light of the blue sky. I must admit that the taste of the clean air of those days has never left my mind. Today when I open the living room door and step out into the backyard with the fragrance of honeysuckle, jasmine and citrus flowers, it brings back fond memories of the big front yard of my childhood home.

Our house was on a circle or roundabout that was surrounded with large houses with very narrow walkways or alleys between them. I assume the house was built before the onset of the First World War during the Ghajar Dynasty. The house was rather large, built with bricks made of cooked mud in the style of French architecture. It had eight large bedrooms; one very large guest room, a dining room, and two living rooms, one on each side of the guest room that had a large, wide balcony and four tall, heavy-looking columns with wrought iron shallow fence areas. It had high plastered ceilings, except in the guest and living rooms, which had drop-ceilings made of delicate wood parquet. Walls in some areas were covered with carpets, occasionally with paintings. The entire building was elevated from the front yard by 12 steps and a wrought iron side fence that was always covered with honeysuckle bushes. Part of the pond and the yard facing the east living room were designated for my father and were across from the entry door of the house; his compound was on one level with four rooms. My father's living room was completely separated from the other part of the house, with a long distance between the two living rooms.

We had male servants to take care of my father's guests because none of the nannies were allowed to help men. The west living room was for my mother, my sister and me. It was adjacent to a hexagonal 36-ft wide enclosed yard with a hexagonal small fishpond in the middle. Tall walls surrounded this area and had a dome-shaped hexagonal ceiling criss-crossed with white board and was covered with sheet metal painted a dirty red color. In the middle of this ceiling a 6-foot hexagonal opening to bring light in was covered with glass. We weren't allowed to touch or use the water because water flowed in from the main source around the clock and was then distributed on to the neighbor's house. From our living room we went down 8 steps to this area, then another 3 steps to the front yard.

Part of the yard was destroyed when the street was widened during the time of Reza Shah. The remainder of the yard and the house were still intact at the onset of the Islamic Revolution. We lost value by selling the house and its remaining beautiful front yard because of my mother's inattention to what my brother Hadi had suggested - to stop the sale for a few days. After the Revolution, I assume the house was occupied by one of the foreign bank offices but I have no idea what happened to it after my 1992 visit to Iran.

Kitchen and Cooking

Our kitchen was built two to three steps down under the house. It was rather dark even during the day because the entrance door was short to prevent the winter cold and the summer heat from getting in. It was equipped with a strong and long chimney to remove the smoke and cooking odors. We had no stove, no refrigerator, no central heat or running water. Food was cooked over wood or sometimes charcoal and water had to be carried up 10–12 steps from the faucet by the water storage tank.

Everything had to be done manually or mechanically, not electrically like today. We had no electrical devices as we didn't have electricity. Whatever was needed had to be made from scratch. For example, salt, pepper, turmeric, cinnamon and many other spices were ground with a mortar and pestle made of stone. The process of grinding the spices usually took place once a year for 3–5 days depending on the number and variety of spices.

Fruits were limited to what was seasonally available. Citrus fruit came to market in February and March and continued until April, then disappeared. Summer fruit like cantaloupe, melons, grapes and cucumbers were brought to our door by shop-less vendors who carried them on the backs of donkeys. These vendors came one after the other, each one singing their special song.

The people inside the houses recognized who was coming and went outside and bought from them. The men selling rock ice came twice a day, at noon and in the late afternoon or evening.

In the summertime when fruit was available, it was made into jam and preserves. Different kinds of vegetables - onions, tomatoes, etc. - anything that you could find in the market today – were dried for later use. But the processes they used were entirely different than today. Whatever they made was stored for wintertime use because when the weather was cold and the roads were rough and muddy they tried not to go shopping as often as in other seasons.

Keeping and raising chickens in the backyard was common because they produced eggs; also they could be butchered and cooked.

In the spring, summer and fall meat was bought daily as needed but in the wintertime meat could be kept frozen under the snow for a few days. Some villagers used to make *Ghormeh* which involved butchering a whole lamb, cooking it first, then frying it to remove excess water, then preserving it and keeping it in a dry, cool and dark place for winter use.

Life was not easy but people didn't know any other way.

Drinking Water

Modern Tehran, the capital of Iran, with its numerous modern high-rises, beautiful French architecture, old houses, fascinating gardens with a constant stream of water, and extensive roads and highways, is located on the slope of the outskirts of Alborz Mountain. Ages ago it was chosen as the capital of Iran by the Ghajar Dynasty. In those days it was a small city surrounded by a very deep ditch and three extremely tall pillars, with huge wrought iron gates to the South, East and West of the city to control the in-and-out movement of people, merchandise and perhaps much more and to provide safety for the city.

The Tehran of those days was well infused with many reservoirs of pure drinking water, especially in the middle and southern parts of the city. This water originated from the snow collected in winter on the peak of Alborz Mountain and melted during the summer, passing through a natural filter (layers of stone, gravel and sand) and running from the higher levels to the lower slopes to form the springs and water reservoirs. One reservoir was close to the Golestan Palace or the Ghajar residence so it was called the Shah's Spring and its water was named Abeh Shah (Shah's water).

This water was brought to the door every day, every other day or every 2-3 days depending on the number of inhabitants in each house. Abeh Shah was carried in a large metal barrel on a wagon pulled by a single horse. The owner of the horse or his coworker started very early in the morning; he arrived at our house at about 4-5 am. By then everyone had left their beds including me because it was time for early morning prayers. The harmonious sound of the horseshoes contacting with the stone blocks of the road was very pleasant, especially during my early morning prayers; it helped me stay awake.

When the man knocked at the door, nanny was ready to open the door and give him the tile containers with big bellies and narrow necks to be filled. The tile containers were kept in a cool area for drinking only. During the hot summer days of Ramadan my mother counseled my sister and me to go to the basement, hide ourselves behind the guest sleeping facilities, and drink as much as we wanted and then ask God to forgive us. She always worried that young children would become dehydrated during the summer fasting period.

There was no bottled water or any soft drinks during my childhood, even my teenage years. Everyone was used to a homemade drink similar to today's *doogh*, which is still a common soft drink for Iranians. Americans may not like or can't tolerate the taste. It is a mixture of yogurt and plain or carbonated water. Another old-fashioned Iranian soft drink was made of sugar syrup flavored with fresh lemon juice or white vinegar and fresh mint; grape syrup and vinegar were also sometimes used. These drinks were made, concentrated and stored in glass bottles as a base for later use and were mixed with water to taste. Today these sweet soft drinks are almost gone from the Iranian menu.

As Reza Shah came to power, the features of Tehran changed drastically. The three gates were demolished; the ditch became a field to expand the surface area of the city; the narrow alleys were changed to two lane streets with wide sidewalks separated by a narrow shallow ditch which always had a stream of water; maple trees were planted on the edge of the sidewalks adjacent to the ditch. This expansion of the city was the perfect decision for the city engineer but a lot of beautiful houses were either demolished completely or part of the house demolished to make room for the street. Such was the case of our house, just three days after my marriage. A few years later, the water pipeline was introduced to Iranian new construction, but it took many years before it was installed in the old houses and before the end of the man who came to the house almost at midnight to direct water to the water storage areas of each house.

With the invention of the water pipeline, the distribution of Abeh Shah was terminated and replaced by the Chamberland filter, a manmade reservoir of layers of gravels, sands and charcoal. At that point in time, one of the very important decisions of the Health Department was the replacement of the public baths with individual units with showers instead of the *khazineh*. Another important decision was separation of male and female bath areas.

However, during my childhood, we had no water pipeline, no special drinking water as is available today. Water came from underground water brought to the surface or from the spring and/or the river. It ran to an open area (*nullah*) exposed to the air and was exposed to dust and sometimes garbage that people would dump into it - resulting in a good growing medium for numerous water-borne organisms and therefore water-borne diseases. Customarily every house had a large drinking water storage area built underneath a room. It had a very short window and a very low door with no light from anywhere. The size of this water storage was the size of the room above it. Usually water would be added to it every month at about midnight by a man whose job it was to direct water flow to the different homes, especially to the water storage. The water never was treated and therefore sometimes became full of daphni and other minute creatures visible with the naked eye. In order to prevent entry of these organisms into drinking glasses, the mouth of the faucet was covered with cheesecloth. Goldfish were added to the water storage units to eat all the daphnis and other organisms. The midnight water was free from all dirt and garbage because no activity occurred after dark.

Every morning in the wintertime, the nanny would make a big pot of boiling water for the kids to use to wash their faces and hands. The hot water was mixed with cold water and poured into a pitcher and was made ready for them. Using a pitcher and its basin was also very common before and after lunch or a dinner party for the guests to wash their hands; a servant usually brought the water to them. The samovar was also a good source of hot water and was used in the morning and afternoon to make tea; samovars are still used today for tea.

Heating Systems

We had no central heating or cooling system. The summer heat was avoided by sleeping in the backyard in a tent or on a bench at night and sleeping in the basement during the daytime. Customarily Iranian ladies used to nap 1-2 hours after lunch, go to bed early at night depending on the season of the year, and wake up early in the morning for prayer. They watered the flowers in the entire back yard to use the "evaporative cooling" effect to bring the temperature down, especially at sunset. As I remember, it was really pleasant when we would get together in the backyard and start chatting and drinking tea or cold drinks and the kids were playing.

In contrast, heat for the winter was controlled by a *korsi* which was a short square table like a coffee table with a wide surface, placed in the center of a room and covered with a very large specially-made blanket. Four special mattresses were laid around it on the floor and at least 3-4 large pillows were placed on the sides of the mattresses. The *korsi* and the blankets were covered with a huge square white sheet. A round container called a *manghal* (half filled with burning charcoal covered with an equal amount of ash) was placed under the *korsi*. The ash prevented sparks and eventual fire. (Japanese people used a similar heating device in the wintertime; I was shown one in 1971 when I visited Tokyo.) Anytime we felt cold we sat on the mattresses under the blanket to get warm and relax. The *manghal* was taken away from the *korsi* every morning; the extra ashes were removed and more charcoal was placed in it again.

Unfortunately every year many children and/or adults were killed by carbon monoxide inhalation, which resulted from the incomplete burning of the charcoal. Therefore the *manghal* was usually kept outside for 1-2 hours every day.

About 40-50 years ago, a Japanese factory invented an electric device to replace the *manghal*; so it was called a Japanese *korsi*. It didn't have the problems of the old *manghal*, replacing ashes with charcoal and keeping it in open air for at least 2 hours to prevent CO inhalation. The Iranian people loved the Japanese *korsi* in the wintertime, especially if their houses were not equipped with central heating. It was very relaxing, pleasant and favorable for retired people to get together to chit-chat and relax, especially when snow was falling from the sky and their activity slowed down.

In those days, generally every house was equipped with a chimney, not only in the kitchen but in the guest rooms as well. A portable fireplace made of black sheet metal with a long wide pipe to take the smoke out to the open air was used in the guest rooms and burned either wood or (rarely) coal.

In school every room used a portable fireplace and coal. They were installed from the beginning of the second month of fall but were never used before the beginning of winter then were removed by the last day of winter.

As time passed by, different kinds of hand mobile fireplaces which burned kerosene oil were imported from Europe. They had no connection to outside air and created carbon monoxide in the room unless a window was left open. And they developed heavy smoke if left unattended in a closed room for long hours. If their tanks got warm, the level of burning increased by itself and produced a heavy smoke. This was also true for kerosene lamps. There were no smoke detectors in those days – they had yet to be invented. It was therefore most important that in every room with a mobile fireplace or where a kerosene lamp was on, a window was left open to let in fresh air.

I vividly remember the time when just a few minutes before guests were to arrive everyone was crying in their hearts because the guest rooms were full of heavy smoke and everyone was coughing. We were forced to open all the doors and windows to get rid of the smoke.

Public Health

The state of public health during my childhood, even during my teenage years, was a terrible mess. Diseases like malaria, whooping cough, small pox, chicken pox, trachoma, leishmaniasis, typhoid, diphtheria, polio, ringworm and many others were common among the children. Whooping cough, measles, polio and chickenpox were definite diseases of the young because in those days no vaccinations existed whatsoever. Small pox pus from infected children was used to inoculate healthy children (the old-fashioned method of vaccination).

Although our parents were very concerned about our health, my sister and I had not been exempt from leishmaniasis and myself from diphtheria. Trachoma and ringworm were common among poor and under-privileged families due to such close contact with each other. Malaria was a common disease before the invention of DDT and the treatment of shallow water to eradicate the mosquitoes and therefore the malaria. Diarrhea and dysentery were often fatal diseases of summer particularly among very young infants due to contamination of food and milk and the lack of refrigeration.

In general, most of the diseases were eradicated after World War II and the discovery of sulfa drugs and antibiotics. The diseases came under control by vaccination of children and eradication of the sources. The death rate, which was 90% during my childhood, dropped to 5-10% after the discovery of two important elements - antibiotics and methods of eradication of the main sources of the disease agents.

Light at Night

No one in the part of town where we were living had any electricity at all. Candles and kerosene lamps were used in rooms and wind (hurricane) lamps were used when moving from one place to the other at night. There were no lights on the streets or alleys. However, in some areas with a higher standard of living, neighbors collectively placed big kerosene lights at the entrance to their walkways. Sometimes a tall lighted candle was placed about every 1-2 yards at the entrance of the alley, especially when there was a wedding or a gathering of mourners. Because of the lack of electricity, everything was generally accomplished before sunset. In general, the town's people were asleep at night except when the moon was full and everything was under bright natural light. According to the children my age, God lighted the city.

Since there were no automobiles, buses, or trains and no factories or machinery to pollute the air, the sky was very clear and the stars were quite visible, especially in the summertime when we would sleep in the backyard under a white sheer tent to prevent mosquito bites and other creatures like scorpions. Before the moon became full or after that the stars appeared so bright, my mother and/or grandmother would explain the power of God in the creation of the universe (even if it was not scientifically correct) instead of reading animal books.

During my childhood and even my teen years, the majority of houses in town had no electricity. The fancy houses were equipped with beautiful chandeliers holding anywhere from 6 to 60 candles or maybe more depending on the size of the room.

Transportation

Comparing transportation of today with the days of my childhood is fascinating. When I was growing up, most men in Tehran had their own horses. Horse-drawn wagons and coaches were used from city to city, pulled by 2 to 6 horses. They were the only "group carriers." Mules and donkeys were used for carrying merchandise of any kind as well as both men and women.

Engines requiring railroads carried large wagons and were establish by a Belgian merchant. It was called the *machine doodi* because of the steam and smoke that poured into the air from the engine. That railroad connected Tehran to the city of Ray where many people went for a pilgrimage to visit the cemeteries located around that holy place. In those days women and children rarely traveled unless they had to, but pilgrimages were a form of recreational activity as there was no radio, TV or movie theater. The most fascinating places to go were the crowded holy places (mosques, Imam Zadeh, and so on).

The first time I saw a car I was five years old. I vividly remember the moment that my mother, with one of my half-sisters, her husband, our sister-in-law and four children, my sister Azam (3?) and my niece Moneer (11), two nephews Morteza (9) and Abbas (2) were traveling for a pilgrimage to Karbala, Iraq. This is where most Imams of the Muslim Shiite sect were buried except for the 8th Imam whose grave is in Mashhad, one of the most famous cities in Iran. I remember the brown car with four doors and a crowd of people around it. In the background I heard the noise of the people crying for the Imams whose graves they were going to visit. I didn't understand their crying until I became much older.

I remember my mother telling me the story of her trip, the places that she visited and the time she spent around the Imam's grave to complete her prayers. Azam had been crying for water that disturbed her prayers. She said the trip from Tehran to Baghdad and back lasted 40 days because it took them seven days to go each way due to the limited power of car engines, the rough and winding roads, and the mountains and canyons. Because of the road bandits, automobile travel was only during the daytime for the safety of the passengers.

The first time that I traveled I was 5? years old. It was summer and all the women on both my paternal and maternal sides decided to go for a pilgrimage with all their children. My mother, sister Azam and one of the nannies and I left our house in a two-horse drawn coach and traveled to Farahzad Farm way beyond the outskirts of Tehran. Today Farahzad is in the middle of Tehran where the most fancy American-style high-rise apartment complexes are located. I bought one of those condos in 1979 but never had a chance to reside in it because of the revolution and my departure from the country; I sold it in 1993.

All the family women gathered at the Farahzad Farm. To me the highlight of the trip was the presence of all my cousins, nieces and nephews to play with. Although only two or three of them were younger than me, those who were older supported me all the time. Dinner was homemade. The food was special and didn't need warming up - meatballs, cutlets, and even mixed rice that when served cold is more tasty than warm rice. After dinner was finished and everyone had their tea, we watched a beautiful flaming sunset while waiting for the guide and his mules.

It was a happy trip. I didn't understand the hardship of traveling. The pilgrimage was to the holy place of the great-great-nephew of either the 5th or 8th Imam (Imam Zadeh Davood). His grave was located on the top of a very high mountain northwest of Tehran.

Although Tehran was the capital of Iran, at that time it was a very small city with no real streets; the few streets present were extremely narrow, rocky, dusty or sometimes muddy; so one can imagine the status of the roads outside the capital. However people believed in making pilgrimages to those holy places at least located in the periphery of Tehran.

The holy places were called Imam Zadeh, meaning descendent of the Prophet Mohammad. I have no idea how these Arab descendents came to Iran and died as soon as they arrived, and who recognized them and certified their ascendancy and registered them as Imam Zadehs and declared their graves as holy places. People like me and a million others had to blindly accept what we had been told.

In those days there were no hotels, motels or other designated rest areas or even restrooms on the road except for an occasional small shop that made special stew in a clay pot; but these were few and far between. Therefore, we had to carry our own food; meal times were like today's potluck. There would be a variety of fresh and crunchy breads, butter, cheese, fruits of the season and different kinds of cookies. We also had to carry various pots and pans, a samovar for boiling water and making tea, kerosene lamps, and sleeping facilities, etc. Our travel plates were made of copper or enameled metals. Two donkeys carried all the food and other supplies and the women and children rode on the mules.

At Farahzad Farm, we all ate dinner and then prepared everything for the trip. I vividly remember the garden where my cousins and nieces and nephews played ball with me. Then we watched the sunset with red flames around the sun as my grandmother always explained to us and we were looking at a real sunset at that time. Meanwhile the sounds of bells hanging on mules' and donkeys' necks attracted all of us. Soon a series of mules, two donkeys and the guide arrived.

As we traveled, every child had to be with a woman when on a mule. I was with my middle half-sister Annis who had no children and loved me dearly. I had on my black sateen chadoor and picheh, as did every other woman, which made me very proud; I felt all grown up instead of feeling like a child. By the time everyone was seated on a mule with a child, the sky was turning dark. But the moon started to glow and made the road shine by the dim light. We started out. Every 2-3 mules were connected by a strap or chain, with the front one's lead in the hand of the guide.

At the time, I didn't understand why we traveled with mules and at night. As I grew up and kept asking why, I learned the reasons. 1) Travel was by mule because these animals were slower and more sure-footed than horses. 2) Travel was at night because the roads were very narrow and winding between high mountains and there were very deep canyons; if the women saw their surroundings they might be very afraid and faint. The guides were local and accustomed to the roads; even so, there were a few casualties every year.

The *kajaveh* was another type of carrier. Horses, mules and camels could carry it. It was important to have two people of the same adjusted weight. They each sat in a basket on either side that was connected in the middle and placed over the regular camel's back (dromedary) or between the Bactrian camel's two humps. Camels were used for special trips through the desert for their tolerance to thirst for long periods.

As we traveled, one of the guides who had a fine voice started singing religious songs and the ladies started to cry even though a child sat on the mule in front of her. As they cried loudly the singing guide made his song stronger. I can't remember what happened then, as I fell asleep as soon as the song started. All I remember about the holy place is a cube inside of a room that was covered by a green sheet; many, many shoes in front of the door; a lot of burning candles; the voice of a mullah; and many crying women.

Kajaveh, an ancient carrier system

That same year my mother took me to the city of Ray where another holy man was buried. We went to the railroad station by horse-drawn coach, then by train (*machine doodi*) to Imam Zadeh Shah Abdolazime. I remember she bought me several different colored glass bracelets that were much larger than my wrist because she was afraid the broken glass of the smaller bracelets might cut my hand. The bracelets were the size of my arm not my wrist.

The first time that I traveled by bus with my mother and her cousins was the summer that I finished 6th grade. A very serious accident occurred on that trip. Later, from the age of 18 or so I used to go to school by bus because all two-horse-drawn coaches were prohibited by order of the mayor; they were replaced by buses and orange-colored taxicabs. Every morning I would walk from home to the school where I worked and returned home at 2 pm, then I went to night school at Tehran University by bus.

But on the days I had to be in laboratory, I had to return home by taxi because our physiology lab (which only occurred once a month) lasted as long as the experiment; it might be midnight or 3 am before it was over. There were no buses running at that time so I had to return home by cab.

The first time that I sat in a plane was when I was 39 years old when I left Iran for London to visit my daughter Minoo who was a student there, then went on to the US for my own further education. It was in October of 1959, before the days of jet plane travel.

I took driving lessons before I went to the US but I didn't buy a car because I was planning to leave Iran. It took me 8 years before I bought my first car, an old Chevrolet in 1960, six months after I arrived in the US. My second car was a 1963 Corvair that I later sold to a student at Wayne State University when I returned to Iran. Two months later I bought a white Paykon, which was assembled in Iran. I was accustomed to an automatic transmission and had never driven a stick shift until I took the Paykon out of the dealership. I tried to learn and practiced shifting for 2-3 hours before I went home and parked the car in front of my house. As soon as I got out, the car started moving because the hand brake wasn't set. I was unable to do anything and the car hit an electric pole so hard that the front part was completely smashed. When I went back to the dealership they all clapped for me and told me, "You are the first prize winner in car wreckage!"

My Religious Life

When I reached the age of nine all religious law now applied to me. I had to follow the adult ways and pray 5 times a day; I had to fast during the month of Ramadan; I had to cover myself from head to toe and could no longer talk freely to any male, even to my two cousins who were almost my age and had been my playmates from an early age. In other words my freedom - to talk, laugh and play, to be a child – had expired. I had to fast and follow the adult path no matter my ability and physical power, especially during the summertime.

During Ramadan school hours were shortened; instead of 8 am – 4 pm we went from 11 am – 4 pm. All government and private businesses had to slow down because everyone was fasting from at least one hour before dawn (about 4 am) until shortly after complete sunset and had to tolerate 12–16 hours of no eating, drinking or smoking during the daylight hours, depending on the length of the day and the season of the year. Fasting was much easier in the winter than in the summer.

People tried to sleep more during the daytime to stabilize the physiological state of their bodies by complete rest. They would visit each other at night or go to the mosque for prayer until late but still allow time for a short nap before the time to eat arrived. The time after midnight and before dawn was called Sahar and the food was called Sahari. The period of eating or breaking the fast started shortly after sunset and was called Ephtar. For 30 days in a row, people could eat and drink anything but alcohol and smoke as much as they liked and as many times as they wished only between Ephtar and Sahari then nothing until the next sunset or Ephtar. Muslims considered Ramadan to be a month of prayers and forgiveness; therefore they tried to visit each other and renew relationships and their friendships. Because of the lack of transportation in those days, it was common for relatives who lived close to the mosque to host those who lived far away from the mosque. Every year my mother's family came to our house, which was rather close to a very famous mosque. They would come on day 17 of Ramadan and stay for ten days until the 27th day.

As my mother was always concerned about my health and that of my sister, she directed us to the basement and told us how we could drink water in the middle of the day or in the hot afternoon. We would secretly go down to the basement and hide in a pile where beds were stored for guests; there we would drink from the container. Supposedly, God could not find us there so our fasting would still be acceptable by God.

A description of a typical day during Ramadan follows. Everyone fasted and slept until late morning. They went to the mosque for noon and afternoon prayers and then returned home for the Ephtar meal. When Ephtar was finished they went back for evening prayer until 9 or 10 pm, then returned home again and would start drinking tea or soft drinks, eating some fruit and special sweets of Ramadan. Then they went to bed and slept until Sahari (dinner) was ready and on the table. They would come to the table to read the Sahar prayer then eat and drink and wash their mouths. Then fasting would start again. After their morning prayer was finished they went to bed and slept until 11 am when they would wake up and the cycle was repeated.

The ten days that we had guests and everyone was very anxious to go to the mosque was the mourning period for Imam Ali who had been assassinated more than 1400 years earlier. During that week all the mosques were full of people for prayer and mourners of Imam Ali. Our guests then returned to and remained in their own homes until the last day of Ramadan, which was followed by a very famous Islamic celebration. In the early morning of that day of celebration, all Muslims were obligated to pay to the especially needy families the equivalent of the average price of most food eaten during Ramadan for each individual in the household, even every infant and newborn child. For this reason everyone liked to be in their own home on that day rather than to be guests and have the host or hostess pay according to Islamic law.

During those ten days (from 17th to 27th) all of my mother's first cousins, their girls and sometimes their own nannies that wished to join the special prayer at that holy period of time came to our house. My mother and grandmother, with the help of our nannies and probably extra help, prepared everything necessary and made it ready as much as the living standard allowed because no refrigerators existed in those days. The group of guests included 15–20 women, with 5-7 in each guest bedroom. People slept on the floor; therefore, in every house one could find plenty of mattresses, blankets, pillows, etc. The guests did nothing except attend prayer in the mosque; the duty of the hostess and the rest of the family was the preparation of Ephtar and Sahari.

As I recall, this process went on at our house until my mother became sick, my grandmother died, and the old nannies that cooked also died. Then, three quarters of our big eight-bedroom house became part of the newly formed street and my parents moved to a five-bedroom house; the Ramadan hosting of family came to an end.

I vividly remember an incident of Sahari and the agony that my poor mother, her guests and the rest of us went through during one of the Ramadan parties on three successive nights. This incident is so vivid that I feel it happened only yesterday. Although I may have forgotten a great many things in my life this story is one I remember well.

In those days the children had no right to ask any questions that were not the relevant to their age, which was especially true in my case. It may have been the age gap between my parents and me or it may have been the same for everyone. Today I believe the latter. Anytime I asked my parents about something that attracted my eyes, the answer was "Your soul is much bigger than your body. This is not for a child to know. God saved you from the evil eye." Then some little seed was poured on the fire followed by my mother's prayers for my health and safety. Every time I asked and faced this process I wished I were grown up and able to do it by myself and not ask any questions.

One of the items that I kept playing with and that I was punished for most of the time until I learned its function myself was my mother's sewing machine. The second item was an alarm clock that had two bells on the top, one on each side of the handle. A third was my father's pocket watch. It had a very delicate key for winding and whenever he wound it and I was around, I dearly wished he would let me insert the key and wind it, even once. I was afraid to ask and if I did he gave me a serious look rather than words. (To be honest, today when I see how parents teach their kids I feel very jealous; it wasn't easy in my day for a kid to kill or bury her desire for learning automatically.)

One snowy and icy cold night when my mother went to the mosque with her cousins, I went to sleep under the *korsi*. All of a sudden I found my father's pocket watch under the *korsi* blanket. My mother borrowed it from my father and left it there so its oil would be warm enough for the large handle to move freely and show the exact time. We had a grandfather clock and one alarm clock that were both frozen. As we had no central heating and the room was so large that the fireplace couldn't warm the entire room, every bedroom was equipped with a *korsi* in the middle and a fireplace in the corner. When I saw the watch in a red velvet box I became so happy and excited that I lost my mind. I took the watch out of the box, opened the back, inserted the key in it and started winding while I was counting from one to seven; it got a bit hard, then eight, then nine and finally ten when it stopped moving. I dared not tell anyone. I was scared to death and left it in the same area so it appeared to be untouched and I went to my bed and slept. My mother and her guests returned from the mosque. The nanny told my mother she'd better go to the kitchen and start cooking the rice. My mother looked at the watch; it showed 11 o'clock. She told the nanny to go to her bed and sleep a bit and she would call her at 2 am. Everything was ready except the rice that had to be cooked in an hour. So the nanny went to bed waiting for my mother to call her. Mother went to her bed and fell asleep; she would wake up every hour or so to check the time and then would fall back asleep knowing she had more time left. Because there was no movement in the house none of the guests woke up until it was too late to eat. They were awakened by a loud sound from a cannon. They came out of their bedrooms, washed their mouths and started their early morning prayers. They had to continue their fasting for 11 more hours.

Everyone suffered through that day. My mother kept apologizing for what had happened. The fasting ended at 5–5:30 pm with the sound of the Ephtar cannon. They all ate and prayed to God. My mother didn't realize why the watch had stopped, so she brought the alarm clock under the *korsi* to get it warm and to wind it. That night they all were tired and didn't go to the mosque. They gathered together and started talking and chatting. It was the kids' bedtime and I went to the bedroom and started looking for my father's watch to see what had happened to it. I found the alarm clock and unconsciously started winding and counting by number for it until it banged and stopped. Once again, I left it in the same place and went to bed. That night again all of them missed their Sahari and started their fasting with no food or drink. My mother took the watch and the alarm clock to the repair shop. The shopkeeper advised her the springs of both were broken due to strong and careless winding.

At that moment my mother realized that only I could have done that. She borrowed a pocket watch, returned home and without any questions or investigation about why I did it she told me I would visit the school principal as soon as the school reopened (they were closed because of Imam Ali's assassination). This was the worst punishment for me, knowing the story would be told to my teacher. In those days, it was common to issue punishment in the presence of all the students during the break. They used a wet stick and the one being punished had to open both fists and receive a certain number of strikes with the flexible wet stick on her palms. To me it was a disaster and that night I was very sad thinking of the next day but I decided to be a good girl and keep quiet and obedient (sometimes I became violent rather than obedient). I did not touch the watch and went to bed very early to show everyone how sad I was. As the watch remained safe and untouched everyone had their Sahari and no more fasting on already empty stomachs for the last two days.

On the last day of prayer everyone, including the nannies, wanted to go to the mosque so my sister and I were left behind all alone at the house. We started thinking and talking to each other to find a way that our mother would forgive me rather than go to the school and complain about me. My sister suggested the best way would be by cleaning the room and sweeping it with a broom. In those days there were no vacuums or other electrical cleaning devices. We had only a 2-foot fine-straw broom for the room and a thick one-foot long dried stem of a special plant with a long handle on it for the yard. We helped each other because our hands were small and couldn't handle the broom easily. We tried our best.

Meanwhile, I found a box with a pocket watch in it, but it was not similar to my father's. My wild curiosity didn't allow me to leave it alone. I opened the box, looked at the watch and put it close to my ear; I couldn't hear any ticking. I started crying and asking God for his genuine help. My sister came to see what was wrong. She couldn't hear any ticking either. Since no one else was home, she took it to the next-door neighbor to ask for her opinion whether the watch was dead or working. She looked at it and told my sister it was working and not to worry. My sister brought the watch back, held very tightly in her two hands. She wanted to thank God so she placed the box between her legs and elevated her arms to point to God and show him her sincere thanks. As she put her hands up, her legs relaxed and the box fell on the concrete. What an accident, how disastrous! After all that, thankfully the watch didn't break and my mother forgave me. I promised her I wouldn't touch anything else … but for how long? Two days later the guests left and our lives returned to normal.

CHAPTER 2

From Birth to Pre-School

I was born in Tehran Iran at 5 am on March 20th 1920 on a very cold and snowy day. I was the 13th child and 6th daughter of my 75-year-old father and the third child of my 35-year-old mother. Both my parents had been married before. Father married at age 16 and had seven live children out of ten from his first marriage, with ages ranging from 50 to 13. He was widowed at the age of 69.

My mother was married at age nine to a very famous jewelry designer for the Ghajar Dynasty palace who had been married for ten years but had no children. In those days they believed infertility was the fault of the mother not the father (the age of the female was considered, not male sterility). My mother became a widow at age 19 without any children. She didn't marry again for ten years. She married my father when she was 29. She always told us she didn't realize how old my father was and assumed that he was not more than 50 years old because he was such a handsome, well-dressed, and soft spoken gentleman as her uncle (my father's close friend) had described to her.

My parents' first child was born a year after they were married. My mother always admired her daughter's beauty and talent; how smart she was at age three. She died seven days after the onset of disease symptoms. Their second child was a boy who died in his cradle 35 days after his birth for unknown reasons. Two years later I was born and after 18 months my sister

Azam was the last born in the family. I had been told that I was so precious to my parents, particularly to my mother, because of the loss of her first two children. In addition my sister and I were the youngest among 14 nieces and nephews. As mother said, I was very happy, calm and quiet during my early years. My teeth started coming in at 4 months and I was walking and talking by my first birthday. My mother was always concerned about my health and well-being as all mothers are; but in addition she was worried all the time because of the loss of her first two children. She made a promise to God that if He would protect me from evil eyes and grant me health, she would sacrifice a mature sheep on my birthday for seven years to make special food to distribute among underprivileged families. You can imagine how crowded our house was, how many workers tried to finish work on that day when the food was distributed among those needy people at the entry door of our house. Mother also always spent a lot of money at the holy shrine (Imam Zadeh) and for poor families 2-3 times a year. But there were no birthday parties, no cakes, no candles, no music and no children of my age as we do today. Instead there were lots of prayers and religious songs that I clearly remember.

Mother strongly believed evil eyes caused her first two children's deaths, so she tried to keep both of us away from exposure to outsiders, especially when unexpected guests came to visit. There was no way to know who was coming to visit to be prepared ahead of time. Nor was it possible to limit the number of guests to suddenly enter the house, especially if they came from a long distance. When the entire family came together they would stay at least 2-3 weeks. This was a common custom in Iran because in those days there were no hotel or motel systems. Even today everyone prefers to stay with their friends or family rather than going to a hotel and staying there alone.

My mother hired a young girl, Nargess, to play with my sister and me and to take care of us as today's babysitters do while my mother and nannies prepared for the guests and the rest of the family.

According to my mother I was a very active and curious child. I never stopped asking questions about new things that I saw. Unless I got the answer I begged her continually, so she suffered from anxiety and worry during the first four years of my life. In contrast, my sister was very manageable during the same age period. Soon I started to pay more attention to my surroundings and became less dependent on my mother, grandmother and nannies. This caused a lot of exhaustion and frustration for them, especially when they realized that I was left-handed.

It was a disaster to have a defective (left handed) daughter. My father tried to convince Mother that many people in this world are left handed but she wouldn't listen to him. She tried hard to find a way to correct this defect. She had been told that in order to shift a left hand to right, the left hand should be so tired that a child unconsciously would shift to the right hand. To do so they recommended that she place a hexagonal pencil between any two fingers of my left hand anytime I tried to use it and to press the pencil until I felt severe pain. My mother had no heart and hated to do so but she had to have a non-defective girl. Grandmother advised her to send me to school to be with other kids to see that they were using their right hand. I was not quite 4? years old. At that time there was no kindergarten, no preschool - and no formal daycare except the maktab existed. Maktab was a private unit run by a Mullah (meaning educated person) for boys and Mullah Baji for girls. It was usually located in the owner's home in a secluded room or basement of the house. The floor of the room was covered with straw and every child had to take her own area rug or blanket to put on top of the straw (kelim) to sit on. The maktab had no chairs, no desks and no blackboards. At first my mother refused to send me to a maktab but the age for acceptance at school was six years old and the newly established preschool close to our house was five. So mother had no choice; she was desperate to correct my handedness and decided to send me to the maktab temporarily until I became eligible for pre-school. In the maktab the Mullah Baji did everything by herself. She taught the

Koran and read loudly from it to the students who had to repeat it after her without understanding the meaning or its alphabetical combinations (spelling).

My mother told the story that when she took me to maktab I refused to go in and started crying. I told her, "Khanoom joon (dear mother), I don't want to go to the bath." I had seen the straw covering the floor similar to the public bath entry area. Mother could not convince me even though there were 5 other girls sitting on their own area rugs or blankets. She tried to persuade me but I refused to let go of her hand and we finally returned home. Mother then decided to bribe me by making me a black sateen chadoor and picheh (a rectangle skillfully made of horsetail hair with a loose design in it. You could see through it because there were spaces between the rows of hair; but no one could recognize your face from the outside) that I was starving for. (I was always trying to wear every black chadoor that I found, regardless of the size).

When the new chadoor and picheh were ready I told my mother that I would go to maktab the next day. I woke up early and asked for my chadoor and picheh. As soon as I put them on I told her, "I'm old enough to go by myself; no one should come with me." My mother finally took me herself although at first I refused. She left me there and Nargess came to take me home. So like other girls I got used to going with Nargess every day – but only for 15 days.

As the story goes, as told by my mother and witnessed by my grandmother and sister-in-law, and as I recollect a very small part of that day … my 15 days in maktab was one of the unique events among my family especially for my grandmother and sister-in-law who were living with us for a short period of time. My mother explained to me what Mullah Baji told her. Today I imagine that the events were funny for everyone but me as I was fighting for my rights even at that young age.

It was a hot late spring or early summer day that Mullah Baji told her six students to bring their area rugs to the porch. We did and while she was reading the Koran and we were repeating her words, a small aircraft suddenly appeared in the sky. I probably became more excited than the other girls and said, "Balloon, look at the balloon in the sky!" The Koran reading was interrupted because everyone became excited and the Mullah Baji could not control us. Since I was the one to disrupt the reading of the Koran she slapped my face. In return I slapped her face, tore her scarf, cried loudly and told her that I didn't want to come to her anymore. The other five girls repeated whatever I said. Just about that time Nargess came to pick me up. She grabbed me while I was still crying hard. As soon as we arrived home my mother took me in her arms. I was still crying and telling her that I didn't want to go to maktab anymore. Mother washed my face, kissed me and comforted me until I fell asleep in her arms.

In the afternoon Mullah Baji came to the house with her torn scarf to apologize for what happened. My mother paid for her scarf and also the dues for one month and promised her that if Mullah Baji lost any students because of the incident she would take care of the dues for that student. This story followed me for years, even in my old age; anytime I criticize something, someone says, "Oh no more; Mullah Baji is dead by now so don't repeat that event!"

Eventually mother found the newly formed preschool, went there and talked to the owner, explaining about my left-handedness. The owner made exception and registered me. I attended the pre-school without incident. I loved my teacher except for the time she worked on my "defect." At least five or six times a day I was tortured so that I would never forget those moments. I loved writing but even today I write with my right hand. Otherwise, I confess that I still remain left-handed no matter how much I suffered.

Another story that I will never forget is the story of my mother's signet ring, which was lost for exactly a year. It happened when I was about four years old. The first part of the story caused a lot of problems and hard times at home for Nargess, the nannies and my mother as well. We had three nannies; one of them was responsible for cooking but my mother never allowed anybody except herself to use their bare hands for mixing food. She always did the hand mixing (in those days no gloves existed for use in the kitchen). One day Mother wanted to make meatballs. As soon as she went to the kitchen I followed her and stood by her. She sat next to a 2 x 2-foot stone mortar and pestle that smashed meat that was in it. She took off her signet ring that was gold with a heart-shaped flat area where her name was engraved on it. She used this ring as her signet and always had it on her finger. She took the ring off and left it on the corner of the mortar. While she was busy mixing meat and vegetables, I sneaked the ring and quickly left the kitchen. It wasn't more than a few minutes before the nanny realized I wasn't in the kitchen. She immediately left the kitchen to look for me and found me returning to the kitchen.

Nanny grabbed me and took me back while asking where I had been. I said that a black crow came to the yard and I wanted to see him (I probably threw the ring for the crow to eat). My mother finished her mixing, washed her hands and then realized her ring was not on her finger. They started looking for the ring everywhere; they even moved the heavy stone mortar. But it wasn't to be found. My mother was very worried because it was her signet ring and anyone could use it since every woman's face was covered and there could be no facial identification. The nannies were upset because they thought they might be accused of the loss. Little by little everyone forgot about the ring. According to my mother, I was 4 years old at the time of the incident and by all means I couldn't remember the moment that I threw the ring toward the crow.

Exactly a year later my mother was invited to my aunt's house for lunch. She took Nargess and me with her. At lunch time, the ladies started talking about different foods, especially meatballs. All of a sudden I told my mother, "I know where your ring is. The crow escaped when I gave it to him." My mother tried to keep me quiet but I didn't stop talking and repeating, "I found it." Nargess, who had been more concerned than the other nannies, asked my mother if she could take me back to the house and look for the ring. But my mother refused and told Nargess that we would all go together. Meanwhile I said, "Khanoom joon, if you want your ring I should go now" and kept insisting. Because the two houses were rather far from each other, Nargess promised my mother that she would carry me on her shoulder and arm and never let me walk. Finally my mother agreed and Nargess carried me on her shoulders back to the house. As soon as we got home she let me down in the front yard and I ran toward the flowerbeds. I told her where the crow was when I threw the ring for him to eat. Nargess had doubts about it but started looking among the leaves and found the ring.

I must say that I strongly believe today that whatever happened during childhood, even very early ages, is engraved in some part of the brain that can be triggered later and every part of that event would appear in front of your eyes as it happened to me today as I am writing this memoir.

The Status of Education during my Childhood

The stories of a girl's education before my birth and during my childhood years are written in detail in the Farsi language that only one of my grandchildren can read, even though all of them including my great-grandchildren can speak Farsi fluently. Therefore in this section I have tried to describe a brief history of the standard of living environment in those days. At this point I prefer to explain how our life was in a primitive state and how we survived that life and came to the present modern style. So the future life-style, when one compares it with the present it will be beyond imagination.

Long before I was born, Tehran housed the first European-style college called Dar-AI Phonone (or Darolfonoon), which means polytechnic institution. This school was designed and established in 1851 by one of the famous prime ministers of the Ghajar Dynasty, Amir Kabir, who was the victim of jealousy of his mother-in-law, the King's very influential mother. He was killed by venipuncture in his private bath by one of his own servants. After his death, the college remained and continued to function but no other formal school was formed except maktabs.

The maktabs were rather primitive unisex schools. Girls generally had little chance to go to a maktab long enough to get much education because the fanatic Muslims never considered a girl as a powerful individual, never contemplated how strong and motivated a girl could be. They believed a girl's duty should be motherhood, housekeeper and a perfectly obedient wife. On the contrary, males had the most freedom for learning whatever subject they desired. Education for girls was very limited because, according to Islamic law, girls should marry at the age of nine. Therefore girls didn't have time to learn more than a few chapters of the Koran or a few pages of religious guidelines and never learned to write. They believed if a girl learned how to write she might write love letters and find a boyfriend. She received her limited knowledge at home with the help of her father, a private female tutor or one of her immediate relatives but usually by word of mouth rather than formal schooling. Girls were not allowed to leave the house without the ever-presence or supervision of the mother or a nanny. In other words the girl looked very cheap in the eyes of other people if she appeared on the street alone.

Education became formal and serious after the fall of the Ghajar Dynasty and the rise of Reza Shah (beginning in 1925) who used his strong power to revolutionize the system of education by ordering compulsory equal education for both genders from the age of seven. Prior to that order, there had been constant fighting between those individuals pro-education and con-education for girls. There was few incident when a school for girls opened and a powerful Mullah ordered it closed. A group of fanatic Muslims invaded the school to prevent entry of the students and their teachers. The owner of the school tried hard to challenge the invaders and sent many, many letters to Ghajar Shah asking for standard education and women's liberation.

It was not an easy task for those pioneer ladies. Some who kept insisting on women's liberation faced punishment and were sent to exile in one of the poor provinces of Iran. One of these brave ladies was Fakhr Affagh Parsay, mother of Dr. Farokhroo Parsay, a pediatrician by education and the Secretary of Education during the reign of Mohammed Reza Shah. Dr. Parsay herself became the victim of religious fanaticism and after the fall of the Shah was executed by the order of Khomeini on May 8, 1980.

The secondary maktab was for mature boys. The main subjects taught were the Koran, religious guidelines, handwriting, math, astrology, literature,poetry and a few other subjects. Young men could choose whatever subjects they desired to learn; their fathers either supported their wishes or dictated what to study. Fathers tried to send their sons abroad, depending on the subject of study. For example, those who wanted to be religious leaders were sent to Al Azhar University in Egypt or Najaf in Iraq. Those who wished to study art and sciences or related subjects usually went to Europe, especially to France or Germany. Some young men whose fathers were merchants and had dealings with Russia sent their sons there. The influence of Germans, French and Russians was the common ground for the modernization in Iran. The level of education among wealthy families was more than 60-fold that of the middle class, 90-fold greater than the under-privileged groups and 100 times more than the farmers and villagers.

During the period of study in foreign countries, some of the men married and brought their wives to Iran. Those foreign ladies were definitely educated but were not used to the Iranian culture and were not allowed to go out of the house alone (in other words, they were house bound). Once they had learned a bit of Farsi they tried first to educate their in-laws and then accepted girls as private students in their own homes, teaching them whatever they wanted to specialize in. Due to the language barrier, the teaching was primarily practical in nature. They taught foreign language, arts and crafts, home economics and decorating, dressmaking and much, much more. Their students could, in-turn, teach other groups of young girls as well. This appeared to be a networking education similar to today's networking style. However, education was performed in individual homes not in a formal school setting.

Educated women were rare, except for some professions like midwifery, nursing, beautician, dressmaker and few others. Women learned either from maternal experience (daughters learned from mothers) or apprenticeship. For example, a practical midwife came from a family whose three generations of ancestors (mother, grand- and great-grandmother) were midwives; but because of the lack of adequate knowledge of hand washing and use of aseptic procedures, the death of a mother a few days after birth was common. It was assumed that it was the act of some invisible creature. In reality it was only microorganisms being transferred from the hands of the midwife to the open wound of the uterus which resulted in septicemia and death of the mother, usually on the sixth night after her delivery.

In those days, no one understood how strong and motivated a girl like me could be because the religious fanatics kept their brainwashing so constant and effective that the girls themselves believed science would be beyond their comprehension.

As Tehran University formed and education changed to co-education where women could attend the same university, the same school, and the same classes as men, the picture of Iran changed drastically.

On January 7th, 1935 the first day of the emancipation of women in Iran, Reza Shah took his wife and two daughters, 16 and 18 years old, out into public without veils for a ceremony that brought all invited guests and their wives out in European style dress without veils. The next day, all the teachers, educators and women students removed their veils or black chadoors and pichehs. The Tehran of yesterday became part of Europe of the day.

In general, the power of Reza Shah could be seen in the modernization of the country. He hired a group of French, British and German professionals to organize and develop a modern system of formal schooling and higher education by establishing teacher training in the colleges and universities. The foundation of the Tehran Universities, the development of a modern system of justice, strong system of security and safety, the railroad system, women's liberation, the change in dress style for both men and women, and much more.

Six years later, fearing that Reza Shah was about to align his petroleum-rich country with Nazi Germany during World War II, the United Kingdom and the Soviet Union occupied Iran and forced Reza Shah to abdicate in favor of his 20 year old son Mohammad Reza Pahlavi. When the war began, Reza Shah had declared Iran neutral. Britain interpreted this as favoring Nazi Germany, especially as the Shah refused the Allies the right to use the trans-Iranian railroad to transport Western supplies to Stalin. Mohammad Reza officially replaced his father on the throne on September 16, 1941. Reza Shah soon went into exile, first to Mauritius, then to Johannesburg, South Africa, where he died on July 26, 1944.

Although the new young Shah followed in his father's footsteps and the country moved toward further modernization, along came the dirty attitude of President Jimmy Carter, who I believe never read about the history of the mullahs' destroying power, and the most unfortunate situation developed with the rise of Khomeini in 1979. The modern country was pulled back at least 50-60 years. All the schools from primary to higher education closed for 5 years; the dress code became Arabic once again and women went back to wearing the black veils by strong force. The first night of Khomeini's power, the highly-educated and experienced people were either executed in groups or were placed in jail. Confiscation, robbery, looting, lack of safety and misery became common all over the country. In general, all mouths were shut, all pens were silenced and broken or one had to spend an unlimited time in jail.

The moral of this story could be summarized in two different directions. If in the first part of my life I faced injustice and discrimination because I was a girl, if my left hand still feels pain because I was born left handed, if I could not continue my education because I was pretty with green eyes, if I faced a forcefully-arranged marriage and had to be punished because I made a hat overnight and wore the hat in a photo shop, if I had to watch the workers while they broke the east wall of our residence in favor of street expansion the same day as my wedding and if I had to face so many other unexpected miseries during my young age, I could overcome all of them one by one and still become a successful person the way I wished.

The other part of the story involved the latest revolution by Khomeini. Not only I but also all Iranians never assumed and never would have expected to see so many disasters. First I lost my motherland and my family residence with great memories of my children as well as my own childhood period; then I lost whatever monies I made and whatever I inherited.

Although I could overcome many difficulties again, there is a considerable difference between the two. The first part brought Iranians a lot of modern changes, a lot of education experience, knowledge and progress and in general a better life. Unfortunately the latest revolution not only pushed the country back 50-60 years but it eradicated all the educated, experienced and knowledgeable people by execution, imprisonment, or disappearance and caused many other miserable situations that are visible to the eyes of the people in the world today. At this point I am grateful to God who has allowed me to have my brain, my consciousness and my memories intact and who has assisted me in writing these memoirs.

Primary School

The private preschool that I attended for one and a half years after my experiences at that crazy maktab meant that my name was automatically registered for the first grade. A primary state school moved from its old place to a newly built facility very close to our house that year. The school was run by the government and had first to sixth grades, with more qualified teachers, a much more extensive educational program, greater atmosphere and more discipline. By the end of the school year my mother applied for my registration and I was admitted to the first not the second grade because I was not yet eight years old, even though my abilities were greater than most of the other students of my age from the learning and discipline I received in preschool. It was my second year in first grade, so I was elected as teacher's aide. I spent five consecutive years in that new school, moving from one grade to the next, skipping fourth, until I graduated.

When I started school it was the beginning of compulsory education for both boys and girls by order of the Reza Shah. Therefore, every child from age seven had to go to school but school was unisex. In the girls' primary school, only three or four workers were male; the rest were female. We called the male workers Baba (papa). The gatekeeper was older and couldn't walk as fast as the other two men who were responsible for all the hard labor at the school. There were four female workers: one was responsible for the student dining room - to warm up the food during winter, keep the room clean and supervise the students at lunch and prayer time; one was responsible for the main office; and the other two were responsible for classes and taking care of cleaning after the students left for the day, and if someone got sick during the day, to take her home and hand her to her family. In those days, few people had telephones so they could not call the parents to take the sick child home. Every Saturday morning (the first day of the week), public health of the students was the main concern.

The school had a very big yard with a large fish pond in the middle and four flower beds around the pond. The classrooms were located around the yard on each side of that square area, about 4-6 stairs above the ground. The dining and praying rooms were 2-3 stairs down the ground. There was no exercise room but we had to exercise in a designated area of the yard. Every class had one hour of exercise per week.

The discipline that was taught to the students from the first grade is still with me, especially the respect shown to the teachers, parents and old people - teaching the children from a very young age to stand when an adult entered the room, say "hello" in the morning and "goodbye" when they left. Also their eating and washing habits were and still are the duty of the parents. At that point of time all the girls had to wear chadoors and cover themselves from head to toe, even the first graders who were only 7 years old.

In the morning when we entered the school, we removed our chadoors, folded them and place them in our school bags. Then all the students of every class gathered in the designated area and formed a two by two line, the shorter girls in front and the taller ones in back. In five to ten minutes, by the first bell, all the students were in line and had stopped talking. Then a short page of Koran was read aloud by a student of one of the upper grades. We all sang the national anthem together; then the bell rang and the lines turned and started moving toward their classrooms, entering the rooms and sitting in designated spots assigned by the teacher's aid. The teacher's aid also managed the harmonious standing up and sitting down when another teacher or other official entered the classroom.

It was also common in those days and I believe it is still the same in all primary schools that all subjects were taught daily by a permanent female teacher except for art, exercise and handwriting practices that were taught by male experts. In high school the presence of hourly male teachers was unavoidable. They had to be married, have children and be more than 30 years old to be eligible to teach girls from secondary to high school. The students had to wear *chadoors namaz* (prayer covers) whenever men were present. In general I had to wear the chadoor in public during all my primary school years and up to the beginning of the 9th grade in high school, the lucky year that women's emancipation took place, January 7th 1935 (according to the Iranian calendar, 17 Dayemahe 1314).

At that point in time the number of students in each classroom did not or was not to exceed thirty, especially in the first and second grades, so the school had multiple classrooms per grade. But by the third grade and above the number of students decreased because they reached age nine. Some had to leave school because of religion and some got married and were not allowed to come to school and contact their classmates, even in the public bath.

The subjects for study were selected and prepared by a group of experts in education and were uniform at each level in all the school systems of the country. The context of the books in each subject increased as the students moved to upper levels but in general the basic subjects continued from first to sixth grade. They included literature, poetry, reading, writing, history, geography, Koran, religious law and dictation. The literature included poem reading in the second grade and above. The other subjects and levels were added to the schedule accordingly. As I remember we always stood up to answer questions and during poem recitation we had to stand in front of the entire class.

During the school year from the second grade on, we had to memorize poems and at night grandmother made us recite poetry. It was very beneficial to students to exercise their memory. When I finished the third grade and was almost nine years old, my parents forced me to pray five times a day and use a chadoor and picheh to cover myself from men (except from my father, my brother and my nephews). When my cousins visited our house they were closely watched; they could no longer come freely and I was not allowed to talk to them and recite poetry as before. The ring of religion around me became tighter and tighter every day; I felt strangled. I couldn't endure to sit and do nothing except pray. My mother tried to teach me weaving, knitting, sewing and doll making.

One of the very happy memories that I have was the art and craft contest that I was nominated for in fifth grade because of my strong background in sewing, woodcarving, embroidery and weaving. I was the winner of the first prize and received a book by Omar Khayyam in addition to a 2-3 year supply of stationery. The book is treasured in my sister's bookshelf and everyone used the stationary for a long time. During the five years that I spent in that school I don't remember any changes in the system. The principal, the teachers and seven workers didn't change; it was a very friendly atmosphere for the students with one exception. Two of the teachers (first and third grade) lived in the same area that we did and used the same public bath that we used every Friday. It was embarrassing to see them and be seen by them in the nude.

Public Bath

In those days none of the Iranian homes had private baths, no matter how modern the house or wealthy the owners were. People did not believe that a shower could make them as clean as religion dictated; they had to be immersed in the water a few times to perform the religious act. Even if they had a bath built in the corner of their backyard, they still preferred to go to the public bath where there was a hot water pool called "*khazineh*" to sink their heads under the water. The *khazineh* pool was very scary for children and very uncomfortable for the elderly because it had a shallow entrance, a deep and waist-high area of warm water with a temperature of close to 39oC. The *khazineh* was built rather elevated from the floor of the bath with at least one step up and a shallow entrance. It had 3-4, maybe 5 sunroofs about the size of dinner plates, which brought light in if it was a sunny day. Otherwise it was rather dark, hazy and hot for the kids and uncomfortable for the elderly to climb up the step and pass through such a shallow entrance door.

In general the basic construction of an Iranian public bath was similar to the Roman or Turkish baths but still with many differences. All the Iranian public baths were built 10-15 or more steps down from the alley (street) level. In other words, the roof of the public baths could easily be seen from the road. They were open from 5 am until 8 am for male customers. Then all the male workers started cleaning the floors in the cold and warm areas and making it ready for the women and their children to use. Then the male workers were replaced with a female manager and workers.

The bath was divided into two separate areas – cold and warm. The warm area was a large area - damp, hazy, steamy, crowded and very noisy with numerous women working semi-nude. They tried to keep their customers happy. A customer would sit in the warm area on a copper tray about 15 cm deep that was placed upside down on the floor of the bath (to meet public health regulations and to prevent any contamination from the contact of their skin to the floor area). Some workers constantly brought a container of warm water and poured it in a big bowl in front of the customer and her children. Other workers washed the long hair of their customers and rubbed their bodies with rough wash gloves to remove dead skin, then washed their children. Until age nine, boys were allowed to come to the bath with their mother.

The cold area was used twice. Once when they entered the public bath, where they took off all their clothes and covered their bodies from the chest to the knee with a piece of cloth decorated with nice lace sewn on the upper and lower part of the cloth that was called a *"long."* Then they went into the warm area. After all the washing and cleaning was done with the help of the woman workers in the bath, they went to the *khazineh* to immerse in the water. The manager or her assistant would bring dry *longs* for the return to the cold area. Then they washed their feet in cold water and sat in the designated area covered with their own bath towels to dry themselves. They would get dressed, pay the manager and leave the public bath.

Every worker had their own customers; they received more tips and extra help from the ones who were their regular customers. From a young age people went to the bath on a certain day every week, so every worker had a certain number of permanent customers plus a few people who went to the bath on an irregular basis. In general, in addition to the permanent jobs serving all the women of a family, the public bath workers also acted as "secret agents" or matchmakers to introduce families who had daughters to families who were anxious to find a good girl to marry their sons.

Going to a public bath in the wintertime wasn't easy, even for healthy people; it was torture for children and especially the elderly who were prone to pneumonia during the fall and particularly in the snowy winter. They had to walk on a rough, rocky and muddy road from the bath to their houses.

My Life at Age 8 and 9

I clearly remember that from the age of 5 or 5? I was very joyful. I was happy, cheerful and a curious child. My two cousins (Mehdi and Mohammad) used to come to our house to play with my sister and me. Anytime my grandmother would come, we all enjoyed her presence because she gathered all of us around her and would tell the stories of her life when she was young. She also told about my mother and my aunts and all the enjoyable events that happened in our family. She always read books to us and made us read children's books like The Fox and The Crow, Cat and Mouse, Cockroach and Mouse, Wolf, Sheep and Lamb, etc. Not only did we read the books, we had to explain the results and what we understood from it. Sometimes she made us "play act" and she would explain the animals' behaviors and ask us to tell about their good and bad attitudes. I believe she was teaching us the way that audio-visuals and cartoons teach our children today. We played during the daytime as much as we could. We would start early morning until noon; then we would have to be quiet until 4 pm because everyone rested for 2 to 3 hours after lunch. We had to be good; otherwise my mother would separate us and send each one of us to a different room.

At night we gathered around grandmother and didn't want to leave her. We kept asking her for more and more stories until she was exhausted. She would promise my cousins they could stay at our house for a few more days (especially during the summertime) if all of us would go to bed and leave her alone for a while.

For the summer the school gave us much homework but not enough for me; I finished one hundred pages of script and one hundred pages of capital letters in one week. I woke up at 5 am and went to a small, secluded balcony where I would start writing, the capital letters first. We used wet ink. To do it fast with wet ink (and my **right** hand), I couldn't start from the right side of the page (as Arabic script is written), so I started from the left and wrote from the top to the bottom of the page. It was handwriting practice so the similar words had to be under each other, like a column. I would divide the two hundred pages by five days, so that every day I finished 20 pages of capital letters and 20 pages of script. For the script, I started from right to left in contrast to the capital letters. The subject matter of the script was whatever story I liked the most. So for me, out of three months of summer "homework," I only had enough for a week or a maximum of two weeks.

I felt really lonely and touchy because I had no one except my sister Azam to talk to and she always disagreed with my ideas. My mother decided to take me to a dressmaker in our neighborhood. I stayed with her only during the summer. I learned a lot from her during that short period of time and whatever I learned became the basic knowledge of dressmaking in my life. I will never forget the day my mother and I, both in black chadoors and picheh, went to the dressmaker's house. My mother tried to advise me not to be a rebel girl and to be polite. "You are grown-up now; don't pay any attention to her life style." I promised her I would follow her advice. Torbat was a tall lady with rather dark skin, black eyes and long black hair woven (braided) and hung on the side of her face. She received my mother then asked my age and said I would be the youngest of her assistants. I was 8? years old and she believed that I couldn't help her. My mother replied that she brought me there to learn not to work. Then Torbat said, "So I don't have to pay her?" My mother said, "No, the only thing I want you to do is not to ignore her." Torbat promised. So my mother left me there and asked her what time the nanny should pick me up.

Torbat Khanoom said, "Every day before sunset except today because she doesn't have her lunch." (Up to the first part of my ninth grade in high school, I never went anywhere alone including the public bath where we all went once a week. Either my mother or the nanny was with me at all times when I was away from the house.)

When my mother left, Torbat Khanoom told me to go to her work place, a rather dark and humid basement of her one-room house. Three girls were working there; I was the fourth. She gave me a V-shaped silk fabric and asked me to hook it (using a long stitch). I did it in a very proper way and then handed it back to her. She looked at the other girls and told them, "Shame on you all, look at the size of her hands and she is left handed; you three can't even do it properly with your right hands." She said whatever she believed about right and left hands (my defect). Because my mother had asked me repeatedly to be polite and I had promised her (she was afraid after what happened with Mullah Baji) I didn't say anything. I obeyed her and kept quiet and didn't react about the left handed statement. Every day I went to her house with my lunch box and stayed until late. I learned a lot from her. But every day I felt really sorry for those three poor girls that she ridiculed and undermined their confidence every hour. Her behavior was even worse toward her mother. I was really afraid of her all the time, even when she tried to encourage me.

She was completely illiterate, unable to read or write, but she was so skilled that no one realized it unless you were in close contact with her. She couldn't read a tape measure, the most basic and necessary element of dressmaking. She cut the edge of the fabric and used it as her measure for her customers. She made a knot between the different measurements and surprisingly never messed up any point. When she would finish a dress it was so fitted and so well made that they appeared to be photocopies from a European fashion magazine. Whatever I learned from her in those days, I use in dressmaking and sewing even today.

One of the most important points that I learned was the art of substituting as she did for the tape measure. She also measured the length of fabric by using her hand from thumb to little finger five times and considered that to be one meter. The second point was the art of visualizing an outfit. She could look at any model and reproduce the outfit without reading a pattern. The third one was the confidence that she conveyed and used to succeed in her work and to duplicate the exact design as in the magazine - without any ability to read. I used those skills twenty-two years later when I made my sister's bridal dress. Because I was a very fast learner and I was familiar with the art of sewing, she let me sit by her and watch the way she cut fabric. Fortunately she kept talking to herself about how to use fabric and in what direction to cut it. It was to my benefit that I learned every point of cutting and sewing. So, every day when I went home I tried to make the exact dress for my doll and would finish it before I went to bed.

I felt I had learned enough and one day when my mother was gone to my oldest half-sister's house for a luncheon, I used 5 out of 9 yards of fabric that she had bought for her *chadoor namaz*. It was a fine cotton fabric with sky blue flowers and pink and yellow dots on a white background. I made a nice dress for myself and wasted a lot of fabric. When my mother came home, before she removed her black chadoor, I entered the room wearing the new dress. She looked and kept watching me as I turned around for her to see the dress. At first she was speechless then she started laughing and asked me if I could make one for my sister. I should use the rest of the fabric because it wouldn't be useful for her chadoor anyway.

Keon and Kevin

I always told my children that I made a dress for myself at the age of nine but I was sure they never were convinced and probably thought I was teasing because they didn't like to sew, especially Nikou.

Recently two of my great-grandsons, Kevin Mortazavi (Shayma's second child) and Keon Rabbani (Shaparak's first child), asked their mothers to buy them sewing machines and register them in sewing school. Keon is very clever and eager about learning any kind of art work but he was more fascinated with the sewing machine and sewing skills. He came to me for a lesson. I taught him how to cut, how to put pieces together and how to make the machine ready for use. It took less than two hours. Then he started cutting and sewing step by step according to what I had taught him. It appeared to all of us that this 9-year-old boy had been practicing every day for more than a year in spite of only two hours of learning. It was unbelievable how he started, how careful and concerned he was in every step of learning and practicing. How amazing to everyone including me that my third generation was acting exactly like myself at the same age. I am extremely proud of both Keon and Kevin today because they are vivid proof of my childhood acts and my claims from seventy-seven years ago.

Keon (9 yrs) cutting and sewing his shirt

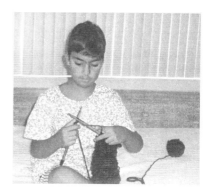

Keon wearing the shirt that he made

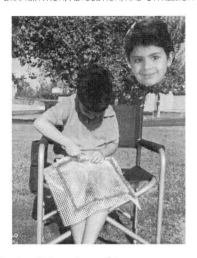

Kevin (11 yrs) crafting on a canvas

Although Shayma's second child Kevin was very active in all aspects of art and was attracted to sewing and other delicate work, I have emphasized Keon's name here because he was the exact same age as I was when I sewed my first dress.

High School

I graduated from primary school at age 11?. Skipping the fourth grade compensated for the extra year that I spent in first grade. I finished the sixth grade and passed the state exam. All girls of the district attended the exam in a designated school wearing chadoor and picheh. The exam took two days, from 9 am to 1 pm. The results were posted in our own schools twenty days later.

I dreamed of going to high school, to continue my education and become a midwife. I clearly remember the moment that a friend of my mother was visiting and asked me what my plan was after I received my high school diploma. I had just finished primary school and my goals were set high. In the presence of my aunt I replied, "To be a midwife." I'll never forget my aunt's red face and the degree of her anger when she said, "Do you think we should be a close relative to a midwife?" My aunt was very much against any education more than primary school for me and reluctant also for her own children's education. She kept telling my mother that primary school was more than enough for a girl like me. She tried to convince mother that if I received any further education my mother would not be able to control me.

At the same time I was trying very hard to convince my mother that everything in the country would soon be changing. Couldn't she see the reforms occurring? If she didn't believe me, I asked her to talk to her stepchildren. Why should my nieces and nephews be able to attend high school and not me? What would be wrong with me attending high school? What did I ever do to her that she was so against me moving forward and registering in school? Mother kept telling me that a good-looking girl like me didn't need to go out of the house every morning and return in the afternoon.

My father left my mother in charge of such things. There was no high school close to our house. She couldn't tolerate the neighbors' criticisms. She was afraid that they would say that my parents were careless and this would ruin our reputation and integrity in the community. I never accepted my mother's ideas. But I knew I wouldn't be able to convince my 87 year-old father; he left all his authority and decisions in the hands of my mother. My oldest half-brother came to our house and visited with father for a short while. He left without trying to see us. My second half-brother Hadi, who really tried to act as my father wasn't successful in helping me because he tried to keep his distance from my mother. Although both of them highly respected each other, Hadi tried not to interfere with his stepmother's ideas. It seemed I was the only one who couldn't yield to her ideas. It took the entire summer of me nagging mother, constantly bringing up the idea and promising her that I would do whatever she said in my life if she would just allow me to go to high school. Finally, after we safely returned from a trip to Mashad and overcame an accident on the trip, she gave in – but not easily. She investigated a private high school, the principal, the teachers and the entire surrounding area to be sure there were no high schools for boys close by and to be sure that no subjects were taught by male teachers. It was impossible to find such a school, but Mother finally agreed - if I kept all my promises and I would be obedient to whatever she said.

The next day we went together and I registered in the 7th grade, the first year of middle school. It is impossible for me to describe my feelings of elation that day. I felt so tall among my primary school classmates that were married during that summer while I was continuing my education. When I met them on Fridays at the public bath, we barely talked to each other because they were married and I was going to school. Their parents and in-laws believed that if they talked to classmates who continued their education, they might also wish to do so. Also, it was not proper for unmarried girls to talk to married ones. (At that time, with the country's socioeconomic reforms, the older religious people were rather confused.)

School started and the students and teachers went to school wearing black chadoors and pichehs on the street. But as they entered the school they changed from black chadoor to a sheer light-colored *chadoor namaz* because of the male teachers (for French, math, physics and chemistry) and other male workers. When male teachers came into a class, the students had to wear the *chadoor namaz*; but covering of face and hair were relaxed at that time.

Although I had to wear a black chadoor even at a very young age, my mother could never force me to cover my face and hair. She always warned me that if a stranger saw my face or hair now, on Eternity Day I would be hung in hell by one strand of hair. I would reply, "My dear mother, let them hang me with a handful of hair so that I will never fall into the hellfire."

*R-L My aunt Marzyeh, her two daughters
Malak and maliheh wearing chadoors*

The school's atmosphere was perfect. The majority of the students brought lunch boxes and remained in school to study or play "pink-pank," the most common exercise of the time. All subjects except math had to be memorized. The foreign language taught was French. Every night until 1 or 2 am I studied in the living room that was lit with a kerosene lamp while everyone else in the house went to bed about 8 pm.

At the end of the school year we had a single exam for each subject. For those who didn't pass, there was another exam at the end of the summer, allowing them to use their summer vacation to study and try to improve their grade. If they failed again, they had to repeat the same class and the same subjects again. For this reason, every student and her parents were very concerned about the exam. I tried to study very hard during the week of exams as I was competing against the other students for the highest grades. When the exam was over, the students were ranked according to their GPA and the one with the highest score was selected to skip the eighth grade and enroll in ninth grade. That year I was the one selected; but I had to get my mother's consent. Although it was a very happy moment for me, it was not easy for me to obtain my mother's consent; she was directly under the influence of her sister. It took me a week to convince her. She tried to think of a thousand excuses; she kept asking me what my plans were; why was I such a naughty person; why couldn't I be obedient to her wishes? I wasn't brave enough to tell her that "her wishes" were not hers but her sister's, who always brainwashed my mother about the country reforms and changes in the lifestyle of Iranians under the modern government. If my mother let me do whatever I asked for, it would be against the family rule.

Finally after begging and nagging again and again, my mother decided to go to school and give her consent personally as she couldn't write (although she could read a bit). She went to school with me but talked privately with the Superintendent. The Superintendent and most of my teachers who were present in the main office did their best to convince my mother to agree. At last she did and I enrolled in the ninth grade.

That year was the beginning of social reform. The Reza Shah brought his wife wearing a French style dress and his two daughters to a ceremony held in the teacher's training school. All high-ranking officials that were invited brought their wives in European style dress, with beautiful French hats and gloves on. From that moment on, the majority (95%) of Iranian women gave up their chadoors and attended ceremonies in European dress; in fact they no longer wore chadoors wherever they went. The remaining minority (5%) who were very religious by heart decided not to leave their homes during the daytime. Wherever they wanted to go, they went after dark wearing long black robes, black scarves under hats and gloves to cover as much as they could. My mother's side of the family was among that minority.

Me wearing a European-style dress in 1936

This reform was so strong, sudden and definite that all religious, old-fashioned parents were under severe shock. They became hard on their girls and tried to control them as much as possible; I was not exempt. I wanted the freedom to tell my mother whatever I thought but she was not receptive. If I insisted, she wouldn't tolerate it and assumed I was being disobedient; she would become sad and touchy. I loved her so much that I didn't want to make her uncomfortable. I tried to accept whatever she wanted; I tried to surrender because I was afraid that I might lose my education.

I was the youngest student in the ninth grade and a follower of the most modern classmates. I wished I had a hat that I could wear every day as my other classmates but I wasn't brave enough to ask for it. Two weeks after school had started, Shirine, one of the girls who sat beside me and became my close friend came to school wearing a beautiful hand-woven black and white hat that attracted my attention. I asked her where she bought it and was told her sister made it for her. She

EMANCIPATION, REVOLUTION, AND OPPRESSION

said she would ask her sister to make one for me and the next day told me I should buy the yarn and take it to her house. Her sister was much older than Shirine. I later came to realize that her main purpose to agree to make the hat was to meet me and somehow to let her brother who was looking for a girl to marry to also see me. Innocently I told my mother I wished for some black and white yarn for my art work. The next day mother brought me the yarn and I took it to school with me.

I waited for Shirine to tell me when I should go see her sister and learn to make the hat. In the middle of the week one of the teachers was sick and our afternoon class was cancelled. Shirine asked me to go home with her; it took only a half hour to learn to make the hat. And since her house was on my way home, I could still be home on time without telling my mother. Her sister taught me to make the hat. That night I neither studied nor went to bed until the hat was finished and decorated. The next morning my mother was quite surprised when she saw the hat. She told me it was beautiful but asked me to promise not to wear it in public. I took the hat to school with me in my school bag to show to Shirine. The teacher was absent again and the class cancelled. We had two hours before the next class started so Shirine and I decided to go to a nearby photo shop and have a photo taken wearing the hats. I didn't have enough money to ask for a photo larger than a 2 x 3. The photo was ready the next week and Shirine brought it to me. I left it in one of my books. Mother almost always searched my books and she found the photo.

Me with my mysterious hat, 1935

At the same time, Shirine's mother sent a message to my mother via one of our neighbors. The message was: If my mother was interested in letting her daughter (me) marry a good Army officer, her son was very much interested in me. My mother had always said she didn't want any of her daughters to marry an Army officer because they might be sent to duty in another city far from Tehran or to the border to fight the enemy and her daughter would be taken away from her. Therefore, her answer to the messenger was "Definitely, no." Especially after she found my photo. She became so mad and frustrated that when I came home that day, without asking me anything or allowing me a chance to explain, for the first time in my life she slapped my face with all her power. I will never forget the multiple colors sparkling before my eyes. She said, "Do you want me to die from shame? Is that what you promised?" She was sure the message from Shirine's mother was related to a conspiracy between me and Shirine's brother. The hat was confiscated and I never ever saw it again. I didn't see the photo again until I found it in my mother's wardrobe ten years later.

Today, seventy years later, I have no idea where Shirine and her brother are living. I can honestly say that the entire incident was in my mother's imagination. I never saw her brother, not even his photo. But the incident caused me such an ugly-arranged marriage. I believe it was my fate, not the result of my mother's frustration, because a year after mother died, my sister married an Army officer and lived like a queen in the Garden of Heaven for 60 consecutive years as happy as anyone could be.

CHAPTER 3

Iranian Political Reform During My Childhood

The first Iranian political reform was started long before my birth. It wasn't an overnight revolution but occurred slowly with step-by-step movements of a simple and ordinary Iranian soldier, Reza Khan who seized political power in 1921, one year after I was born. On December 15, 1925, four years after the coup d'etat that ended the Ghajar Dynasty, he took his imperial oath and became the first Shah of the Pahlavi dynasty. With this reform, Iran moved toward modernization, resulting in very great changes in the infrastructure of the country as well as the life style of the Iranian people.

From January 7th, 1935 onward, when Reza Shah took his family out in public in Western dress - without veils - the new modern dress code applied to both men and women. Men wore suits and French style hats (chapeaux) instead of long robes and turbans or Egyptian hats. The school uniforms were a gray cotton material with white bow, collar and cuffs for girls and white shirt for boys. There was no compulsory uniform requirement for the students in higher education. In a country where women in public were usually covered from head to toe by chadoors, where their hair was never exposed to the eyes of men other than family members (father, brothers, nephews), the new Western dress code ordered by the Reza Shah was unpleasant for the more religious people, including my mother and her very religious relatives.

In contrast, all of my father's family was in favor of the new dress code and modernization and I loved their attitude but it was entirely against my mother's wishes. This was a big area of family controversy at an early stage of my life (between 10 and 12) with two antagonistic family groups. Since I was very young, I was the follower of modern style with my father; but I couldn't say anything derogatory about the old ways in the presence of my mother's side of the family, especially in front of my aunt who believed I was a rebel girl, not acceptable to the public eye in those days. That fact caused me to be pressed into an arranged marriage shortly thereafter.

In general, women who were very religious decided to remain in the confinement of their homes and wouldn't go into public unless they had to, and then only with their own style of cover. Religious ladies like my mother made a long robe and a round fabric hat with fabric pleated around to cover her face and wore black gloves to cover her hands instead of scarf or chadoor, which was now forbidden. Although my half-sisters and -brothers and their families admired my attitude (I was almost the youngest among them), they all preferred to remain silent and play neutral and not to interfere with my mother's opinion. My middle brother (Hadi) whom I loved dearly acted as my father and tried to convince my mother that I should be allowed to adopt the Western dress. But she assumed he wanted to take me into his custody as his own and separate me from her. This was another and probably the most important reason for my arranged marriage. My mother never accepted his idea; although they had high respect for each other they tried to keep their distance from each other.

My brother Hadi in his 1930s-style clothes

As I clearly remember, at that period the entire country became active and moved toward modernization. By the expansion of narrow paths into two- or three-lane streets from the north to the south and east to west in Tehran and the arrival of the railroad connecting the Caspian Sea in the north to the Persian Gulf in the south, the country changed from an underdeveloped to a modern country in a short period of time. Electricity, telephone and telegraph systems were developed for the first time, paralleling the development of higher education and the establishment of Tehran University, modern hospitals, a nursing school, compulsory education and the formation of different banks and other modern businesses - all required a well-educated populace specialized in every aspect. Therefore the Iranian government decided to send a group of high school graduates abroad for higher education in different specialized areas and for the first time to pay their expenses and scholarships.

Although many Iranian aristocrats and businessmen used to send their sons for higher education to Russia, France,

Germany and England and paid their expenses themselves, these individuals were usually descendents of the Ghajar Dynasty merchants or landowners, not ordinary people. Persian carpets, turquoise, caviar and similar products were common exports while imports including sugar, wheat and other such goods were also very important. The importation of wheat, regular sugar and sugar cubes from Russia and Belgium was a very hot subject at home during my childhood. Every year the country's progress was very obvious. Fortunately I could read the newspaper and understand the activity of the government all over the country. The control of the internal war as well as the considerable progress of the government in all directions made the younger generation proud of whatever had been accomplished by Reza Shah.

During this first reformation, which I believe was more constructive than the second revolution (entirely destructive), my parents lost a considerable amount of money, which indirectly affected my sister Azam and me. In those days neither modern court nor banking systems were established in Iran. The court system was based on mediation and the majority of the mediators were clergies. People were conducting business transactions based on their verbal promises. The bank system was based on individual trust. There was no printed note for currency. Only silver and gold coins were used. The money exchange was accomplished through a group of merchants called "Sarafs;" people would bring their silver coins for exchange with gold coins or vice versa. People kept small amounts of money at home but they handed larger sums of money to trustworthy individuals (usually friends) who had large safe areas in their homes and were just keeping the sealed bags in their safes as a favor. The recipient never counted the deposited money; nor was a receipt note handed to the owner. My father sold a very valuable property and took the proceeds to one of his close friends who was a member of the Ghajar Dynasty and a very famous and trustworthy individual. Two days later his friend died unexpectedly of a heart attack in his sleep. He had four sons and two daughters who collectively denied my father's claims and threatened him that "if you pursue your claim you will receive a hot bullet in your cold head. When my mother said my 76 years old father went to mediators, he was told to think of his safety rather than his money and they discouraged him to follow-up. The second incident happened when I was fifteen and my sister Azam was thirteen, part of our land and home was confiscated by the government to widen the adjacent street. During this disastrous period, I have no idea whether the government did not attempt to pay for the loss or my mother was unaware she could have applied for it. She was influenced by some neighbors who told her not to go close to the city government office. They told her if she did, the government would fine her and charge her a lot of money for the upgrade of our house because the building was left intact. Therefore she tried to remain silent. In my unhappy state, unaware of my surroundings, I tried to convince mother to consult someone else rather than the neighbor; I suggested she ask the three neighbors who lost their houses completely but unfortunately no one knew where they had moved. There was no way to find them to learn about their fate with the city officials. My 92-year-old father worried over this and developed severe asthma that we all believed would cause him to suffocate at any moment. Finally my mother decided to sell the house and get rid of all the problems. My middle brother (Hadi) decided not to interfere personally so he sent a message to my father and advised him not to be in a hurry to sell the property. But my parents, especially my mother, ignored his advice and decided to put an end to the stream of realtors that came one after the other to try to convince them to sell. The house had historical value and still exists but it was sold for one-tenth the amount of its value and the first buyer sold it one week later for ten times more.

My brother Hadi in new style clothes, 1936

How the times have changed. It is hard to imagine the extent of damage due to the amount of pride and the lack of knowledge of my parents, refusing the advice of their children regardless of their ages and the level of their responsibilities (in contrast to the present status of parents who often consider their children's proposals no matter how young they are). This wasn't the only episode in those confusing days when their minds were occupied with whatever had happened around them one after the other. I believe it was a lack of their ability to think in the right way, to consult with knowledgeable people and then take action.

I clearly remember the day that my mother was talking to my aunt about an investment; I was 18 years old and had two children. I told them I had read in the newspaper that a piece of land in the northern part of Tehran was for sale for one hundred tooman (equivalent to thirty five dollars) for every 10,000 square meters. I had collected and saved enough money to buy a section. They both laughed and told me, "You are still a child, how can you think about such big business?" I was not allowed to make the purchase.

A few months later my mother took a good chunk of money (maybe twenty times more than what I told them) and invested it. She took a large house as collateral and agreed to receive the interest in the Islamic way, which meant she should receive interest as "rent" because in Islam interest is forbidden. After a year, the monthly rent payment was no longer sent to my mother. When she asked why, the person told her to take the case to court. My mother, who was against the modern dress code and didn't want to appear in public, hired an attorney who was also a mullah and the one who recommended the investment to her. After about six months and payment of large attorney fees, Mother was convinced that all her money was gone with the wind. In addition, it was determined that the house used as collateral belonged to someone else rather than the person to whom she loaned her money. The entire "Islamic" business was nothing more than a trick. She became sad, frustrated and disappointed for a few days. Then she accepted the big loss and said, "This was my faith and I am sure God will eventually punish them."

Iran Post World War II

While Iran was rapidly growing, developing and making real progress, the Second World War had its effects on Iran. Although the Reza Shah's government announced its neutrality, the United Kingdom and the Soviet Union feared that Reza Shah was about to align his petroleum-rich country with Nazi Germany during the war so they occupied Iran and forced Reza Shah to abdicate in favor of his son. The political necessity of replacing the very wise and powerful Reza Shah with his twenty-year old son Mohammad Reza (the late Shah) resulted in serious but silent turmoil. Reza Shah went into exile in Mauritius, then Johannesburg, South Africa, where he died in 1944.

About that time numerous European and Russian ladies with their children immigrated to Iran and Coalition Army soldiers invaded Tehran and other cities. The population increased considerably in a country whose style depended on many imported items from abroad. This caused not only a serious food ration but also the spread of many diseases including serious typhoid and typhus that killed many Iranians including my twenty-one year old cousin Mohammad, who was my best friend and childhood playmate. UNICEF, the Red Cross and other American organizations tried to help the Iranian people but the Iranians weren't used to the kind of food offered, and they believed real Muslims should not accept any donations from non-Muslims.

I clearly remember two incidents concerning food rationing. One was bread that the government distributed to schools for the students, staff and teachers. The bread was so rough and hard to chew; you could see all the seeds that were mixed with the flour. I recognized canary seed as well as chicken seeds of different colors. The kids loved bread and we used to have a special food recipe that sometimes required bread. One of our nannies used to make bread for us at home. My mother and my husband decided to buy some rice and flour and store it in case the situation got worse; then we could use it. Because we had a big back yard, we tried to keep some hens and a rooster for eggs, so we had to feed them, too. My sister and I decided to accept our share of the distributed "loaf of bread" to feed to the chickens. One morning the nanny came to my mother and reported all the birds appeared to be dead. With great surprise we went to their cages and found them breathing but entirely asleep and inactive. We thought that either a scorpion or a snake bit them and my mother told us to let them die in peace.

My sister and I left the house and went to school. I was the school record-keeper in high school and my sister was a third grade teacher at the primary school. Our schools were located in two different parts of town. On that specific day my school had a lot more absentees than any other day and in my sister's area many students were sleeping in the classrooms while their teachers were lecturing. I usually returned home at 2:30 and my sister at 4:30. That day when I returned home I found my sister had come home early. She was crying hard and telling the story of her students in class - most of them fell asleep so their parents or the school keepers were called to take them home. We were all wondering why this was happening. That evening, the radio announced ergot seed had been found in the bread flour that caused a deep sleep and all the schools would be closed for one week. Because of the situation with the children, we forgot all about the birds. The next morning we found them in the back yard eating and playing happily. Fortunately in this terrible incident, all the children came out safely.

The second food problem that I was directly involved with was the distribution of egg yolk powder from UNICEF for all the staff, school keepers, and their families. This is such a vivid memory it seems like it happened only yesterday. I was in charge of the distribution of egg yolk powder. I wrote 2-3 kinds of recipes and started distributing them with the powder. I had to offer the yolk powder according to the number of family members. I first called Mr. Jamshidi who had ten children and told him he could take as much as he and his children could consume. I handed him three pages of hand-written recipes. (In those days there were no copy machines in Iran.) He said, "I cannot read the recipes but I will ask my son to read them to my wife. What kind of food is it?" I said, "It's egg-yolk powder." He looked at me and said, "Thank you, but we don't know how to eat powdered yolk." I told him the three pages of recipes in his hand explained how to use it. He said, "Lady, we don't want to eat and go to sleep forever this time." He refused because after the bread incident, he was afraid to try anything else. I kept calling the other gatekeepers; but they also refused to take any. So I had to report to the school principal. She told me that we couldn't send it back; if we did they might never give us anything else that the people might need in the future. And so we decided to keep it a secret and discarded it in the trash.

During World War II Iran became known as the "Turquoise Bridge" because railroads and surface roads were developed linking the Persian Gulf to the Caspian Sea as a major route for American help to reach Russia until the war ended. It took between 10 and 12 years to repair all the damage that resulted from the development of that transportation network. At the end of the war Iran again reached for a level of stability one day at a time. The period of progress began and continued for 27 years. Then the second revolution started. In fact, this revolution caused nothing but destruction, bloodshed, execution, confiscation and many, many more atrocities like no one could imagine. If comparing the reform and the revolutions with the 56-57 intervening years - in the first, a simple ordinary soldier Reza Khan pushed and pulled a bankrupt third-world country with an almost 98% illiterate, fanatic and inactive population with only one school of higher education ("Dar Al Phanoon") toward modernization and industrial development. It is hard to imagine the second revolution, where a rich country with all forms of construction, development and performance, with numerous schools of higher education, universities and modern hospitals and millions of educated and well-trained people could be pulled **back** in time 50 or 60 years and how a handful of revolutionaries were able to mentally destroy the well-educated masses so they didn't understand the difference. During the first revolution, those who were political opponents of the system were trapped in difficulty. During the second revolution, many thousands of well-educated, well-trained, well-known, innocent people were executed with no trial. Their families were forced to evacuate and the revolutionaries were able to confiscate their valuables. The confiscated goods were not for the benefit of the poor but to increase the wealth of the revolutionaries. Those who became aware of the savage situation escaped the country and left everything behind; they believed that some day this uncivilized storm would slow down and they could go back and save whatever they had. But as soon as the revolutionaries found that the owners had left Iran, they plundered property and confiscated whatever they wanted. I know this to be true, as it happened to some of my closest relatives by other close ex-relatives. I have a link to one cruel person who did such unforgettable, shameful actions. I myself was not exempt from the savage victory of the revolutionaries. Five days after the execution of my friend Dr. Farokhroo Parsay, a pediatrician and the Secretary of Education, I had to leave Tehran in a very fearful, sad and unpleasant manner. I left on May 13, 1980 on an Iran Air flight from Tehran to London. My two granddaughters Shaparak (11?) and Shayma (10?) accompanied me.

CHAPTER 4

Marriage Drama

It was the winter of 1935, the same year that we faced so many complicated dramas that happened one after another in a chain of events. My oldest cousin gave birth to her first child and got a severe infection caused by her irresponsible midwife. She became so ill that her mother (my aunt) had to leave her 8 children behind and went to take care of them, both child and mother. In those days there were no antibiotics available; therefore the mortality rate among mothers after childbirth was very great. My healthy grandmother went to her daughter's house to take care of her 8 grandchildren. Unfortunately, after 2 weeks she became sick. When my mother got the news about her mom, she decided to go to her sister's house to take care of her sick mother and 8 nieces and nephews. The status of Grandma became worse day after day and she died from pneumonia 2 weeks later. Meanwhile my mother came down with severe zoster (hives). In that horrible situation my older cousin (17) and I (13) were the only ones to accept the care-taking responsibilities. She started taking care of her two younger sisters and four brothers and I took care of my sick mother, younger sister and old father - **and** went to school and attended classes every day.

While we had enough maids to do the cooking, cleaning, entertaining, etc., I don't think we were that rich. The general situation was so poor that most people were happy if they could just live with a good family in a nice place to work, receive free room and board and collect some money for their future life. In such a stormy and disastrous family time, during Grandma's funeral and after, one of my mother's cousins (Grandma's niece) who was looking for a good girl to marry her son, kept visiting my mother day after day, brainwashing her by telling so many good things about her son. My mother who always suffered from malaria and now from severe zoster, the recent loss of her mother and the illness of her beloved niece became so depressed and weak she assumed she would die soon. If this happened, her stepchildren would try to take care of her husband (our father) and leave her two daughters (me and my sister) behind. I am sure she lost her abilities to make up her mind, especially about her cousin's proposal. She consulted her sister (my aunt) who herself was trapped in the middle of her daughter's life and death situation. My aunt was a very old-fashioned, religious fanatic, always against education and very much pro-arranged marriage. Therefore, she agreed with my mother about their cousin's idea (for an arranged marriage for me).

Arranged marriages were very common, especially among religious families. They believed love developed after marriage not before; if it occurred before it would be satanic love. The boy was introduced to the girl by showing his photo and the mother, sisters and the rest of his family described the girl's character to the boy. Girls should not have any photos of themselves. I had a photo of myself with a fancy hat on that was confiscated by my mother for many years and I am sure it was the basis of the punishment for such an unwanted, forceful arranged marriage. Mother was so convinced that she did not want to talk to anyone except her sister. My father gave up all his authority, power and decision and left everything to my mother's hand; therefore, she was the only one to decide about my future life. My brother Hadi, who really acted as father to me, kept talking to my mother to convince her to stop this process; but she was adamant. Since Hadi failed, he left us with great anger and didn't come to visit our father for rather a long period of time. Other brothers, sisters and the rest of father's family protested the marriage and didn't attend the wedding ceremony.

At that point in time - the end of the school year and beginning of state exams - I was like an active bird trapped in a strong cage, no door to escape, no place to go and no one to talk to. Everyone believed that because of the government reform I became a rebel while in truth I had no heart to argue and disagree with my mother at that stage of her convalescence. I tried to keep myself busy with exams and ignore all their activity but it wasn't possible. Thinking of my future going down the drain made me terribly ill, frustrated and angry. I was so depressed, crying all the time; I stopped eating for three weeks. I lost a lot of weight; my skin color became pale and yellow. Finally I found they were talking about hiring an exorcist to bring me down and take the anger out of me. At that point I thought I'd better surrender and cooperate with them at least temporarily until I found a way to get out, which I eventually did. Everyone was surprised and believed a miracle happened before their horrible exorcism was performed. They set the wedding date and sent their invitations.

In those days no invitation cards were available. The customary way to invite guests was to have a non-relative deliver invitations to each person by presenting a small plate filled with white sugar-coated fine pieces of almond with a few jasmine flowers on top of the plate, covered with a very nice hand-embroidered napkin. There were no telephones to use to call and make an appointment. The person delivering the invitations would just knock at the door of every person, enter the house and sit with the lady of the house after having tea or a soft drink. She opened the napkin in front of lady and told her who was going to marry whom on such a date and indicated that the lady and her family were invited. This process took at least 10-15 days because the poor women had to go from one family to the other by foot and were only able to visit 8-10 families a day.

According to Iranian custom, one of the big rooms of the house was decorated for the wedding. The bride and groom who never met or talked to each other would sit in front of a tall mirror and a mullah would read some Arabic words to marry them. There were always two wedding days, one for the bride and one for the groom. The groom had to go alone to the male reception to be introduced to the male guests. The next day the female reception took place and the bride and the groom had to go together to that reception to receive the female guests. They had to sit on chairs decorated with flowers and placed at a designated spot. In the woman's reception, the only male was the groom. In my case the male and the female receptions took place on the same day and at the same time because of the city street construction and the destruction of our property. We arranged to have the male reception held at the next-door neighbors' house.

Meantime my father received government notice that he should give up half of the backyard for expansion of the main street passing from east to west of town. The demolition date overlapped with the wedding date. It was another sad day for all of us. We used to live in a very spacious French architecture house with a big garden and pond. The building remained intact and it still is. It was crucial to convince the demolition group to postpone their plans. My father decided to go himself, to bribe them to stop for a few days. They accepted my father's request but insisted on demolishing the most upper part of the east side wall to show that the government order was being applied. Three days before the wedding that part of the wall went down. The next day a group of workers started to hand wash all the trees and bushes and collect all the dirt from the backyard and to make it ready for the ceremony.

After much continuous crying and 21 days of complete hunger strike, I lost my ability fight my fate. I had to surrender because no one could convince my mother to change her mind about my marriage. Finally I decided to accept her order, say yes to my destiny and marry the stranger I had never met or spoken to. According to Iranian customs of the day, a room was decorated for the wedding and the front yard was arranged and well prepared for the reception. While the preparation of the wedding room is still a common custom, a lot of modern ideas have been added to it in recent times.

On that horrendous wedding day, I felt more like a robot than a bride. The groom, Hossain Amir Hessami, a complete stranger to me, entered the room where I was seated all alone in a chair in front of a very tall and wide mirror. He sat on the chair next to me and said "Hello." That was our first communication of any kind. I answered with a deep and shaky voice without looking at him or turning my face toward him. The room was so quiet that it appeared to be vacant but it was my heart not the room that was so empty of feeling except for hate and anger. His niece who was about 5-6 years old, good-looking, talkative and well dressed like a doll entered the room, jumped on his lap and started talking to him. For a moment I felt the taste of freedom from such an ugly moment but it wasn't long before the mullah starting reading some Arabic to prepare us for the dreaded wedding vows. No photos were taken of the wedding because it was not common to do so at that time.

After the wedding prayer was finished we had to go to the front yard where all 300 invited guests were seated in chairs in a single circle around the yard. We walked around and greeted them all, then went to sit on our two designated chairs next to each other. As we sat down I preferred to talk to my friend Shirine who was seated next to me rather than to him. While I was talking to her, the groom, the only male among all the female guests, felt ignored and silently left – I didn't even notice. When I finally heard whispering and laughing, I turned my face and saw his vacant chair.

Today, it is more than 70 years or over 25,550 days since that crazy day. I have to be honest to say that he was very handsome - but not in my eyes. He was from a very prominent family - but that was no reason to create love in my heart. He was very kind and generous - but to me he appeared tough and touchy. He was reserved and easy going - I was very active and serious. He loved to enjoy his life free from the duties and responsibilities of his family and his business - I was anxious to make everything occur on time and to challenge all the barriers of life.

The next day after the wedding, the demolition started again. The polluted dusty environment forced everyone to leave their properties. My parents decided to go to my aunt's house temporarily; I had to go to my husband's house. The 5-room house was very clean and had been recently painted. Three rooms were furnished with the furniture my mother sent for my husband and me, the other two rooms were for my in-laws (mother, her other son and a young girl servant). After three months, about the time I was feeling the first signs of pregnancy, I overheard talk that we had to move to a small old house. I asked my husband why we had to move out and he told me the landlord wanted to move in; we had no other choice. My mother found out that the house had only been rented for three months. Surprisingly, my mother became remorseful, disappointed and sad, but it was too late - I was pregnant. She decided to take my husband and me to her own home. Therefore we moved to my parents' house, where I lived permanently. Nine months later my first daughter, Minoo, was born on June 6, 1937. A year later I lost my father who died of pneumonia at age 94.

Two years after my father's death, I decided to apply for a teaching job. I had only a ninth grade or middle school diploma. But due to the shortage of teachers and the new method of teaching, middle school graduates could have a year of training and be eligible for teaching first graders. Everyone in the family was against my idea except my husband. I tried hard to convince them of my idea to register for training. In the meantime, I became pregnant with my second daughter Nikou. It wasn't an easy pregnancy. After three months I developed asthma, which consumed me for 5 months with much coughing and uncomfortable breathing. No antibiotics were available in Iran. Finally, I recovered during the last month of the pregnancy and had an easy delivery.

After a year I felt miserable. I couldn't tolerate sitting home doing nothing day after day. I tried to keep myself busy making dresses for the children, weaving, doing embroidery and artwork, but it wasn't enough for me. Although everyone was against my idea, I applied for a teaching job and became a first grade teacher. Minoo was 5 years old and had finished kindergarten. I registered her in my class - I became her first grade teacher.

During this period of time Mother became ill, suffering from liver disease after a four month pilgrimage to the holy city of Karbalah, Iraq. Then Nanny (Nikou's babysitter) that we all trusted highly died suddenly. This caused a great deal of sadness and it was very difficult to find a replacement for her, so I decided to apply for the position of school record-keeper because of my responsibilities at home. Meanwhile, I became pregnant for the third time. It was an easy pregnancy but not an easy delivery. I was close to death due to serious bleeding resulting from placenta previa that happened at home not at the hospital. Fortunately, the baby was delivered safely and named Nikrou. As a result, I was bedridden for a month.

After three months leave of absence, I went back to work. The school principal was easy on me; she wanted the work done and the results completed on time, so I would bring the paperwork home with me to finish while I was taking care of my mother and children, supervising nannies, etc.. Life was going on; the children were growing up. My sister finished her teacher's training and became a third grade teacher. Instead of me sending Nikou to kindergarten, my sister took care of her at her school. At age five Nikou passed first grade with the highest grade. But according to the education law she was too young (not yet six) and they didn't accept her in the second grade. I tried hard to get a waiver for her and I finally did. Since then, that age law has been abolished.

During this period my mother felt rather well for some time; but during the fall and especially winter she suffered from asthma, edema, kidney failure and a heart problem. Her physician, our next-door neighbor, used to visit her every other day; I was at her service day and night. My sister was taking care of the other matters at home. After six years of this situation and a rather long period of chronic illness, Mother suffered a serious stroke one morning at breakfast. Her doctor visited her immediately but she was in a deep coma that lasted 21 days. When she came out of it and became fully conscious, we found that the left side of her body was paralyzed. There was no physical therapy or similar treatment in those days to assist in her recovery. With time, she recovered and became functional again, but she continued to suffer from liver, kidney and heart discomfort all the time. She died at age 62 after eight years of suffering. During that same week I lost one of my nephews at age 29 who suffered from a congenital heart defect. It was not easy to lose two members of the family in one week.

My Married Life

In general, my husband and I were at opposite ends of the earth. When I became pregnant, I told myself he could no longer be a stranger; I'd better love him because he would be the father of my child. But the distance between us was so great that no sign of love whatsoever appeared in my heart. There was not a single bit of his attitude that I could tolerate, so I didn't mind how he spent his time. At night he would spend a number of quiet hours in a bar drinking vodka (prohibited in the home) and often came home after midnight to face my ignoring him. I never asked him why he came home so late or why he arranged trips with his friends and their families. He knew that I didn't like to mingle with them. I was very happy to spend time with my children and my mother and sister Azam under the old rule of our house. His easygoing manner and kind heart especially toward less fortunate people made him spend or give away much of his money without questioning or investigating the situation of anyone who asked for help. He often lost all his money without questioning or follow-up with the borrower. Whenever this happened our standard of living fluctuated. That was very hard on me but he didn't seem to mind. He always said, "God is great. He will compensate someday some way." This was repeated time after time. At first I tried not to argue with him because of my mother. We were living in her house and I was afraid she would overhear us, despite the fact that the house was very large with five bedrooms, two living rooms, a dining room, a guest room and two furnished basements.

Hossain Amir Hessami, 1944

I didn't want our children to know anything about the lousy relationship between us. So I had no choice but to cope with whatever happened. I tried to keep my face strong and my mind active enough to handle it all and let no one know my internal problems - rather hard to do. My mother understood more than any other member of the family what was going on in my life; it was on her mind. She kept asking and sometimes begging me not to think of divorce before she died. She felt a heavy guilt because she had ignored my constant crying and my three-week hunger strike in the middle of state exams; she had ignored the repeated demands of my half-brother Hadi to stop the damn arranged marriage. She realized her mistake just 3 months after the marriage was finalized.

I felt I was trapped in the net of nature and tried to cope with it and not cause any more shame and frustration for my mother toward her step family, especially her step-son Hadi. On the other hand, I wanted my girls to grow up to be able to take care of themselves in case of my separation or divorce. Above all I didn't want my job and especially my education to be interrupted again. Therefore, I tried hard to keep the family structure intact in a very smooth and quiet way with a great dignity – an eventual impossibility.

My husband was very kind but extremely naïve with regard to his friends and the less-fortunate people who worked for him. He spent as much money as he wanted with no limitation or budgeting. He was in the business of exporting Persian carpets to Europe, especially to Germany. This business thrived after the Second World War. But due to his mishandling he became bankrupt three times in the 15 years we were married. Each time that it happened it was very hard on me and it took a long time to recover. Because of his male chauvinistic nature and our age difference, he never believed in me. I tried to convince him to be more careful in business, to limit his trust of those middlemen who were experts in ripping people off and not to deal with

Our two daughters: Nikou (L) age 3 and Minoo (R) age 6

those who wanted to buy today and pay later. But unfortunately he didn't seem to learn from past mistakes. Little by little I was worn down and finally lost my patience after my mother's death and his third bankruptcy. I decided to ask for a divorce. Because of his laid-back manner, it took more than two years. In the end, in a very courteous manner with regard to the supervision of our children's education in my hand, the divorce was finalized in February 1952.

Our friendship continued. My family and I accepted him and his family. In the summer of 1963 I returned to Iran and he came to visit me. In March 1966 he sent me a Noruz card and asked me to take care of our three daughters more than ever. It was his last communication with me. He died of cancer less than a month later. God bless his soul.

About My Sister

Six months after my mother's death, my cousin Mehdi, one of my closest friends and childhood playmates, called and invited my sister and me to his house. I asked him what the occasion was to be. He laughed and replied "matching." I asked him who with whom. He replied, "A good friend of mine to your sister Azam." I kept questioning him, "Please tell me more about your friend." He said, "Don't be afraid, it's only an introduction of a young man to a young woman. Please tell me what you're so worried about." I told him I was nervous about the decision that his mother might make in the absence of my mother. He promised that he would never let what happened to me to be repeated again. He said the gentleman that I would meet that day was an Iranian military attaché in Baghdad. His name was Abbas and he had come to Tehran to pick up his formal military uniform because the Shah of Iran had accepted a formal invitation from King Faisel of Jordan to attend a regional meeting which would be held in April 1950. Abbas was to accompany the Shah from Baghdad to Jordan.

So at 4:30 in the afternoon on March 16, 1950, my sister and I went to my aunt's house. My cousin's friend Abbas arrived shortly afterward. He was young, rather tall – an attractive man in military uniform. We greeted each other formally and talked about many different things including world politics for about 45 minutes. Then he said he had to go pick up some things before the shops closed. He stood up and said goodbye in a military fashion and left. After a while, without any comments or advice from my aunt, my sister and I returned home, walking the long way and talking about the guy we had met, but not in a serious manner.

About 9:30 my cousin called and asked lots of questions about the afternoon's meeting. I asked him to be more specific in his questions, not vague and confusing. He asked me what Azam thought about his friend. I told him that she liked him and she thought their chemistry was compatible – he would be a "good catch." My cousin said that the reason he called was that Abbas said he was 50% sure at first glance. If Azam felt the same way and accepted his time limitations, it would be a perfect match. I told him that it would be better for Abbas to talk to Azam directly.

In a few minutes Abbas called and talked with my sister until midnight. They decided to get married in five days because he had to leave Tehran on March 27th. This was only four days before the beginning of Noruz, the Iranian New Year, and two or three days before the entire city started New Year's vacation, which often lasted thirteen days. During this period all schools, universities, offices and main businesses remained closed. So they only had two days to buy their bands, her wedding ring and other customary items. And I had only five days to arrange the wedding ceremony at home, including the wedding dress, dinner party, and the invitations.

Fortunately by this time we had a telephone so I asked my mother-in-law to come to the house and start preparing the invitations for the intimate (close) family members. I called the cook who used to come to the house and prepare meals for special occasions. He prepared a very delicious Iranian wedding meal complete with desserts.

In those days there were no ready-made wedding dresses. Because it was Noruz, the seamstresses that we knew were on vacation. I made Azam's wedding dress, which was sky blue silk lace, complimented with long gloves made from the same lace.

Despite the timing, things worked out. A total of fifty close personal friends and relatives, including all our brothers and sisters (who protested and boycotted my arranged marriage), attended the wedding ceremony on March 23rd. Everything was perfect except for the wedding bands. My husband had volunteered to take the bands to the jeweler to have the names engraved inside. I think both of them were drunk and didn't notice the difference in the ring sizes. So my sister's name was engraved in both rings. They didn't notice it at first and when they did, they never attempted to correct it.

The wedding ceremony started at 4 pm on March 23rd and ended at 2 am the following morning. At that time, everyone including the groom left the house. (It is customary for the bride and groom to stay apart until after the **entire** wedding ceremony and reception have been completed before they live together as man and wife.) My sister told me that Abbas would come for breakfast at 10 am so we had to clean the house. I suggested that we go to bed – I needed to get some sleep. Then with the help of the nannies, we made the house spotless before 10 am. The cook slept over that night and managed to clean up the kitchen mess and prepare a fancy breakfast. I asked him to stay for two more days to prepare lunch and dinner for our guests who came to the house. In those days high-class restaurants were rare in Tehran, at least I didn't know of any. Besides, the Persian custom didn't allow entertaining guests in restaurants. Everything was put in order. Many members of our family kept calling on the phone, asking why I had kept Azam's wedding a secret. I had to answer the question so many times every day, telling them that it was not a secret, it just happened all of a sudden.

Abbas had to return to Baghdad on March 27th, so the two of them had to make plans for their wedding reception. Early on March 26th, the morning news sympathized with the Jordanian nation because of the assignation of King Faisel during early morning prayers. The announcement of a 40-day period of mourning for the nation resulted in the cancellation of the April regional meeting. A single bullet from a crazy assassin destroyed whatever had been planned between the two countries. The Shah's trip was cancelled. The King of Jordan flew to the infinite. My new brother-in-law Abbas extended his stay to include a 15-day vacation and left Tehran April 12th instead of March 27th.

Finally Abbas and Azam found ample time to talk, to make up their minds and decide what their future plans would be, including their September 10th wedding reception. Our brother, who always acted as a father to us, proposed having the party in his beautiful rose garden outside of Tehran. Once again I made my sister's wedding gown, copied from a friend's wedding dress made by one of the most famous French-educated seamstresses. That year the color sky blue was the "in" color for bridal dresses. Therefore both of Azam's dresses were sky blue; the first one was made of silk lace and rather short; the second one was silk satin with a long skirt and glittered top. That summer, I did nothing but sew from early morning to late afternoon. Besides the wedding gown, I made a beautiful light pink satin dress for myself and three shades of pink taffeta dresses for my three daughters. I also made all the embroidered accessories and decorations for Azam's bedroom for her to take with her to Baghdad.

The wedding reception was held in a Japanese-style rose garden decorated with small electric lights around the trees and among the bushes. According to the style of that period, the bride and groom stood by the entrance door to welcome their guests. When the friend whose gown I copied entered and saw my sister's dress, she was in shock and started stuttering as she congratulated my sister. A week later, her sister-in-law (one of my closest friends then and even now) came to visit me to find out how I copied the dress. My friend had agreed to let me have the dress to copy but when I went to pick it up she reluctantly told me she had changed her mind. I explained to my friend that it had been very insulting to me. So I used what I had learned from the seamstress Tarbat Khanoom, looked closely at the dress, made a copy of it in my mind and used it immediately. My friend asked for a better, more detailed explanation. I told her that when she brought the dress and left in on the couch while she went to the kitchen to get me a cup of tea, I looked at it very carefully to see the style, the color, and the sleeve and not the rest of the dress. As soon as I got home I made a copy of the top with regular material and had my sister try it on. It was a good fit. The next day when I was completely relaxed, I started making the wedding dress. It fit perfectly. I told myself that I must forgive my friend for changing her mind and I did so.

Unfortunately there were no photographers to document those unforgettable moments – I have only memories. I always blamed myself for not calling the photographer. But at the time I was overwhelmed with all the things that had to be accomplished. To answer my children's questions and satisfy them; to take care of all the criticisms coming constantly from my mother's side of the family, protesting the mixed party, the French music and French food, and so many other points. No one realized that I was not the only one making the decisions. No one believed that most of this party was what my brother-in-law Abbas wanted to do, not me. Despite everything, the most beautiful wedding party was held in my brother's garden. All my mother's family with their critical, religious opinions and beliefs attended the ceremony. But they were relegated to the second floor living room where they could watch the entire garden party through tall glass windows on three sides of the room.

On September 20th my sister and her husband left Tehran for Baghdad in his Volkswagen. Fortunately they returned to Iran after only eight months due to government budget cuts based on the new Prime Minister's decision. This was very beneficial to me because my sister supervised my kids' homework and lived in the same house until their own home was built.

My sister was married to an exceptional person and lived in a very comfortable standard for 60 years. Every minute of that time was full of joy and happiness. Looking back, I want to emphasize that no one could predict some part of our future and analyze the power of fate in the qualities of everyone's living standards.

My sister Azam, son Faroukh,
daughter Firoozeh, and husband Abbas

My sister had two children and four grandchildren. Her three grandsons live in Iran at the present time. Her grand-daughter, Negar, lives with me in the US. She is my third adopted child.

CHAPTER 5

Adult Education

Although my children's education was at the top of my priority list, I could not just sit and think of my own future education without doing something. I had only a middle school diploma, a certificate for teaching first graders and a job as a record-keeper for the rest of my life. But I didn't want that nor did I want to be like other married housewives, sitting at home sewing and caring for the children, etc. And I certainly never **ever** wished to be a beautiful pigeon with a wrapped wing in a golden cage. I always wanted and challenged the ability to fly. But without further education how could I? In this case I had no wings to open and no strong muscles to contract to make flight easy, so I had to make a strong and determined decision to go for further education at the appropriate time.

By then, the children had grown up (12, 8, 4) enough to take care of themselves and each other; my sister supervised their homework at night with the help of two nannies who had lived with us for so many years. They were treated as members of the family and took care of the housekeeping and cooking, not easy tasks in those days. Everything was prepared from scratch and housekeeping was just as hard, too. There was no electricity and no electrical devices, no refrigerator, no hot water and no washing machine. Everything was done by hand.

At that time, I was working at a school as bookkeeper. The school was a combination of preschool, primary, secondary and high school with a total of 950 students. The school hours were 8-

12 am and 2-4 pm, in other words, no classes and no teachers from 12-2. Many students brought their lunch boxes and stayed at school at lunchtime, so they needed constant supervision. The school ruled that every office staff member had to remain one day from 12-2 pm and leave at 2 pm instead of 4, which was closing time.

I was always starving for additional education. At that point, I found enough time to go for it. I decided to attend adult night school and I registered in 12th grade for a home economics diploma. I had not completed 10th or 11th grade and I had been out of school for 12 years, so I had to work as hard as possible. The adult school was 6-10 pm for 5 successive nights each

Minoo   Nikou   Nikrou
My daughters in the fourth grade school uniforms

Teachers and staff of high school Parvin Ettsami where I worked and was also a student in adult school, 1950

week for 9 months, with a one-time state exam at the end of the year. In order to manage this, I first requested to stay all five days at lunchtime and leave my job at 2 instead of 4 pm. All my colleagues gave me a positive response. Today I am most grateful to them. Although most of them have passed away, I will never forget their help that provided a successful life for me today.

When classes started I had to attend from 6-10 pm for 9 months. I had to go by bus - but not directly; I had to walk one hour each way from home to the bus stop and from the bus station to school. After four months of going to school every night, one day with no reason I fell down on a smooth, flat surface and wound up with a broken metatarsus and stretched tendon, with a cast from my knee to my toes. It reduced the power of fast and easy walking; I had to use a cane. After this accident, instead of one hour it took me 2 hours to walk each way.

Working every day from 8-2, studying from 3-5, then leaving home again for night class from 5-11, I needed a lot of courage and energy. Looking back, I cannot imagine how I did it. The last three months of the school year passed without the cast on my foot but with a lot of pain and agony in walking. Finally the year ended, the state exam was set up for a week and the results announced after two weeks. I passed the exam with an acceptable GPA. Immediately I applied for Midwifery College that had always accepted home economics graduates. But after a few days I found out my application was denied because of a change in the acceptance policies. All applicants now had to be science graduates. I did not lose my hope and courage; I submitted my diploma to the educational division main office and requested a change of position from bookkeeping to assistant superintendent that had higher pay and greater status. It might be hard to believe, but despite all the responsibility and agony, I felt thirstier for further education.

Once again, I talked to my colleagues for help and they agreed. Fortunately, at that time because of government budget cuts, my sister and her husband returned to Iran. She was pregnant and they came to live in the same house where we both had lived for a long period of time. Although both nannies were still healthy and active, she started supervising the entire family again. She gave me a lot of encouragement and support that enabled me to continue my education. I registered for a science diploma in the adult school. This course of study was much harder than the year before. I had to study all subjects plus math, physics and chemistry from the 10th and 11th grades in order to understand what was taught in 12th grade. In other words, I had to study 3 years of high school subjects in one year. I hired 3 private tutors, one for each subject, and dedicated Thursday and Friday afternoons (the weekend) for studying math, physics and chemistry. My daughter Minoo was studying the same subjects with me because she was in the 11th grade. After six months of hard work at my job and in class I came down with pyelonephritis and had to be in complete bed rest at home for one month. I felt miserable. I couldn't think of anything except the classes that I was missing. I kept my books under my blanket and pretended I needed a quiet room to go to sleep. I started reading and memorizing as much as I could. This helped to occupy my thoughts, although I couldn't do as much as I was expected to. As soon as I recovered and was allowed to move around, I started going to class until the school year ended. State exams started and finished in one week. I was lucky enough to pass with an acceptable GPA to sit for the University entrance examination. At this time my sister gave birth to a wonderful daughter, Firoozeh, who is my best friend today.

I was not brave enough to announce my future plan to anyone except my sister and my children. I was afraid that if I didn't succeed I would have to face great criticism from everyone in my entire family. It was school summer vacation for 3 months and the best time for me to study all subjects from 7-12th grade. I read and memorized day and night until mid-summer. The University entrance exam was and still is very hard; it is like horseback riding or car racing - hard to compete with thousands of young, active recent high school graduate applicants when 99.5% of them were the same age as my daughter, Minoo. I registered for the biological sciences entrance exam that was held for three consecutive days. The results were announced in the newspaper and on the radio after thirty-five days. I was so hopeless that I forgot about it. Then one morning when I entered the school the doorkeeper congratulated me. I was so surprised. I asked him what for; he replied, "Don't you know? I heard on radio Tehran a while ago, you've been accepted at Tehran University College of Biology. You are #8 among a class of 150 accepted applicants." I became so thrilled when all my colleagues congratulated me. It was a great day for my family and me but I started worrying about how I could handle it. The University was far from my home and the school; I had to go by bus. All lecture classes were held in the morning and laboratories in the afternoon. Due to a recession and the bankruptcy of my husband I didn't want to quit my job. On the other hand, it was my only chance to enter the University. If I didn't register immediately I might lose my chance forever. I couldn't decide what to do, so I went to one of my private tutors who was one of the top authorities in the educational division and asked for advice. He told me, "Stop thinking. First go and register. You will receive the college schedule; then take it from there. Don't think of resignation from your work but manage it. There are many college students working quietly." I will be forever grateful to him.

Tehran University

In September of 1953, I registered at the University in the College of Biology and managed my working hours. I studied as hard as possible and passed all exams with great success and became class valedictorian. I must confess that it was not an easy job during that period. The school principal became hard on me. Sometimes she made my life miserable especially after Minoo graduated and left Iran for her nursing education in London. I gave the principal my college schedule at the beginning of every year. She knew my exam time, which was so crucial to me. Today, I only remember a few remarks she made. For example, all of a sudden she told me, "We have to announce all the exam results tomorrow at 8 o'clock. Therefore, all report cards must be ready and on my desk at 7 am." On another occasion she told me at 4 pm that all report cards had to be handed to the students before noon the next day, while she knew that I had to sit for exams in two subjects the day after. I replied, "No problem, if you let me take all cards and exam sheet results with me now." She agreed but I am sure she never believed I could do it in that short period of time, because there was not even a basic calculator available in those days. I started working at 5 pm and finished at 6 am. I didn't go to sleep for even five minutes. At 6:45 am when I sat in the bus on the way to work to leave all 950 report cards on her desk, I fell asleep so deeply that the person next to me had to wake me when we got to my bus stop.

Yet another unforgettable occasion happened during my last year of college. The principal assigned me as supervisor of the 12th grade final exams for two successive weeks that overlapped with the exact weeks of college final exams. This time I had no choice except to get help from the person above her. I asked for a short meeting with her master (supervisor). While I was waiting, the supervisor's assistant came out and called me by name. I went in and he told me, "Your job is suspended." I asked him why and he replied, "You spend all the time at the University; your daughter has gone to England and you never took your job seriously. Therefore you wasted government money." With great surprise I asked him, "Who gave you this report?" He told me, "You'd better ask yourself then me why you are here today." I replied, "With all honesty I worked as hard as one can and she is as hard as no one can imagine. I am here because I am desperate for help. She assigned me to be supervisor of the 12th grade exams while at the same exact time I have my last year finals at the University. If this is the case, I prefer to submit my resignation right away and go home to have peace of mind for my final exams." At that moment my eyes were full of tears and I was trying not to let them drop. He kindly told me there was nothing to worry about since the letter of suspension had not yet been signed. "When the report reached the main office, I was appointed to investigate. I found the truth of the matter. So I suggest you go see Mr. Kossari, the General Director for the Division of High School Education and tell him about this." I went to Mr. Kossari's office and asked his secretary for a 10-minute immediate appointment. Mr. Kossari was in his office but the door was closed. His secretary told me it was impossible to see him for even one minute. I asked "Why?" The secretary asked me didn't I know that state final examinations were in progress all over the country that month and Mr. Kossari was extremely busy and didn't want to be disturbed – no matter what. I tried to convince the secretary to let me have five minutes but he told me not to waste my time; I should come back the next month when Mr. Kossari would be free. Once again I faced another hard, rocky road to climb; I had to go forward. I told myself to be strong, not to be afraid, to make up my mind and find a way to pass smoothly. But I couldn't decide what to do. I was being pushed in two different directions – either lose my job and continue my education for a better future – or keep the job while dreaming for better, further education. I needed to keep my job to be in a better financial position. I also had to finish my exams according to schedule; otherwise I might lose countless opportunities.

While I was sitting on the bus to go see someone and ask for help, my mind was in a whirl. Suddenly I noticed two gentlemen seated next to me talking and criticizing the mayor's office. One of them advised the other, "Why don't you go to Mr. R. Hirad, the Shah's secretary; his office is open to everyone. Plus he himself helps make sure whose rights are in jeopardy and who is still eligible for his or her achievement." As soon as I heard that, I got off the bus at the next stop and changed my direction; I headed to his office. It was about 11 am. I called a taxi and went directly to Mr. Hirad's secretary, Mr. Kazemi, a polite young man. I requested five minutes for an urgent meeting with Mr. Hirad. He took my name to Mr. Hirad. About ten minutes later he came out and guided me into the office of the Shah's secretary, Mr. Hirad, a very respectable and rather old man, standing in the middle of the room. I greeted him and he kindly responded, then asked me what my problem was. I tearfully summarized the story. As I talked, he slowly moved toward his desk and picked up one of his business cards. He handed it to me and told me to go to Kossari's office right away and give the card to him. "The doorkeeper may not let you in, but you give him this card and tell him this is for Mr. Kossari. Then call my assistant Mr. Kazemi and let him know the results of your meeting." With much appreciation, I left his office. While walking toward the exit I looked at the card – it was blank, except for his name; he had written nothing on it. With great surprise and disappointment I left, called a cab, and gave directions to Mr. Kossari's office. When I got to the office it was 1:30 pm. His door was still closed and he was inside. I told the doorkeeper I wanted to go in and talk to him; I was referred to the secretary. I said. "I talked to him this morning. I am back again to talk to Mr. Kossari." He told me he was not allowed to let anyone in. I handed him the blank card and politely asked him to give the card to Mr. Kossari. He promised to place it on Mr. Kossari's desk. Then he looked at both sides of the card, realized the card was blank and asked me to write my name on it. I told him to take it as it was. He went inside the room and immediately came back and let me in. I told Mr. Kossari my story. He advised me to go to school and keep my job.

The next day I found that one of my colleagues replaced me for those two weeks of exams and I received four weeks leave of absence with full pay. I owe a great deal to Mr. Hirad for all my success, also to the gentleman who talked to me first and pointed me in the right direction. I don't remember his name; I didn't know him and I never met him again but I have never forgotten his true help, great concern and unforgettable kindness. I also owe Mr. Kossari for his prompt action.

I graduated as valedictorian in a class of 150 students in 1957. I received the gold Medal of Honor and a six-year government scholarship for further study abroad. Because of my personal experience, I always made a point to let my secretary know that I had an open door policy to let anyone in who wanted to see me without questioning, especially during the period that I was the Director General for Office of Teachers' Health and Welfare.

Valedictorian award certificate written in Farsi with a gold medal on the left corner, 1957

After all these happy moments, one day I felt a lump in my right breast. As you know how upsetting it may be, I decided to keep it to myself and made an appointment with our family physician that was a surgeon and university professor. He was the only one who had treated the entire family including myself since I was very young. When I met him he recommended immediate surgery. I agreed but not immediately because Nikou was preparing for University entrance exams that were to take place during the next two weeks. Those two weeks were a great hell for me. By the end of the first week I told my sister and prepared myself for the next week's surgery. Fortunately, the pathology report was a blue dome cyst not cancer. I happily recovered very fast and went back to work.

High School Principal

After a while the main educational division called and offered me a principal position, a very prestigious job. It was very special working as principal in a combined sciences and literature degree high school containing 7th – 12th grades in each division and 1200 students, 50 teachers, 12 classrooms, 3 dining rooms, 3 offices and 18 workers. I decided to accept the job since there was a great probability that the law approving the scholarships would never pass parliament or it would take a few years to be approved. I started working and proposed a lot of changes in the system of teaching, as well as necessary repairs and modernization of the classes, laboratories, and dining room, etc. I developed extracurricular activities and a training division for students who were working to go to college. In other words, students attended extra classes after school hours in preparation for University entrance exams. Parents were appreciative and the students were really happy.

After two years in this position the law and budget for government scholarships was passed by the parliament and announced to the government. I was one of the recipients of that scholarship award. It was the most important event of my life. I had to leave my two daughters behind (Minoo was already a student in England). I had to give up my position and definitely my job. I had to go somewhere that I was blind to its culture and mute to its language. How could I handle all the criticism, discouragement and many other fearful things imaginable? If I could not learn the language and challenge the higher education I would lose both my job and the award. I had to decide against all odds, regardless of all criticism and controversial ideas received from my old fashioned and religious family. Some predicted that I was ignoring my two daughters and I would lose them forever. Others said, "What is wrong with such a beautiful and prestigious position with great income?" I was diagnosed with grandiose ideas. The third group who were old age relatives said, "She has been out of her mind since her childhood." After all the discouragement that was sent directly or indirectly, I told myself, "Why should I lose this opportunity? God is going to help me as he did up to this point." So I made my final decision by giving up the job, leaving my two girls with my mother-in-law and their father and went to the United States to be a student once again.

Speaking to the students.
Wishing them success and saying goodbye, October 1959

101

I applied for acceptance on a form called an I-20 "Certificate of Eligibility for Nonimmigrant (F-1) Student Status" that I received from the University of Toledo (Ohio) for an English language course from the English Language Institute at the University of Michigan-Ann Arbor. I had no idea where I was going. I didn't know anything about the weather in the region; I had no one to ask about it. I decided to go wherever my fate took me. I must confess that I was unable to complete my own application; someone else did it for me. I realized I had no knowledge of any foreign language, so I hired a private teacher to teach me English. He was Iranian but had studied in England. He never taught me the every-day needs to communicate; his main area of teaching was grammar only and therefore I was completely at a loss for daily conversational English. Meanwhile I gave my 30-day notice of resignation and made an announcement to the students. My colleagues at the school gave me a very nice farewell party and invited the Secretary of Education as a surprise for me.

Three days before I left Tehran I had a car accident that resulted in two broken metacarpals in my right hand and a bloody nose. It was the other driver's fault; he drove too close to the bus and paid no attention to the stop sign. He took me to the closest hospital, left me in the emergency room and disappeared. The doctor fixed my hand by placing it in a cast, then hanging it around my neck.

Farewell gathering at high school. Dr. Mehran, Secretary of Education was present. October 1959.

Gathering in the office of Undersecretary Mr. Yzadon Far who facilitated our journey to the US, October 1959

CHAPTER 6

My Journey to America

After all the agony of intended separation, my family and I went to the Tehran airport. I planned to go to London and spend some time with Minoo who was a student there, then go from London to Paris to join the rest of the group of students. The airport was crowded with all the relatives and friends. Everybody brought a box of special candy or pistachios. No one considered how I would carry them all with me, regardless of my broken hand that they didn't know about. My sister, my two girls and other close relatives collected all the boxes to take home because I had no room and no use for them. Meanwhile, one of my professors appeared with two suede jackets made in France for his two daughters who were living somewhere in the United States. He wrote their addresses on a piece of paper, handed everything to me and asked me to mail them from the US. Then a lady that I knew ever since I became a principal appeared with a bag ready to mail containing a suit for her son. I told her, "I can't take it; you see one of my hands is in a cast." She started begging and crying and kept telling me, "Assume he is your son; you should do it." I gave up and I took it. Although my main luggage was gone, they put the 2 jackets and her bag in my overnight bag.

On October 8, 1959, I boarded the four-engine propeller-driven plane and left Tehran for London's Heathrow airport. After flying for too many hours to remember, I got to London and met with Minoo. She took me to the hotel. I planned to stay in London two weeks to spend some time with her and have a bit of rest after all the hard work. During that two weeks I started learning every-day communication by talking to Minoo and her friends, writing sentences on a piece of paper, memorizing them, then going for a walk on the street and practicing with people who were shopkeepers trying to sell their merchandise.

At the end of two weeks I went to Paris' Charles DeGaulle airport to join the group of eleven graduate students of Tehran University who had received scholarship awards. We were the first group; therefore Iran Air Company covered all expenses for seven days. The company entertained us beautifully. We lived in one of the most famous and prestigious hotels very close to the Arc de Triomphe de l'Etoile and they provided us a mini bus with a Persian-speaking tour guide to take us everywhere possible. I spent fifteen days in London and one week in Paris looking for the most fascinating thing to see. As I remember, it was early Thursday morning November 1st, 1959 that we all left Paris for Brussels and spent some time at a close-by hotel, then left Europe for the US. We arrived at the New York international airport, which amazed all of us, particularly the automatic glass doors. We had to change airports to fly to Washington, DC. I was so tired and exhausted; I don't remember the name of the airline. But today I can clearly visualize the moment that I saw four individual dress hangars wrapped in clean white paper on the ground. Although both my hands were completely occupied and my right hand was still in a cast, at that moment I was wondering how I was going to hang up my dresses when I got to my room and how could I find a shop that sold that kind of hangars. Unconsciously I grabbed those hangars on the ground and carried them all the way with me to my final destination in Ann Arbor, Michigan. Imagine my surprise when I arrived in my own room and opened the closet to hang up my dresses; I laughed at myself because I found 25 similar hangars in that closet!

When we arrived in Washington, DC, an Iranian gentleman welcomed us and told us, "The Iranian consulate office invites you to stay in Washington, D.C. for a formal dinner tomorrow night and for four days to visit the famous areas of the town." He took Nejla and me to the YWCA and the boys to the YMCA. Early the next morning Nejla and I woke up and didn't know where to go for breakfast. We were really hungry. I asked Nejla to help me to get to the post office - she could speak English well. We went for breakfast first, then asked directions to the post office. I bought a box from the post office, placed the 2 suede jackets in it and wrote the address that their father handed to me at the Tehran airport. It was our first time writing an address in English. Nejla copied it the way that the other package was written. (Reversed the sender and the recipient's addresses). So, after all the trouble and heavy weight carry-on, especially with my broken hand, the post office sent them back to Tehran according to the address.

English Language Institute

It was November 1959 and the weather was very cold but sunny in Washington, DC. All the parting with family and friends was over and we had to face the reality of life as foreign students abroad. On Sunday morning we all headed by plane to Detroit, Michigan's Ann Arbor airport. A young Iranian student from the language center met us, welcomed us to Michigan and guided us to the airport bus going to Ann Arbor, our final destination. We observed a heavy clouded sky, almost a foot of snow on the ground, and a thick fog in between. The young man explained to us on the bus the temperature was so many degrees below zero. We all felt miserable due to the extreme cold. He guided us to our homes, gave us written directions (address note) from our house to the class and advised us to go in and out of the shops along the way, to warm up and prevent frost bite. Then he left us and said, "See you tomorrow at the Language Center at 8 o'clock."

All the boys were placed in one large apartment; Nejla and I in a big house with 10 rooms, most of them occupied by other girls going to college. Monday morning Nejla and I left the house to walk to class. We didn't see any pedestrians. Everyone was riding in cars but we had to walk while we took the English language course because we were not allowed to buy a car for six months. As had been suggested, we went into a store at one door and out another door. Inside, each store was warm enough to reduce the cold from our hands and face. When we got to class we were miserably cold but it didn't last long. After a while we took our coats and scarves off as we were feeling warm and comfortable. We all registered and sat for the placement test. As was the usual habit of Iranian boys, they had had a party for themselves the night before and had drunk as much booze as they could. Therefore, they were drunk enough that all except two of them, plus Nejla, were placed in fifth grade. The others and I were placed in the first grade, as we didn't know any English and I couldn't even spell my last name.

Left to right: Me, Baharlu, Forough, Atta and Daryush at the English Institute lounge, 1960. (Forough and Atta later got married.)

I tried to study as hard as possible. Our teachers didn't leave us alone. They tried to be with us all during the day in class and at night at the dinner table or other gatherings. We were in constant contact with our teachers day and night. We tried very hard not to speak Farsi (our native language) in order to accustom our minds to the sounds of the new language, in the hopes of improving our accents. I definitely failed and have never been able to overcome my strong accent. On the other hand shifting the direction of writing (Farsi is written from right to left) and translating English words or sentences into Farsi were easy skills that we picked up quickly. We had our new lives in a new world with a new life style. On a Friday morning exactly 33 days after we arrived we had our mid-term exam. That night shortly after dinner we went to an ice skating rink; it had been arranged by the English center. I was very anxious to see the ice skating rink and to see how skating was performed. None of us had ever been exposed to such a place before. In Iran skiing was common but not ice-skating. We went to the rink in the school bus. As we entered I saw the row of bladed boots, organized on a wooden stand; it reminded me of the entrance to the holy shrine of Imam Zadeh where everyone had to take their shoes off and put them on a stand. But these boots were for rent for $3 a pair for 4 hours of use; the entrance fee to the rink had been taken care of by the English Department. Mr. Michael, the head of the school, was standing by the main door, helping the students and teaching them the basics. When I got my skates and had a close look at the blades, I paused for a while wondering how I could wear them and walk on them. If I broke my ankle or twisted my knee what would happen? How could I go to school in such cold, cold weather? While I was thinking, Mr. Michael came forward and told me to put my skates on. He wanted to teach me how to dance on the ice. He took my hand and told me to go. It was impossible for me to keep my balance; I was swinging like a grandfather clock's pendulum. It was out of my control. He came close, grabbed my waist and started dancing with me while I was swinging to the right and left. On Monday morning when we got to school we found him in bad shape; he couldn't walk straight because he was suffering from severe back pain. My classmates started teasing him and kept telling him, "Mr. Michael, we could have danced with her but we were thinking of the back pain!"

Housing

The first months passed and I got a satisfactory grade on the exam so I was happy in class but very sad at home. I asked for a private room and paid twice as much for four months in advance. The room was like an attic (it was right under the roof) with insufficient heat. At night I couldn't sleep because of the ice-cold draft coming from the unsealed window. Anytime I complained to the landlady, she told me, "You'd better go to the pharmacy, buy some bandages and cover your knees and then you'll feel warm." Finally I talked to the student advisor and asked for help. He promised to find me another place and talked to the landlady to get my advance payment back. During the fifth week of class I had a very bad headache while attending lecture. Suddenly I fainted and ended up in the hospital. I spent three days there while they did all the required tests. Fortunately, the results were negative. I missed a week of class but my very nice teacher told me, "I'll cover the material for you if you stay after class" and I did. Meanwhile I found a perfect room in a small four-bedroom house closer to every place that I needed to go by foot. Margi, the landlady, was so nice, so kind and so clean and the room was really warm and pleasant, located on the first floor on the west side. Every night she took me to her TV room and explained what was going on; she made me talk and corrected my mistakes; I learned a lot from her. I have forgotten her last name but never her glorious face. She let me read her magazines and recommended the advertising portion. Everyday when I came home I picked up one or two of them. First I looked at the pictures then I read the ads. One day I found a card in the Time magazine. I read it but I didn't understand what was free. I wrote my name and address on the card and mailed it. It was Saturday morning that someone knocked at the door and asked for Massy. I went to the door and saw a very tall, good looking, well dressed gentleman. I introduced myself and he introduced himself. I was wondering who he was. He said I am a life insurance representative, here to explain and sell it to you. I replied I did not ask for it. He showed me the card with my name and address on it. I asked, "What is free?" He told me, "I am." I said no thanks and he then said goodbye and left. The landlady, who understood my mistake, laughed and told the story to her other tenants.

Post Office

I usually received a letter from home at least once a week and I tried to reply as soon as I could. Such correspondence acted as a tranquilizer for someone really homesick like I was, but it was like a sharp knife entering my heart when I received a letter accusing me of something I never wanted to do. I can't forget the pain and the shame that I suffered because of someone's mistake. I mailed the package that Azghandi handed to me in the Tehran airport, supposedly "ready to mail." It was ready except for the reversed sender and receiver addresses. I had copied the way she did it on the package for my professor's daughters. As a result, both packages were sent back to Iran and arrived at the customs office. These packages were small and remained somewhere unnoticed for a long period of time while the expected recipients notified their parents and complained about not receiving anything. The parents kept writing to me and asking for a reason why I didn't mail the packages and bothered my sister to know what happened to their gifts. I didn't know what to do. I had no evidence from the post office that I mailed them because I sent the packages by regular mail. It was very hard for me. So no reasons and no answers, although I replied to their letters with repeated apologies. Finally I got so tired that I decided to send them letters and ask for the price to repay them. I talked to one of my friends and asked for his advice. He told me, "You'd better go to the Washington, DC post office and ask if the mailman couldn't read your handwriting. Instead of sending it overseas he might have sent it to the dead letter room." His advice seemed so difficult for me; going from Michigan to DC cost a lot of money and how could I find the exact post office? I asked him if he really meant it; he told me, "Yes, it is easy to do. The English

Department class is out for four days and two of my friends are going to DC with their car. You could go with them. They can take you to the post office and are willing to help you. Also it's only one hour by plane and 6-7 hours by car. You'd only have to pay for gas and I'm sure they will share the costs with you." I accepted the deal. I met his friends beforehand and the three of us got into a big Lincoln car and headed toward DC. In the middle of the highway, a snowstorm hit. The visibility became almost zero, so the flow of traffic was greatly reduced. I was sitting in the back and every two hours they changed places, taking turns driving. I don't remember what time of day it was; I only recall it was windy, snowy and dark. I tried to sleep because I was afraid of the weather and the road and I didn't want them to know I was afraid. All of a sudden I heard a pop and the car stopped. They went out and told me the left tire was flat. "We are very close to a rest area. We can't move the car and you can't walk in the snow so you stay in the car and we'll be back soon." They hitchhiked from the car.

Little by little the car got cold. I tried to curl up in the fetal position to make myself warm and I fell asleep. I don't know for how long; I was awakened by a noise at the window. There were two policemen with a bright flashlight. Inside the car it was almost freezing and so was I. They asked me to get out of the car and I told them I was so cold I couldn't move. They brought their car close and helped me into their car. On the way they asked me what happened. I explained with my broken accent; I was shivering to death. They took me to a very big and very warm area. It seemed to me it was a part of a car repair shop with four or more fireplaces, all with active glow. They brought me a big cup of hot chocolate. My hands were almost freezing and I warmed them by holding the hot cup in my hands. After two hours the boys came back to the area and told me, "We have to stay here tonight because they asked for cash and we have none. If you have some, we are willing to borrow it." I asked, "How much do you need?" They told me $250. I didn't know the price of a tire, which wasn't more than $10 - $15 in those days. I trusted them and paid. They left me there where the policemen left me before. In such a huge area I sat on the bench by myself. It was so warm and pleasant that I didn't feel lonely or scared. It was about 6:30 the next morning when they came to pick me up with another cup of hot chocolate that they paid 10 cents for from a vending machine. I again sat in the back of the car and we headed on to DC. We arrived at about 1 pm and went directly to the main post office. An employee took me to the dead letter area to look for my packages, but as much as I looked, I didn't find them. After all the agony of the cold, the car trouble, sleeping on the bench and spending one night in a strange area, I went to the YWCA to stay for two nights and the boys went where they had made reservations. The next day they went to the Iranian embassy to take care of their business, whatever it was. Because the weather was so cold and stormy I preferred to stay at the YWCA and spend time in the library. They came to pick me up the next day to return to Michigan. They started driving as they did before, changing places every 1-2 hour and talked about filling the gas tank. Once again they asked me for $100 cash as a loan. I told them I only had some traveler's checks left with me and they told me, "That's as good as cash." I signed a traveler's check for one hundred dollars and gave it to them and invited them for lunch in a restaurant on the way back to show my appreciation for the ride to DC and back. I thanked them again and told them to please take my share of gas from the $350 they owed me. I never saw them again and they never paid their debt. When I sent them a message, they replied, "We treated her like a queen not an ordinary person and the $350 is government money not her own."

Christmas Vacation

The English Department made arrangements for all students to have two weeks Christmas vacation and we were assigned to American families who were willing to take foreign students as guests. It was beneficial for the students to become acquainted with American customs in general, to learn conversation, and to avoid feeling lonely, especially a week before Christmas. A note explaining the start and end date of vacation was distributed to each of us. The note included the name of the host and hostess, the city and the reason for the vacation. I'm sure a similar note with identification, character and interests of each of the students was sent to each host and hostess beforehand. We all gathered together during the usual school hours; the bus was ready; the student advisor, one of our teachers and another gentleman joined us on the bus headed for one of the churches. After a short mass, all the hosts and hostesses arrived. They called us by name and we introduced ourselves to each other. My hostess' name was Mary Johansen. She was a very modern, good looking, well dressed, middle-aged woman with a beige four-door Chevrolet. She was a librarian and her husband was a merchant in Jackson City, Michigan. On our way home she told me about the distance, city population and its landmarks. We arrived at her beautiful large house, well decorated with modern furniture, a lot of antiques, woodcrafts and so on. The most amazing thing was the Christmas tree with all the lights on, glittering angels, gold stars, red, blue and green bulbs hanging and a lot of nicely wrapped boxes under it. I had never seen a Christmas tree before and I had no idea what those boxes were for (in those days, Muslim people knew nothing about the Christmas celebration). She took me to the bedroom assigned for me. The room had a beautiful view, a shining brass bed with pink satin cover, a nice wardrobe, a big vanity and a desk. The house was located in the middle of the woods; I couldn't see any homes around it, so it was a bit scary for me. I didn't like the big dog that always followed me and rubbed his nose on my legs. Mary prepared sandwiches for lunch and placed dog food in the dog's bowl. Her dog started eating in the kitchen, which really surprised me. In Iran, religious people don't deal with dogs, shouldn't drink booze or eat certain foods, or do so many other things that I cannot talk about. Since I was from a religious family I believed some of those ideas but not anymore.

Mary prepared a nice dinner; it was meat and different vegetables. She kept asking me about the kind and variety of foods at home and I tried to explain to her with my thick broken accent. I helped her set the dinner table. About 5:00 pm her husband Bill entered the house He came to me and kindly introduced himself and I did the same. He was almost the same age as his wife. Later Mary told me they had been classmates in high school and married after college graduation at the age of 21, forty-eight years ago; they had no children. At the dinner table Bill talked to me and asked me how I afforded the living expenses, how far away my country was, the route of travel and a few other questions like that. I tried to answer as well as I could. Mary asked about my two friends, Mr. Fakoori and Mr. Atta who were guests of two other families in Jackson City, on the other side of town. Mr. Atta was my classmate the first year at Tehran University; he changed his field from Biology to Geology. I met Mr. Fakoori in Paris. He graduated from Shiraz University and his field was Literature.

I suggested to Bill and Mary that I wash the dishes and they accepted. I was glad that dishwashers didn't exist. I started to wash and rinse as much as I could and when I believed it was complete, I washed the dog's dish at the end.

Every day Mary left the house at 9 am and came back at 4 pm. Her husband Bill left at 7:30 and came back at 5:30. He had to drive a long distance. I was alone in the house watching TV or reading a conversation book given me by an Iranian priest who lived in the same city. His wife came to the house and taught me how to write short essays, official letters, letters of intent and request letters. She spent 2 hours with me every day I was there and charged me $40 a day.

Mary showed me how to make lunch for myself. I loved peanut butter and toast the most and I still do. The first Saturday and Sunday, Mary took me on a tour of the city and showed me all the city landmarks. On Christmas Day, Mary and Bill arranged a dinner party and invited four couples and a single woman, which made a total of 12 around the dinner table.

She prepared a pork leg, lamb chops, mashed potatoes, yams and Uncle Ben's rice, with apple and pumpkin pie for dessert. She made rice because when she asked about the food and its varieties in Iran, I mentioned rice and lamb. I also told her eating pig meat is forbidden in Islam. Their guests spoke to me a lot so I was comfortable and felt I could communicate with them and believed I was well understood; but today I realize that they didn't understand what I was talking about; they never laughed or repeated their questions. If they didn't understand my reply, they repeated my answer not their question. After dinner we all sat around the Christmas tree with Mary and Bill sitting on a bench. She opened the boxes very carefully and kept the cards and threw the nice wrapping paper and the bows in the fireplace. I asked her, "Don't you want to keep the bows and intact paper?" She told me, "If I keep them, how will the manufacturer run his business?" The next day Mary told me, "My aunt and her husband have invited you and your boyfriend for New Year's Eve." I had no boyfriend but didn't want to refuse the party. I started thinking that I should call Atta or Fakoori. I told myself, "Atta is young and my classmate; it is better to call Fakoori who is closer to me in age." I called him and asked him to join me for New Year's Eve. He told me that his hosts were going to the same party and he had refused to go with them. He said, "I have no desire to go to the New Year's Eve party but I will join you," and he did. The afternoon of New Year's Eve, Mr. Fakoori came to the door with his host. Mr. Johansen promised to give him a ride back to his house after 1 am. Bill and Mary welcomed him, and we left for Mr. and Mrs. John Howell's (Mary's aunt). Their house was rather far away and we arrived around 5 pm. This house was a British style home and much smaller than the Johansen's. As I remember, the kitchen and dining room were on the first floor; the living room and bedroom were upstairs. Mr. and Mrs. John Howell welcomed us at the door. We entered the kitchen; then Bill, John and Fakoori went to the dining room. Mary and I started helping Ann to get all the food ready to go to the table. She made ham, baked potatoes, meatballs and rice. Ann told me that the rice and meatballs were especially "for you and your boyfriend. I heard you are Muslim and don't eat pork." I replied, "Ham is OK but not pork;" she didn't say a word and didn't tell me that ham was pork. Finally Mary and I took all the dishes and Ann placed them on the table. There were two bottles of white and red wine on the dinner table. We all sat around the table according to Ann's seating order. Then John asked us, "Do you like red or white wine?" We both replied, "No, thank you." Then John sat in the armchair at the head of the table and started praying. I am sure neither of us could follow him. Then he asked how Muslims prayed at dinner. I replied, "We thank God after eating not before." Shortly after dinner all the dirty dishes were moved to the kitchen sink. I asked Ann if I might wash; she said, "Yes, you wash, Mary can dry and I will put the dishes away." Then we all went back to the dinner table where the three gentlemen were chatting. Ann served a very delicious homemade apple pie with tea and/or coffee. It was almost 9:30 when John said, "Let's all move to the living room and enjoy the music." We went upstairs and entered a rather big room with dim lights and slow music. I saw a bookshelf filled with the Encyclopedia Britannica and an armchair next to it on one side; a dark red and white sofa and two chairs and a rectangular coffee table on the other side of the room. We all sat on the sofa or chairs but Mr. Fakoori sat on the chair next to the bookshelf and started to read some of the books. Meanwhile, John served after dinner cognac, offering it to Mr. Fakoori and received the words, "No, thank you." The couples started dancing. I was watching them and Fakoori reading the book. They changed partners a few times in the middle of dancing; I am sure they were whispering about us. Anytime the music was interrupted, one of the two men asked Mr. Fakoori if he wanted to dance; he replied, "Later on." I was annoyed; why weren't we participating with them and why should we sit silently during their happy moment?

The grandfather clock hanging on the wall showed that midnight was close. John told Mr. Fakoori that it was time for dancing again and he said, "Later on." John then came to me and asked if I wanted to dance with him. While we were dancing he moved me to the middle of the room and when the clock banged 12, he kissed my cheek and said "Happy New Year" and everyone kissed each other, shook hands and repeated Happy New Year. We went downstairs wearing our coats, said goodbye and got in the car. We gave Mr. Fakoori a ride home first. He and I sat in the back seat of the car; Bill was driving and Mary was next to him. I found Mr. Fakoori very angry and quiet. When I started to talk to him, he didn't want to reply. When the car arrived at his driveway, he got out of the car and said goodbye to Mr. and Mrs. Johansen, not me. I was ashamed of his actions and attitude after such a nice party. When we got home, everyone went directly to bed and slept. In the morning, New Year's Day was an entirely white day - about 10" of snow had fallen during the night. At breakfast they asked me why Mr. Fakoori was unhappy the night before. I said it wasn't clear to me at all; since I had known him I had found him to always be quiet and indifferent. Mary suggested I call and ask him about it in my own language. So at 9:30 I called him and started talking about the party; then I asked him why he was so quiet and what was bothering him. He angrily responded, "What do you expect; don't you realize what you did?" I thought he was angry because I was helping them. I said that it wasn't bad at all. When you are in a strange place you shouldn't present yourself as a stranger sitting at the table of strangers. I was happy and comfortable; what was wrong with this. Again he angrily told me, "Don't beat around the bush. It was very bad and shameful." I said, "What was so bad and shameful - for you or for me?" He replied, "For a lady like you." Then he said again, "For you, your host and also the one that made the ugly proposal." The more I talked to him the more confused I became. I didn't understand what he meant, so I hung up and lay on my bed and started to review all the events of the previous evening to find what it was.

About 30 minutes later the phone rang and Mary called me to the telephone. I grabbed the receiver and Mr. Fakoori was talking to me about my wrong doings. Once again I asked Mr. Fakoori what was wrong. He replied, "The kiss." With great surprise I said, "What?" He said, "You forgot all about it. Don't you remember he played a trick; he took you under the mistletoe and kissed you." I started laughing and he asked, "Why are you laughing? Instead of being ashamed, how soon you become American." I said, "Honestly, I invited you to this party to kiss me, but by reading the Encyclopedia Britannica, you missed your chance forever. I feel John is like my father, not a religious fanatic friend like you." After the holiday we went back to our language classes.

After English classes were over we all went to different universities; I never saw Mr. Fakoori again but I heard he married an American woman, had two children and switched from literature to law.

On August 1st, 1992, in Norman City, Oklahoma, Atta who was my first year classmate at Tehran University married Forough, my closest girlfriend and house-mate in Ann Arbor, while they were both students at the University of Oklahoma. Forough received her PhD in physiology and Atta a PhD in petroleum geology. They returned to Iran in 1968 where Forough began teaching at the university and Atta worked for the National Iranian Oil Company. In 1972 after the Institute of Paramedical Sciences was established, Forough accepted a part time teaching position there in addition to her job at the university. They now live in Los Angeles and have two children and two grandchildren. We meet quite often.

Church Speaking

On January 5th, 1960, the second part of English language started. The Iranian educational attaché in Washington, DC realized that our acceptance time for regular university coursework was either summer or fall of 1960. There was time to spare. He told us we could register for English class for one more term and the Iranian government would pay the tuition because the Office of Student Affairs in Tehran hadn't realized there would be a considerable time gap in between courses. It was a blessing for all of us. We were introduced to the American Universities as graduate students of Tehran University regardless of the fact that English was not our native language. So we all registered for English immediately. In the middle of the term I received a notice from Mrs. Margaret Brown, a foreign student advisor in the English Center. I met with her right after class. She told me that one of her friends was an active member of a Christian society and was looking for a Muslim person to go to their society and explain the Islamic information about the birth of Jesus. If I was willing to do so she could introduce me to her Christian friend. I replied I would do it with pleasure. Then she said it would be during Easter vacation. A week later I received a formal invitation letter from the Christian society including a handwritten note that a car would come to the English center to pick me up at 5:10 on Tuesday, February 15, 1960. I tried to be prepared as much as I could, collecting the information about the ancient story of the life and the pregnancy of Mary and her husband Joseph, the respect of Persian religious leaders who went from far away to be present and witness the presence of the angel at the moment of delivery. I made myself presentable by wearing a tailor-made black formal suit that I brought from Iran, a lime green scarf and matching shoes that I bought in London and an overcoat.

I was picked up by the church liaison, Mark, and his assistant. During the drive, a strong storm and heavy rain prevented me from seeing the road. We arrived at 6 pm and entered the church. Mark introduced me to the audience: "Massy is an Iranian Muslim graduate student at the English Center who plans to go to Toledo University for further education." There were about 30 people in the audience. I had thought the group would be young Christian students or adult students like I had been in Iran while in high school. They were neither. They were a group of hard-liner Christians, as prejudiced as one could imagine, and much older than I was at the time. I started talking and explained about the Muslim beliefs of what was written in the Koran; that of the 124,000 prophets, Muslim people worship five (Noah, Jacob, Moses, Jesus, and Abraham) plus the last of all prophets, Mohammad, that all Muslims in this world would be his followers. One of the audience raised his hand and asked me why Muslims worship five not all of them. I replied because they present the same written religious documents. Like the Bible for Christians, the Koran is for Muslims. I was very proud of myself because I felt they understood me well. The subject appeared to be interesting to them because they were listening very carefully. I continued talking about the Koran and Christianity. Again one of the audience asked me about the relation of Jesus to God. In reply I said as far as I was concerned their relationship would be like yours or mine with God. The other person tried to clarify the point and said, "Do you believe God is the father of Jesus?" I responded, "No, never, God is not a mass, a substance or any other thing that could be thought of or touched or could be seen. God is above all nature and is invisible. Jesus is a saint, a human being created by God." Then again another question arose. "Don't you believe Mary was a virgin?" I said, "Yes, for sure I believe it. One hundred percent. It's written in the Koran." Then the other gentleman loudly said, "If you believe in her virginity, how come you don't believe He is the son of God?" I said according to what is written in the Koran, Mary was a virgin at the time of her son's birth, no question about it. But parthenogenesis was common among certain species of lower animals; it might also occur in humans. If we assume Mary's pregnancy was a result of parthenogenesis, why was her baby a boy not a girl with XX chromosomes? Jesus was definitely a boy with XY-chromosomes. Therefore it is proven scientifically that Joseph was the father of Jesus not the invisible, untouchable, supernatural God. All of a sudden all the audience stood up, raised their fists in the air and angrily shouted words of which I could only recognize a few. "Kick this #-@*%#- scientist out of this holy church; she is a naturalist not a real religious Muslim." Mark and his assistant grabbed my arm and took me out of the church in a matter of seconds and then took me to the car and left the scene. My over-coat, umbrella and scarf were left behind in such a heavy rain that I arrived home entirely wet. Surprisingly, the next day I found my stuff in a box in the Student Advisor's Office in the English Center, including an envelope with a Thank You card and $20 for "services rendered."

Second Term of English Class

After Christmas vacation, the class started again and finished in March 1960. My University acceptance was not until June, so through a student advisor and one of our English teachers I got a chance to attend Biology and Physiology classes at the University of Michigan-Ann Arbor until then. This was very helpful for my summer classes. Meanwhile, I bought a series of children's encyclopedias and started reading one after the other. I used four dictionaries; one was Farsi to English, the second one English to Farsi (I brought this one from Iran), the third was Webster's and the fourth was a medical dictionary. I used them all to understand the meaning of a single word. During that peri-od I was happy, living in the same clean room. Often my desk was decorated with a bouquet of lily of the valley flowers grown in the backyard outside of my window and brought to my room by a wonderful, very kind and lovely landlady who always tried to help me. I never forgot her cleaning and shining the house, par-ticularly her attention to the tenant. Every single week she changed my sheets with very soft, well-ironed sheets that had a beautiful fragrance. I believe she is in Heaven now, so God bless her soul forever.

Graduation photo, 1960

Toledo University

The last week of May I had to leave Ann Arbor and go to Ohio to start classes at the University there. I went by United Airlines. On arrival I saw my name on a placard and introduced myself to the young man standing there. His abbreviated name was Mori (Morteza), a student from the Engineering department. He took my two suitcases, my book box and me to his car and started driving toward the University dormitory. He told me so many things - about the University and its dormitory, the number of Iranian students at the University, etc. At the dorm gate he took one suitcase and book box and I carried the other suitcase (those days we had to carry them; none of the suitcases had wheels on them). I introduced myself to the attendant who was sitting at the front desk. I signed in, then she let us go in the elevator. The attendant herself accompanied us to the fourth floor to show me my room. The room was relatively large with only one very small window. The wall of the room was made of cement block with no plaster cover. It was dark, damp and had no way to get airflow. I was shocked, looking around the room;

then I asked Mori if every place was like this. He replied, "You are lucky to get this room; there is a shortage of rooms in this area." It was open only for the summer and I had no choice. I had no way to return to Michigan so I had to go forward. Mori realized how unhappy I was. He asked me to have dinner at his house. He said, "I live close to campus; I'll go home to tell my wife while you settle yourself in. I'll be back to pick you up." I started hanging my dresses up and placing my books (the series of children's encyclopedias and four dictionaries) on my desk. An hour later the intercom called my name: "Massy, your ride is here." When I went down I saw Mori with a young, good-looking pregnant wife by the name of Lila. We walked toward their house. Mori told me they were living in a shelter area remaining from the Second World War. They had one bedroom, one bath, one very small kitchen and a living room. They had a dark green sofa, a very small square dining table, two chairs and one side lamp. I didn't see the bedroom and bath. They served barbequed chicken, hot dogs and ice cream for desert. After dinner we chatted, mostly about my life at school the next day. At 9 pm they both accompanied me to the dorm. Lila very kindly told me not to be upset about my place; I could come to their house anytime I liked. She was home every day preparing for her new arrival.

At 8 am the next morning I walked to my advisor's office to discuss the courses and the schedule for which I was to register. He advised me to take Microbiology lab and lecture for 6 weeks from 7 am to 2 pm, Monday through Friday. I bought two course books and a lab workbook, then went home and started looking at page after page. I found the glossary and the sample exam questionnaire and started reading, trying to find the words' meanings using the many dictionaries so I would be prepared for the Monday class that started right at 7 am. The professor taught the first two 45-minute sessions; then his assistant ran the lab. We had a 15-minute break every hour. The lab assistant lectured and explained what we were to do step-by-step; then we started working. We had short quizzes every day, about 5-8 questions, and a long test at the end of each period.

One Monday morning I woke up and looked at my watch; it read 7:30 am instead of 5:30. In a rush, I left the room, ran out of the dorm, walking as fast as possible. It was normally 10 minutes from the dormitory to class. I entered the college hallway and saw the clock in front of me - it was 12 minutes to 6 am. The janitor was sweeping the floor. He looked at me with great surprise and asked me, "Did you not go to the dorm last night? It is too early, go home." I went back to the dorm but the door was locked and I couldn't get in; so I sat on the doorstep and started reading. At 6:05 am the cleaning lady came; she asked me if my boyfriend knew that I couldn't get in after 11 pm. She also asked me, "Where did you sleep last night?" With great shame I replied, "I read my watch wrong, so instead of leaving at 6:45 am I left at 5:40 am." She let me in and I went to my room, tired and sleepy, and lay down on my bed. I fell asleep until 9 am. When I went back to school, the first lecture and exam were already finished. I went to the lab and the lab assistant asked me where I had been; I missed the exam. I told him I was sorry. Then again at the end of the hour he asked me if I was all right; I said yes. Finally he realized that I didn't understand what he meant. At dinnertime I went to a nearby restaurant where all the students living at the dorm went to eat. That day two of my classmates came to me and talked to me about the exam that I missed. They were wondering why I wasn't there on time. I explained everything to them and they advised me go to the professor and let him know what happened and ask if he would give me a makeup exam. Every day when I went to class, I wasn't brave enough to ask the professor; instead I asked the lab instructor for a makeup exam. He was a young man with a strange accent (from Texas). He told me that it was up to me. Unfortunately I didn't understand what he meant. As much as I searched the dictionaries I couldn't find the meaning, so I asked one of my classmates what "up to you" meant. She said "any day, any time you select." The next morning I sat through my makeup exam.

At dinnertime, the only nearby restaurant was a place that all the students from the dorm went for dinner and to talk, especially with new foreign students like me (I was the only Iranian there). Everyone was interested in finding out who I was and how I got to the US. Did I come by camel, by bus or did I walk over the seas? In those days young people were not familiar with Iran and its culture. They considered Iranians to be the same as Arabs; I was surprised at that.

The night after mid-term exams, Suzanne, a mature young lady who was a biology teacher attending the summer courses as her in-service requirement, sat next to me and started asking about my life in Iran, my marital status and the number of children I had. I explained to her in my very broken English. Suzanne told me how lucky I was. "You left your children behind in such a far distant place for the purpose of further education." She assured me that the University never allowed a married woman to go beyond a Master's degree. Her application for a PhD program was rejected because she had three children living in the proximity of the University while mine were living on the other side of the globe. This conversation triggered my thoughts about how my personal life was a copy of hers. If the University denied my application for the PhD program I would lose my scholarship forever, regardless of my good reputation, my position, my job; above all how would I handle all the criticism and strong gossip of my entire family. I became so depressed about my goals and what I had in mind for the future that I couldn't sleep for two nights and felt agitated whenever I started thinking about it. Finally I decided to keep my personal problems to myself — I had no other choice. I had to continue forward for whatever destiny might bring me in the future.

My second course started on July 6th. I was happy. I learned the town and my surroundings. I made a few friends. I was busy going to school, spending time with friends, particularly Mori and Lila and also Faramarz, whose father was one of our close family friends in Iran.

Two weeks after the second term started, I found a lump in the same breast as in Tehran two years before. I was scared to death; I thought it was growing out of the cyst previously removed. I went immediately to the student health center to see a doctor. The lady at the front desk asked me a few questions and my purpose for the doctor visit. I explained everything to her. She told me, "If it's cancer, they ship you home." I was really shocked. I had trouble breathing for a moment. When I met with the doctor he suggested I see Dr. Burenhimer, an oncologist who specialized in breast cancer and asked his nurse to make an appointment for me. I went back to the dormitory very sad, almost crying. One of the nursing students living at the dorm told me she would take me to Dr. Burenhimer, but that I should let my advisor know. The next day after class, I met with my advisor and explained my situation. He told me that Dr. Burenhimer was the best in town and that his wife had had the same problem but it wasn't cancer. He said, "Go see him and let me know the results."

My friend took me to Dr. Burenhimer's office in her car. After reviewing my history of surgery and the examination, he suggested aspiration first then a further discussion later on after the results were known. I agreed. He inserted the needle and aspirated 2 cc of clear fluid. He explained the anatomy of the breast and this kind of benign lump, which will happen in 80% of women regardless of race and color of skin. He told me that it might appear every 2 years and that any time it happened I should go back to him to have it aspirated. Once again I became happy and cheerful. I continued my studies until the end of the summer course. The lecture and lab exams were over; with a great relief, I got an A in both courses.

I went to the dormitory assuming I could now rest and relax but when I went inside I found the elevator not working and my belongings sitting next to the elevator. With great surprise I wondered what had happened, why no one was at the front desk and whom I should talk to. After a while the front desk clerk came and told me that the dormitory closed at 12 noon that day, so no one could go upstairs. She said, "I tried to find you and couldn't so I personally collected everything from your room. I checked all the closets, drawers, etc. and nothing is left behind." I asked her why she didn't tell me before. She replied that it was written on the top of the agreement that I signed; didn't I remember? I started worrying about what I was going to do - call Lila? Go to the student advisor? Or what else? I asked the clerk if I could leave my things here and go find some help. She said she was sorry but I had to remove everything and get out of the dorm. At that moment I felt so very tired, sleepy, miserable and lonely. I needed someone to give me an idea of what to do, to help me move from here and to find a place to live. It was almost 2 pm and I had to be out before 4 pm. Mori appeared in the hallway. His baby had been born 8 days before and I didn't know about it yet. He was laughing, telling me about his son's weight, height and how quiet he was. I was embarrassed that I didn't know about his wife and child but I had been busy with the course and dealing with my lack of language abilities. He said, "Let's take care of your stuff first; then you can come home with us until you find a place." I didn't want him to think that I was helpless; I collected my suitcases and bookcase and he helped me carry them to his car. He told me, "You can stay in my house as long as you like, but as you know, there is only one bath and no extra bedroom; you will have to sleep on the couch and take your shower later on in the day." He was a great friend. If he hadn't come to help me that day I wonder how I would have managed. I am most grateful to him, his wife and all his children wherever they live today.

As I entered his home, Lila came to me with her son in her arms and welcomed me on behalf of her son. I piled my stuff in the corner of her room and started asking how I could go about finding a place to live. Mori told me he would take me to the student center in his car. There were always announcements on the bulletin board. I could also talk to my advisor; he might know of a place. He gave me a ride to the student center. I went to the bulletin board and found a room for rent in an apartment complex. I wrote the address down, then went to the student advisor and explained my situation. He gave me the name of someone close to the University and advised me to go there and see about a room. He gave me the directions to the house.

I knocked on the door and a very good-looking woman with a tiny baby in her arms opened the door. She welcomed me in and I followed her to the living room. She asked me some questions about myself - what I was doing, what part of the world I came from, what were my beliefs, my native language and finally my religion? Then she told me she had 9 children from the ages of 13 to the baby who would soon be 6 months old. She told me if I could give her a hand at night and be with the children on Sunday while she went to church, she would give me free room and board. This was such a miserable event for me that I felt dizzy. I politely responded that I couldn't accept her offer and that I didn't need free room and board. I left her and cried all the way to the apartment for rent, which was rather far from the University. The 12-story building was located among beautiful woods and the apartment located on the 7th floor. I went up on the elevator to the 7th floor and walked a short distance to the apartment. I rang the doorbell and an old but good looking, well dressed, tall woman with white hair opened the door. I introduced myself. She welcomed me and showed me the room, which was well decorated with a white bedspread, a vanity decorated with many little dolls, a desk and a chair, and a good spacious closet. The room also had a beautiful view of the woods. I explained my situation. She told me the rent was $45 per month but that I had to pay for 4 months in advance plus one month as damage deposit. I accepted and gave her a check for $225 and told her I would move in the next day. She gave me a key to the apartment. Once again I was very happy. On my way back to Mori's house I bought a box of donuts for them, also hamburgers for all of us. I was really happy that night. I asked Mori how to call a cab to go to my place and he gave me the number. I slept on a couch for the first time in my life. Early the next morning I woke up and called a cab and by 9 am I was out of their door. (I promised them that as soon as I got settled I would invite them to have a Persian dinner with me at my house, but it never happened.) I arrived at 9:40 am carrying all my stuff to the elevator and then to the apartment. Happily I arranged it all in my room. Suddenly I noticed that the bedspread was not there. Then I looked around and found that all the decorations on the vanity were gone. I went to the landlady and told her, "My dear lady, I can see some changes in the room." She replied, "Call me Mary, not 'dear lady.' The changes you see today are correct. I sent the bedspread to the laundry; you don't need it. I also collected all the decorative items because my late husband bought them and they have sentimental value for me." I felt it was dishonest to take a check from me for four months in advance then collect all the decorations. But I told myself I had to accept the situation. There wasn't any other choice.

Later on I found the landlady to be a very fussy and unhappy person. She told me not to touch anything in the kitchen unless she gave me her permission. I believe she was concerned about the electricity bill. She told me no visitors were allowed in the apartment. Today when I think about it, I tell myself that she might not have been acquainted with any people of other nationalities or it might have been due to her age but my calculations do not match what-so-ever, particularly when I compared Mr. and Mrs. Johansen in Jackson City, Michigan and even my landlady in Ann Arbor. All of them were very concerned about me and they talked to me with respect and tried to introduce me to their neighbors and friends. I spent the next ten days going downtown and to other areas of Toledo doing nothing from morning to night except walking and window-shopping. I would come back home in the late afternoons and read stories from the children's encyclopedia books. I kept myself busy to overcome my loneliness. I was terribly homesick and depressed. I received a note from some of my Michigan friends. They were planning to go on a mini-vacation in Detroit. I immediately called and told them I would go if they could come to Toledo and pick me up or tell me how I could get to them. They told me they would come and get me. They did and we all went to Detroit.

On the way I explained my housing situation in Toledo. They suggested that I transfer to Michigan State University; there were plenty of dormitories and beautiful living spaces. As soon as we arrived in East Lansing (around 10 am), I went to the admissions office and applied for a transfer. The officer told me they needed my transcripts and student file sent directly from Toledo University to MSU; it might take 2–3 weeks, so I couldn't be admitted for the fall term. I begged her for another scenario and told her I could go to Toledo and ask them for the transcripts if she would give me a letter. She kindly prepared the letter and handed it to me in a sealed envelope, then explained the way I should bring my file from Toledo University to MSU and hand it to her personally. Meanwhile she advised me to apply for the graduate dormitory. I did immediately and became so happy. Early the next day we left for Toledo and arrived at 11 am. I went to my advisor to explain my situation to him and to ask him for help. He made a few telephone calls and told me to whom I should hand the sealed envelope. I picked up my file and transcripts from Toledo University in a sealed envelope.

It was almost 2 pm when I went to my apartment with the idea of paying two months rent and apologizing for the inconvenience that I had caused the landlady. While I was waiting for the elevator, a young man carrying a suitcase arrived. As the elevator door opened we both got in and pushed the 7th floor button. The elevator stopped, we both got out and walked in the same direction, reaching the same door with the same key in our hands. He opened the door and let me in first, and then he followed me in to my room. I said, "Oh no, this is my room," and he said, "No, I already rented it." I opened the closet to show him my dresses and my books and found it empty. I was so upset but I am sure he understood the situation. He called Mary who was watching TV in her living room. Mary came in and told me, "All your belongings are in the hallway closet." I asked her, "Why? Didn't you rent to me for four months plus one-month deposit? Didn't I pay you in full?" She replied, "Yes, you did, but I changed my mind because I believe a boy is better than a girl." Once again I had no choice but to accept the situation, but this time with a happy mind. I thanked God many times for such a successful outcome, although I was very angry at her dishonesty. I tried to remain calm and quiet. I asked her for the return of my payment. She counted 17 days and subtracted that from the total and gave me the rest. With the help of that young man, I gathered up my belongings and said goodbye to Toledo forever.

CHAPTER 7

Michigan State University

I arrived in East Lansing and went directly to the MSU Admissions Office with the sealed envelope in my hand. The lady in charge welcomed me to MSU and guided me to the dormitory admissions division. From there they took me to the building and showed me the room, which was under my name. It was on the 5th floor facing the Red Cider River with numerous MSU students riding in canoes and singing campus songs. It is difficult for me to explain my feelings at that moment and the extent of my happiness. I can only say I found myself in Heaven after the miserable events of being alone, homesick and - the saddest part of all - the feeling of homelessness.

It was not long before the fall semester started. I was accepted as a graduate student and found a few more Iranian graduate students in different fields of study. We are still close friends as are our children and grandchildren. I remained at MSU for six years until I received my Ph.D. in Physiology and Embryology. During the six-year period I lived at 118 Woodmir Avenue, Apt. #2, East Lansing, Michigan. So many good and bad things happened while there.

In 1961 I lost my half-brother Jaffar, who I loved very much. He died of a heart attack, as had his older brother. My family decided to keep his death a complete secret from me. However, after two weeks I received a letter from my youngest daughter, Nikrou, who was 13 at that time. She innocently sent her condolences without knowing of the family's decision. It was very hard for me to accept. And with the difficulties in making over-seas phone calls, I didn't speak to my relatives. There were no direct telephone lines between houses as there are today. You had to call through operators and phone companies and with the time difference it might be 48-72 hours of constant contact before you would be able to talk to someone. I was so upset that I couldn't function as well as I did before; I couldn't stop my tears and no one asked me what was wrong. I had to continue my studies no matter what. My weekdays started from 6 am until 5 pm; there was no lecture after 5 pm. I came home to eat dinner and watch the 6 o'clock news; then I went back to work from 7:30 pm to 2:30 am every night except Sunday. The Endocrine Unit laboratory where I did all my research was rather far from my house (approximately 25 miles). I also worked all Saturdays and most Sundays preparing myself either for an exam or collecting data for my Masters' thesis.

In the fall of 1962 I registered for statistics and two upper level classes in Biochemistry (human and plant). I was so busy I had no time to think about anything else. Meanwhile, I received very good news; Minoo graduated from the London nursing school and received a certificate of midwifery as well as registered nurse. She was planning to go to Iran and start her career there. I convinced her to come to the US for post-graduate study. I sent her the necessary form, but the US consulate in London denied her visa application and told her she would probably just stay with her mother instead of attending school.

*Minoo graduated from nursing
and midwifery college, London, 1963*

Her final decision was to return to Iran. I was very disappointed but once again I had no other choice except to continue
my work hoping to finish my studies as soon as possible. Minoo
was hired by one of the most famous hospitals in Tehran and kept
corresponding with me as did my other two daughters, Nikou
and Nikrou, and my sister. The most exciting moments of my life
were receiving letters from any of them and relaxing while I reading them. I would read the letters again and again, especially on
days when I was depressed.

One Sunday while I was home studying and preparing for an
open book Plant Biochemistry exam, I was surprised to find
another lump in my right breast. At first I felt so hot then so cold
that I started shivering. I felt the entire building spinning
around. It was Sunday and there was no way to contact any
physician. I thought the best thing would be for me to study, but
study for what? This was the third time I felt this lump. I might
become crippled; if I didn't die, I might remain in bed for the rest

of my life. I'd better stop reading; I will surely die before I receive my degree. If not, then how could I handle it by myself, alone. No one could come to the US; they had refused Minoo's visa. There were so many other thoughts that were running through my head; how could I go through such a disastrous period? Once again, I stood up and told myself, "Wake up, who knows everything in the world? Stop thinking, stand up and go forward, you cannot predict your entire future." Meanwhile, one of my classmates came in to study with me. It was a blessing for me. On Monday morning, I called Dr. Bernheimer's office in Toledo. Fortunately he was in and talked to me personally. He suggested aspiration again and if I could get to Toledo he would do it free of charge. He was so kind and considerate, but it was impossible for me to do so.

I tried to find a local specialist. I met with him the next day. His advice was surgery not aspiration and he explained to me the benefits of surgery. I accepted his idea, but I had two problems. In the first place, I only had student insurance so I had to provide other insurance to take care of the medical expenses, which required 90 days of coverage prior to the surgery to be eligible for receiving medical payments. My second problem was the interruption in my studies that I could not afford because of the time limitations of my scholarship. In addition, I was in the middle of the semester's course work. I asked my physician what would happen if the surgery were postponed for 3 months. He said, "Nothing, if you don't occupy your brain by thinking about the surgery." I promised not to think, but as soon as I left his office, I felt a terrible pain in my right hand and shoulder. The pain was unbearable, especially at night. Today it is difficult to think back and imagine how hard it was to be alone by myself, worrying day and night about the future life of my children and myself.

Meanwhile, in the spring of 1963, I received three letters from Iran. The first one was from my sister, who wrote a long letter for the first time in her life. She explained Minoo's plan to get married to one of the famous mullah's sons in the very near future and asked me to come home for the wedding. Nikou, my second daughter was begging for my blessing and asking me to come home at least for a week to attend the wedding. Minoo's letter was a short letter to tell me about her future husband, an Iranian-educated chemical engineer working in Tehran. Much to my chagrin, I was unable to attend due to the necessity of my surgery. I replied to my sister explaining my situation and the reason it was impossible for me to go home. The surgery was scheduled for the same day as Minoo's wedding. I begged my sister to keep my surgery completely confidential.

Minoo and Mohsen's wedding, Tehran, Iran, 1963

By the end of the semester I was admitted to Sparrow Hospital in Lansing, Michigan and surgery was performed. After 2 weeks, I returned to MSU and finished the last stage of my thesis by defending it and received my Masters' degree. Since most of my course work for my Ph.D. program was completed, I decided it to go to Iran during the summer. It was time for a vacation after four years of continuous work.

Me going to Saad Abbad Palace to meet with the Shah, Tehran, summer of 1963

As I had promised to go home to attend Minoo's wedding reception, I applied for a long summer vacation (3 months). It was a very joyful trip, especially since I found a chance to meet with the Shah to ask for an extended period of study from 4 to 6 years. I also arranged to bring my youngest daughter Nikrou back with me. She was a 12th grade high school student. We came back to the US together in September of 1963. She registered in the 12th grade at Lansing High School and I returned to my studies to continue my research and prepare my PhD thesis.

Nikrou registering in the 12th grade, Lansing High School, 1963

Nikrou and Ali's wedding photo, 1964

In 1964, Nikrou married a young Iranian student (Ali Mousavi Nasle) and moved to Detroit, Michigan as soon as the school year was over. Although they had a very simple wedding, they have enjoyed a very high standard of living since then. Their son Adib was born on March 24, 1969.

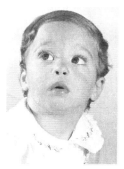

Adib, my first grandson, Tehran

In the spring of 1964 I received an unexpected letter from the Government of Iran signed by the Undersecretary of Education. It stated that the group-one scholarship would be terminated by September 10, 1964. It was shocking news, as I was one of that group. Once again, I had to find a solution. Meanwhile, all my English language classmates that formed group-one called me from different Universities and consulted with me as to what they could do to extend at least two more years to finish their PhD degrees.

I decided to go to Toronto as a representative of group-one to meet the Shah of Iran who had been invited to one of the Canadian Universities to receive an honorary doctorate degree. I planned to stay in the same hotel, so I made a reservation. I left MSU at 4 pm, right after my final exam, which was held at 2 pm. Nikrou accompanied me and we arrived in Detroit, Michigan at 6 pm. I had a 1963 black Corvair. I asked for directions to Canada and Toronto; the estimated arrival time to the hotel would be 1 am. According to the Shah's formal schedule, he was to arrive at 4 pm the next day, so I had plenty of time to rest. My appointment was at 7:30 am the following day in the lobby on the 12th floor. I was driving very carefully; the car radio was on but I was trying to keep Nikrou awake. I asked her to sing a song for me. I looked at the car clock; it was 10 past 11. Then all of a sudden we found ourselves in the middle of a sparkling shower. Someone hit me from the back and threw my car off the road into a field surrounded by barbed wire. The car stopped in the field and we got out of the car and called for help. When we finally arrived at the front door of the hotel with a smashed car, it was 5:30 am. We had spent four hours in the hospital emergency room. It was hard to believe that this terrible accident happened with no fatalities. I met with the Shah on time with successful results (i.e. two more years' extension). However, as a result of the accident, I suffered a great deal due to severe neck whiplash; my left hand became numb; my neck was in a collar for one month, so I couldn't work in the summer as I had planned to do. Instead I registered for more courses. I couldn't get any compensation from the Canadian insurance for the lost job because my contract was not finalized, but my car was well repaired by them.

In September of 1965, my second daughter Nikou who had graduated from Tehran University's College of Veterinary Medicine joined me at MSU. She had been accepted for a

Master's program in Microbiology and Public Health. At the same time we both registered for a medical Mycology certificate. We became classmates for 9 months, twice a week, and received our certification at the same time.

Both Nikou and I were very busy with our work; but I was much busier with my doctoral thesis as well as working full time in Embryology and Histology. On most Friday afternoons Nikou and I traveled to Detroit to visit Nikrou and her husband. We spent time with them and did some shopping. We returned to East Lansing Sunday afternoon. In May 1965 Nikrou's husband, Ali, was invited to join the newly formed University in Tehran. Therefore they planned to return home and I was looking for a post-doctoral position.

Minoo kept writing and explaining about her pregnancy and we were counting the days until her delivery. It was early morning September 13, 1966 when the phone rang; the operator told me I had a telegram from Iran, informed me of the great news and congratulated me on a newborn girl named Shaparak. I cannot describe the degree of my excitement and happiness that day. I like to say my first grandchild and my Doctorate degree have the same age, but my diplomas are silently hanging on the wall while Shaparak is an active successful physician in her own private practice with three sons aged 10 to 5. In the middle of September, Nikrou and her husband returned to Iran permanently and at the end of October 1966, I moved to Wayne State University Medical School for post-doctoral study. The subject of my post-doctoral research was platelet-leukocyte aggregation and micro-clot formation *in vitro*, which caused myocardial infarction *in vivo*.

Walking on Wayne State University campus, 1966

I left MSU after six successful years but Nikou was still tied up with her Masters' program for one more semester. I rented an apartment across the street where Nikrou and Ali had been living for two years; they left 15 days before I got there. Once again I was alone, by myself; I was busy with my new work at a new place with new people in a new town – in crowded downtown Detroit where the medical school was located. They told me not to go to the library at night, as I used to go every night and study until very late; so again there was no choice. The only thing that made me happy was the time I talked to Nikou; she reported her days' activities and I did the same. I was fortunate enough to receive an invitation from Detroit Technical College to teach Biology in the evening from 6-8 pm and from the Medical School to assist the human anatomy course every Wednesday afternoon from 2-5 pm in addition to my research project. These two classes kept me so busy at home that I didn't feel lonely. Every Friday afternoon I drove to the MSU campus and stayed with Nikou until late Sunday when I returned to Detroit. At the end of the semester, Nikou finished her Master's

Michigan State University

Upon the Nomination of the Faculty has conferred upon

Masoum M. Montakhabolayaleh

the Degree of

Doctor of Philosophy

Physiology

Given under the Seal of the University at East Lansing in the
State of Michigan on this eighteenth day of March.
in the year Nineteen Hundred and Sixty-seven.

Michigan State University

Upon the Nomination of the Faculty has conferred upon

Masoum M. Montakhabolayaleh

the Diploma for

Advanced Graduate Study

Given under the Seal of the University at East Lansing in the
State of Michigan on this twelfth day of June. in the year
Nineteen Hundred and Sixty-five.

Michigan State University

Upon the Nomination of the Faculty has conferred upon

Masum Montakhabolayaleh

the Degree of

Master of Science

Given under the Seal of the University at East Lansing in the
State of Michigan on this twenty-first day of March.
in the year Nineteen Hundred and Sixty-four.

My three certificates from MSU, 1964, 1965, and 1967

142

degree and got a job in the Henry Ford Hospital in Detroit. She joined me in the same apartment. Time was passing by; we were busy planning to return to Iran the next year, 1967.

I had no news about their father's illness; no one told me until I suddenly received a letter from Minoo informing me of her father's serious condition and asking me not to tell Nikou before her final exam. It wasn't easy to call home in those days because there was no direct telephone line. I was dependent on the letters to give me family news. I realized how busy Minoo was, working as a matron in a big hospital, having a new baby in one hand and caring for her sick father with the other hand, so I was not expecting any letter from her regularly. I was completely blind about what was going on in the family. Although Nikrou and her husband Ali were in Tehran in those days, she didn't send me bad news. My sister didn't write to me because she thought it might take my time. Finally, one day I received a letter from Minoo, explaining her father's condition and asking me to arrange a temporary trip for Nikou to go to Iran and visit her father. It was obvious what would happen in a short time. I talked to Nikou and prepared everything including her return visa to the US. The flight was scheduled for late one Friday afternoon; I received a telegram early that same morning saying, "Our father passed away." Therefore there was no reason for her to leave in a hurry any more. According to Islamic rule a dead Muslim must be buried as soon as possible. It wasn't easy for us but we had no choice except to accept our faith, get over such a disaster and continue our work as usual.

My Life in Endocrine Research Unit (ERU)

In the course of six consecutive years at Michigan State University, I met many people and I became very familiar with most of the professors, their assistants, the staff and the secretaries in the Physiology, Pharmacology and specifically the Endocrinology department. I never felt any discrimination or dislike except in the ERU where I felt one person somehow didn't like me or maybe was jealous of me. Her name was Ann, a technician, who was also a student in the Master's program. She was rather young, tall and slim, good looking with ocean blue eyes and silver blonde hair. This young woman had some personal problems; she was very prejudiced and proud. She was a drinker, easy going and very eager. There were ten people in the ERU lab. Joan was the laboratory manager, Nancy worked in histology, Ann was responsible for blood testing, Mary was a part-time ERU secretary, Gayle D. Riegl, Abu Shaikh and I were PhD candidates, Mark, Dick, Charles, and Ann were Master's students, and Fred and David were lab assistants. Joan tried to help everyone and keep a distance between Ann and the other students.

One Friday at coffee break during my first year in the ERU, everyone was talking about MSU football and making bets. I didn't understand American football; it was very different from the Iranian game. I tried not to discuss it but followed the way they bet. I dropped my one dollar and said "MSU." On Monday morning at 10:30 I went to the ERU after two hours at an embryology lecture. I found Ann and John Nellor discussing the winner. Ann tried to explain that Monta's bet (my bet) wasn't valid; it was only by chance and not an understanding of the concept of football that I had won. Dr. Nellor said, "Ann, I told you once, now it's the second time; she is the winner. Don't pick on her accent or her nationality. She won the bet and we have to give it to her." I went to the room that I shared with Mark, Dick and Abu. Ann came to the room and slid the contents of the pool envelope, ten single dollar bills, toward me. The others sitting at their desks told me it was insulting. I said never mind; the winner had no time to pay attention to every tiny incident.

The second event was during an organic chemistry class in which we all were enrolled. All of us, including Ann, made a plan to study together at the ERU every night for 2-3 hours. It was very helpful and satisfactory until the midterm exam; afterwards the situation changed. Ann bluntly told me, "Monta, you go and study some place else. Don't come to the lab at night; we can't suffer anymore." (The 'suffering' was the result of her poor grade that John Nellor had just notified her about.)

The third event was the criticism about not reading the Lansing Evening News. Ann kept asking me about it. One day an icy rain was falling on top of at least two feet of snow. Despite my car having snow tires and chains, it skidded and spun in circles 3 or 4 times. I was lucky that no car was close to me when it happened. I was scared to death. This was the first time that I faced such a horrible incident. The ERU was located in the middle of a big farm away from everything. My apartment was 25 miles away. I entered the ERU with a very pale face and a dry mouth and went directly to my office to relax a bit.

Ann came out of the lab with a newspaper in her hand. She placed the first page in front of me and said, "Do you have more of this crap to bring to this country to ruin American girls? Do you recognize this Iranian girl?" Then she left the room. I thought, "My God, what is up today?" I started working on my own research and didn't pay any attention to the paper. I told myself I would read it that night. At coffee break Ann asked me again about the paper. I replied that I hadn't yet looked at it. Then she asked me to tell her who the Iranian girl in Lansing High School was. I explained that she was living with me and going to school; that in the summer of 1963, I went to Iran and in September returned to the US with her. I had introduced her as my youngest daughter. Angered, Ann said, "You'd better stop talking about her; go and bring me the newspaper." Finally, I went to my office, grabbed the newspaper and returned to the basement where we took our coffee breaks. On my way, I saw Nikrou's photo; she was in a red suit and white silk blouse with lace ruffles on the cuffs, collar and chest area. She had made the suit herself during a school sewing contest. I didn't realize it but she was elected the champion by the judges, so her photo was on the front page of the Lansing Evening News.

Nikrou's photo in Lansing newspaper, 1964, in winning outfit from sewing contest

In each one of the above cases, I tried to pretend that I didn't understand what was going on, showing no reaction and asking no questions as to why Ann didn't like me, why she was always angry at me, what I had done to upset her. I just tried to stay away from her to prevent face-to-face criticism and keep the place peaceful and friendly.

The last incident happened on John Nellor's last day at the ERU and my last week at MSU. John was going to Washington, DC for a two-year sabbatical. I was going to Wayne State University for my post-doctoral research. I tried to organize my leftover research and the histology slide boxes that I worked on for a living because my scholarship was terminated at the end of six years. That day I left my apartment for the ERU at 7 am. As I left; I saw the mail from the day before on the table. I grabbed it and rushed to the car. At the first stoplight, I found the bank envelope. At the second stoplight, I opened it and took a quick look. At the third or fourth stoplight I picked out four of the cancelled checks to make sure I didn't owe any money to the secretary before I left East Lansing. I arrived at the ERU at 7:30 and went directly to the histology room. I left my handbag next to the sink and started arranging the slide boxes.

It was about 8:15 when Dr. Nellor entered the lab and found me in the histology room. As he entered the room, I greeted him as usual, but he didn't respond. He was frustrated and very angry. He said, "Massoum, I'm not going to sign the final documents for you. I'm going to keep you in this lab for another six years. I'll never ever recommend you to anyone. If you go anywhere I will sue you. Don't you realize the consequences of your misuse?" I wondered what I had done wrong. Was I accused of some crime? If not, what had happened? He was walking and talking nonstop and I was unable to think of anything that could have caused him this much anger and frustration. I felt so dizzy that I couldn't stand straight. I had to lean on the table for support. He was circling around and continued talking and attacking me. I became more and more speechless. Finally, his glance hit my eyes and he paused and perhaps realized how devastated I was. At that moment I grabbed a chair and asked him to sit. Then I sat on another chair facing him and almost in tears I asked him to please tell me what had happened. His silence gave me time to relax a bit and ask him what I had done wrong. He said, "You misused my secretary in the Physiology Department." I stood up, locked the door, slid my chair behind it, grabbed my purse and said, "Dr. Nellor, with all due respect, I won't allow you to leave this room until you pay close attention to my questions and answer them one by one." He was still silent. I began speaking, "Don't you remember you yourself told me to go to the Physiology Department and talk to your secretary and ask if she could type for me? Did you not tell me that she is more familiar with your wording and your handwriting? Didn't you?" In reply he said, "Yes, Massoum, I told you to do that, but I didn't tell you to misuse her. Why didn't you pay her?" It was then I realized how lucky I was that day and at that specific moment. In spite of my hurry to get to the lab, I had seen the mail on the table and had grabbed it. In fact, I had my cancelled checks in my hand. I took the cancelled checks, placed them on the back of a histology book and asked John to notice that a check was made out to his secretary. He said, "Yes, it is." Then I asked him, "Should I pay her more than $400?" He replied, "You overpaid her, but what is the $120 for?" I said, "She didn't have a typewriter at home, so she asked me to rent an electric IBM and I did. This voided check was for the security deposit." He stood up and told me, "Massoum, I beg your pardon. After such a long period of good working relations, I always trusted you. Please forgive me. Your patience and honesty will be unforgettable forever." He kissed my forehead and again asked for forgiveness. Then he asked me to please let him out. About two hours later, while I was still working in the room, he brought me all the signed documents for my graduation. I will never forget that specific day. Whenever I think of that situation I feel so thankful, because if I hadn't had those cancelled checks in my hand, how could I have proven to him that I had always been honest? At the end, he said, "Massoum; let's stay good and close friends forever." And so we remained.

Untold Story

From 1972-1977, John Nellor came to Iran four times and visited most parts of Iran as time allowed. He had been very interested in developing an institution of higher education similar to the American University in Beirut, Lebanon in some developing country around the world, but he was most interested in Iran. He strongly believed that if he could talk to the Shah of Iran as an educator, not a politician, he could convince him to build such a university in the south or central part of Iran, no matter how deserted the land or how salty its water might be. Such things could be corrected in a short period of time. He always talked about the potential of such an organization in that region because the Gulf countries and Arab nations used to send their younger generations far distances to Europe or America for study. Whenever he talked to me he tried to convince me to arrange a meeting with the Shah when he came to the US. In turn, I tried hard to convince him that this wasn't an easy or simple request for me to complete. I was a simple student, he was His Imperial Majesty. John Nellor was never satisfied with my response and kept telling me this Iranian group of valedictorians could be classified as the nobility and must be brave enough to talk about education and modern technology in Iran. It wasn't an easy or simple process; it required an experienced person that couldn't be me. Such a person should have close proximity with the Palace, specifically with the Shah when he traveled, and should be able to recognize the right moment when the Shah was in a good mood and excellent spirit to present a meeting request.

As much as I was reluctant, John affirmed his idea more and more. When I tried to explain the financial state and its related bureaucracy in Iran, he told me, "Massoum, you are a chicken. The Shah and his family could fund such a university to start, and then collect their share after five to ten years with ten percent interest. This is the main purpose; I wish I could have a chance to talk to him." When John was in DC and we were in Michigan, he called me and asked if I had heard the news. I said, "What news?"

He said, "Massoum, it is time for you to grab the chance. The Shah of Iran is coming to DC in ten days and will be the guest of honor at the White House. (It was President Johnson's era.) I decided to take a chance and call His Majesty's special physician, Dr. Ayadi, who always traveled with him. I explained my request as well as the purpose of this meeting. I told him that John Nellor, my major professor, wanted to suggest the establishment of a university similar to the American University in Beirut to be founded by His Majesty and the entire Pahlavi family.

Dr. Ayadi asked, "Did you not tell him that he had numerous advisors?" I replied, "I tried my best." Then Dr. Ayadi told me he would try his best too, but there would be no guarantee. Two days later, I received a telex from the Embassy of Iran informing me that on Thursday April 10, 1967, John Nellor, Nikou and I would have the honor of meeting with His Imperial Majesty at 3 pm local time in the Crystal Room in Washington, D.C. I was extremely happy, envisioning being in the middle of a beautiful garden of an imaginary Imperial University in Iran. What a pleasant thought and wonderful moment! I called John Nellor and told him about the date, time and place of the meeting. I told him we would be in his office at 12 noon sharp; we should introduce ourselves at the front desk of the Crystal Room by 2:30 to be ready for the 3 pm meeting.

April 10th arrived and Nikou and I got ready to go. We left Detroit at 4 am and arrived in Washington, DC at 11:30. We rushed to Dr. Nellor's office and arrived at noon, entering a beautiful lobby with a cathedral ceiling. Nikou said she would stay there so I went to his office, which was very elegant. After greeting each other he directed me to an armchair at the upper part of his conference table. I found him dressed in a very informal outfit. He asked me if I had come alone.

"No, John, Nikou came with me."

"Where is she?

"In the lobby"

"Why didn't she come up?"

"She wanted to relax a bit."

"Massoum, would you care for a glass of ice water?"

"No, thank you."

While he was asking me these questions I felt there was something he didn't want to tell me at once. I said, "Dr. Nellor, what time should we leave and how far is the Crystal Room from here?"

He reluctantly said, "Not far; you can be there on time." After a pause he said, "Massoum, are you OK?"

"Yes, I am."

"I suggest taking a taxi; it would be much easier than going by car and finding no parking space." Then he turned his chair and started reading some papers that were on his desk. With great surprise I asked him, "Are you reviewing your proposal?"

In reply he said, "What proposal?"

I told him, "The Imperial University of Iran that you made sketches of from A-Z."

John turned his chair toward me and said, "Massoum, all I wanted to know is one word, yes or no." I started thinking what had happened to him; all his questions appeared to be irrelevant to our upcoming meeting.

"What is going on?" I said, "John, please give me a clue. It has been more than thirty minutes and you keep asking me trite questions; I am unable to solve this puzzle. Time is limited we have to be there by 2:30."

He said, "Massoum, I hope this situation doesn't hurt you, does it?"

I said, "No."

He said, "To tell you the truth, I can't make it." I desperately asked him what he meant. e said, "Sorry. I am not able to go with you to visit with the Shah. I would be liable to lose my job and my position." I asked him again with anger, "Why?" Dr. Nellor remarked about his stupid enthusiasm and then explained that if President Johnson realized John's involvement, not only would he be mad at John but John would fall into the FBI's net. I could only say, "Oh, my God." Can you imagine my feelings at that moment? I felt like the room was full of steam and smoke mixed and I was unable to breath. There was no point to talk more or ask more; I had to go forward to find a solution. At that terrible moment I recalled my mother's advice when I succeeded in catching something odd. She always warned me, "Don't play with the tiger's tail." At that moment, even I felt how scary it would be; but later it proved to be otherwise. At that moment I had no mind to think and no strength to move. Somehow I managed to get to the lobby by the elevator. I can't describe the details of that beautiful place because when I arrived I only saw the cathedral ceiling and when I returned to the lobby everything I saw was through a haze. Nikou was waiting for Nellor and me. When she found me alone, she came forward, grabbed my arm and directed me to the powder room. I was so disturbed, helpless, angry and mad that I lay down on the sofa. Nikou tried to comfort me; to reduce my anger and frustration she kept bringing a cold towel and applying it to my face, which was deep purple in color. We were limited in time and had to go forward. Finally, we left by taxi to the Crystal Room. On the way, Nikou kept her charming phrase, "Thank God, we didn't have an accident, we didn't kill anyone on the road, we are still alive, breathing and going to meet with the first person of Iran; not many have such a great chance."

Finally, we arrived on time and went to the front desk of the Crystal Room. Dr. Ayadi was walking down the hall; we greeted him and he asked where the professor was. Suddenly and out of my conscience I replied, "He and his wife had a car accident this morning and both are hospitalized." He asked me if I had visited them. I replied, "Not yet, I am not familiar with this city."

As the moment of the honorary event approached, we moved to the Crystal Room and the Shah entered. We both bowed and he shook hands with us. Dr. Ayadi introduced Nikou as my daughter. Then the Shah said, "Iran needs people like you. I heard about your professor's plan. You should follow his path." We bowed again while he moved to the other room. The meeting was over.

This meeting was the first stone block of the Institute of Paramedical Sciences and it was the reason that I sent the plan of its establishment to the Shah's office before I sent it to the Ministry of Science and Higher Education for approval. The Board of Trustees of the Institute later also had the honor to meet with His Majesty.

It was 3:30 P.M. when we got a cab to my car and left Washington DC. On the highway, as it got dark and reading the signs became difficult, Nikou told me she would watch for all the signs, specifically exits and intersections; my duty was driving and hers was reading the signs. Little by little, she became drowsy; we had left Detroit at 4 am, had driven to D.C. non-stop, and now were returning to Detroit. We both were tired but I myself felt mentally and physically exhausted. I couldn't blame her; she was young, so she slept. Once in a while she moved a bit, opened her eyes and told me not to worry because I was on the right route. I kept looking at the signs; the area appeared unfamiliar; so I called, "Hey, Nikou, am I going toward Detroit?"

Nikou said, "Yes, I am watching you."

I told her, "Nikou, I don't need someone to watch me, I am desperate for directions."

Once again she said, "Trust me; I know you are going toward Detroit."

After about five hours of driving, I looked at the gas gauge and said, "We need gas." (I didn't exit earlier as I wasn't sure if I exited I would be able to get back on the same route.) Finally, I had no choice but to exit. I found a gas station and asked the shopkeeper if we were on the right route.

He said, "Sorry, you are about one hundred miles away from the junction that will take you to Detroit." He advised me to set the mileage reader to zero, then return to the junction I had taken and go toward Washington, D.C. He said, "You can't miss it. When you see 100 miles you should see a junction that will tell you which way you should go."

So on that night I drove 200 extra miles. Instead of arriving in Detroit at midnight, we arrived at 4 am - but we arrived safely. We slept for three hours and went to work at 8 am as usual.

In August 1977 the International Association of University Presidents (IAUP) was held in Tehran and John Nellor represented the University of Nevada-Reno and the cooperative program with the Institute of Paramedical Sciences of Tehran. Dr. Nellor and his wife had the honor of meeting with the Shah of Iran at Saad Abbad Palace. But he had lost his chance to propose the establishment of an Imperial University in Iran similar to the one in Beirut.

*Shah of Iran shaking hands with
John Nellor at the Saad Abbad Palace, 1977*

CHAPTER 8

Return to Iran for Good

I received a job offer from the Tehran University Medical School, Department of Anatomy, Pathology and Cell Culture at the same time the Wayne State Department of Physiology and Pharmacology where I was working for my post-doc offered me their help if I wished to apply for permanent residency. My ego, stupid prejudices and the most important one, my family ties, masked my logic and proper thinking. I never believed it would be a golden opportunity to have permanent US residency. I had no one to consult with and get advice about it. I never imagined what would happen if the country underwent a revolution. I never dreamed how much I would lose and how I would be when I had to leave my country in a rush and how much I might suffer. But I wanted to go home, to be with my family and pay back my obligation to my country and the younger generation. I thought if I applied for permanent residency in the US, I might not be able to do what I always dreamed for in Iran (i.e. establish an institution of higher education).

Finally on September 11, 1967, I left the US with Nikou after 8 years of consecutive study. We left Detroit on KLM to Amsterdam and from there via Iran Air to Tehran. We arrived at the Tehran airport at 6 pm and then went on to my sister's house, arriving at 8:30. I met my first grandchild, Shaparak, when she was twelve months and eight days old.

The first time I met my first grandchild Shaparak, Tehran, 1967

She looked like an angel in a pink and white dress, a gold and pearl necklace and matching bracelet. She entered the room in Nikrou's arms, looked at me with her brown eyes and wondered who I was. After a while she accepted me; she came to my lap and became my closest friend up to the present time where she is my wonderful and concerned private physician.

After a week of rest and meeting with all the relatives and friends, I faced the reality of life and started looking for an apartment to rent and a job to work. I had a job offer from Tehran University but according to law, my previous job which had been suspended during my period of study was still pending. Therefore, the Education Department had to reactivate my job and then make an agreement with the Tehran University to allow me to transfer. It took me thirty working days to go every morning to the office of the gentleman who was in charge of signing the agreement letter until I could transfer to the higher education division. This gentleman was angry enough to resist signing the agreement letter. He kept asking many questions about my scholarship – how had I obtained it? Who had helped me from "behind the curtain?" He couldn't believe that I had received it on merit due to my high grade point average. When he had a few visitors in his office, he told me, "You spent ten years abroad, enjoyed yourself and now expect everything to be done in 10 days which is not possible. Look at these people, they are all waiting for a position; you have a lot of support, while they don't have any. It isn't fair for them." He tried to make me mad by insulting me as much as he could and in as many ways as possible. In contrast, I tried to be calm, quiet and polite, not to respond. I knew if I became angry and said something he would make me a fat file and ruin my reputation. Today it is hard for me to believe the degree of my tolerance at the time. While I was quiet and ignored his nonsense he became upper handed one day; I decided to challenge him, but how could I do it?

On my last visit to the man's office, an old gentleman came in with a job offer paper in his hand. He advised me not to be angry, to pay no attention to this letter, it is just office formality. It was written, "You must teach Arabic literature to 8th graders in so and so high school." He kept telling me, "Go home and spend time with your children. I know you well. My daughter who is now in her last year as a medical student at National University was a student in the 9th grade when you resigned from the high school superintendent position and went to the United States. Be sure, I will do my best to facilitate your transfer to Tehran University Medical School." I must admit that I have forgotten the man's name but will always remember his kind attitude and innocent face. I am sure God likes him wherever he is, either in this world or the infinite sky.

After about thirty days I shifted from going to the Educational Department to the real estate office to find an apartment to live in. I finally received a copy of the agreement letter to Tehran University Medical School. It was a great relief, but I didn't realize that this was just the first challenge I had to face. There would be more and more challenges, in higher rather than lower education, in government and private sectors.

The day after I went to the University hiring department with my job offer and transfer agreement letter, they welcomed me and I met with the head of the department to introduce myself. He kindly introduced me to everybody in the laboratory and showed me my office. I started my work the next day. It was quite a challenging task, with a group of French-educated doctors who were strongly against an American-educated person. During breaks they would talk to each other loudly. They believed American-educated people had no knowledge; they are too proud of themselves, pretentious and easy going. If someone asked them a question, they told the person to go ask the American-educated person, he knows everything except the answer to your question. They tried to tell the story about an American-educated gynecologist who could not find anyone in the system to hire him, so he finally took a job in the Veterinary Department taking care of pregnant cows, sheep, pigs, etc. Later on I found out that he was in military service for two years and had no choice. Their criticism never ended. I tried to keep myself busy and as strong as possible, to never lose my temper and to answer their questions properly. One day one of the pulmonary specialists from a great and famous family talked about his mother who always told him that all good-looking girls were uneducated because they married at an early age; in contrast ugly girls were well-educated, working in different areas, as teachers, dress-makers, etc. "Today it's just the opposite; how come a person like you is working in this department with us?" I started laughing and told him not to be surprised; I was returned to my parents. It was not easy to tolerate all the different and unpleasant ideas of male verses female with equal levels of education.

A few months later, I received a letter from the National University of Iran about a teaching position in the College of Biology. After an interview with the Dean, I accepted the position to teach Physiology to sophomores and Medical Mycology to senior students from 5-9 pm twice a week. I continued this teaching position at the National University of Iran for six consecutive years. There was no criticism and no challenges with the opposite gender, my colleagues all were American-educated. Six months later my second granddaughter Shayma was born.

Shayma, my second granddaughter, 1969

Although delivery took place in a modern hospital, Minoo suffered severe septicemia. Today Shayma is a successful banker and has two sons 12 and 10 years old.

Two years after my transfer from the Educational Division to the Tehran University Medical School I received a telephone call from the office of the Secretary of Education about a meeting with Dr. F. Parsay who had graduated from the Tehran University Medical School. I met with her and accepted the position of "Director General for Teachers' Health and Welfare." She told me, "This office needs new blood, so the committee selected you." I accepted the position and returned to where I belonged - education. In this position, I got closer to my dream of "higher education." I wrote a letter of proposal to establish a school of Associate Diploma, specifically training in nursing for primary and secondary schools. The plan was approved and I received a 45 day-grant from UNESCO to go to Tokyo, Japan to review their system, which was unique in the world.

Meanwhile, in February 1969 Nikou married a British-educated civil engineer in Tehran. Today her 23-year marriage has been ended by the return of her husband to Iran and his marriage to a select revolutionary woman. Their son Hessam was born March 18, 1971. He is my youngest grandchild.

Nasser and Nikou married, 1969

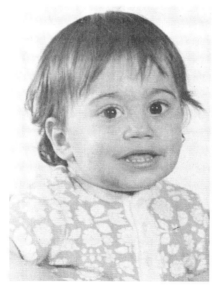

Their son, Hessam, 1971

Preview of IPS

Since 1957 when I received my BSC degree, was elected high school principal and started working in a semi-private high school with 1200 students, I felt the need for a better, stronger and more modern system of education and I wished to undertake it myself by establishing a private high school. But at that point in time my mind was working toward my own future education. During that two-year period (1957-1959) I made advances toward modernization with a most successful education program by establishing evening classes for senior students who planned to go to college. In spite of my mind being occupied by so much change in all directions for that private school, whatever I had in mind appeared to be far off in the future.

I tried my best anyway, even after four years when I returned to Iran in the summer of 1963 for Minoo's wedding reception. I spent at least 5 days a week in the Ministry of Education to testify that those who where hired as private rather than government personnel should be considered government employees because they had higher benefits while private employees had none. As soon as the law sending valedictorian graduates abroad was passed by parliament and was sent to the senate, I started to pack my suitcases and prepare myself for a trip to the US to start my own advanced education despite a strong fear of not knowing the language.

Whatever I was thinking, I had to leave it behind and look forward to an invisible horizon. I did it. In other words, I "walked on a completely dark and strange road." When I went to the US and faced a lot of difficulties with so many strange and unfamiliar events I completely forgot whatever I had been thinking before. I became so busy with my own personal problems that I forgot my past. I'm sure in the course of life everyone must face such things at least once or twice. From October of 1959 when I left Iran to July of 1967 when I was engaged in my post-doctoral research at Wayne State University in Michigan and the time that Dr. John Nellor called me from

Bethesda, Maryland to pick him up at the Detroit airport, I never ever recalled what had been in my mind before I came to the United States. I met Dr. Nellor at the airport and I handed the car keys to him to drive. Dr. Nellor had planned to go to the Endocrine Research Unit (ERU) that he was in charge of and spend some time there. While he was driving from Detroit to East Lansing we talked about so many different areas of interest. He told me, "Massoum, someday I wish to come to your country and with your help and effort set up an American University similar to the one in Beirut." Then he said if for some political reason he couldn't do it, he suggested that I go for it and he promised to help me as much as possible. At that moment it appeared to be nothing but sweet talk on the road. We arrived at the ERU and he made a surprise entry to the lab. I went in for a short time to visit my friends Joann and Shirley and then returned to Detroit. On my way back I started thinking and reviewing our conversation and his suggestion but it appeared to be far from reality. Whenever I started thinking and planning for my future life in Iran his idea came back to my mind then was forgotten again.

In April 1968 I went to memorial service for Mr. Yazdonfar, the Undersecretary of Education, in charge of student affairs in foreign countries. His few close friends started talking about his character, his education and his personal life. One of the speakers admired his kindness and his great concern for others. He explained his personal life in detail and said Mr. Yazdonfar had nothing until he became a partner with one of the private schools of higher education that resulted in a great change in his life style and brought him a lot of money and fame as well.

At that moment the dormant seed that Dr. Nellor planted in my mind in July 1967 started to germinate and grow day after day. But I hadn't a well-developed source to study an allied health program of the same design that I had in my mind. And so it was that I submitted the letter of proposal for the establishment of a school for an associate degree in special nursing program for primary and secondary schools and I received a 45-

day grant from UNESCO to go to Tokyo, Japan to review their unique system developed after World War II.

This was a great opportunity for me. While I visited the Japanese health care network system at the primary and secondary school levels, I also had a chance to visit the allied heath system of Tokyo University upon the recommendation of Professor Takeo Wada. As it turned out, the 45 days were almost doubled time-wise because from 8-12 am I was visiting primary and secondary schools in different locations with the interpreter from the Ministry of Education and from 2-6 pm I was at Tokyo University's Allied Health College. It was a great time for me to be in close contact with the people of another nation to learn from their experience and expertise, to see their creation and courage, to understand their culture, attitudes, life style and their mannerisms. Furthermore it was a very fruitful trip because on my return I had a chance to establish two separate programs of higher education - the first one was an associate degree special nurse training program for primary and secondary schools affiliated with the Ministry of Education; the other one was a private college of allied health or paramedical sciences.

As this trip was a mission trip, I had to follow protocol and introduce myself personally to the Iranian ambassador to report my arrival and departure time, telephone number, residence address, the purpose for the trip and my area of interest. I had an English interpreter in charge of the UNESCO program. She picked me up every morning at 8 am with a black car belonging to the Minister of Education. The driver wore a black suit and long white gloves. The inside of the car was covered with white cotton fabric decorated with beautiful lace. My interpreter Midori explained everything to me. The driver dropped us back at my hotel at exactly 1 pm. At 2 pm a similar car from the Tokyo University came to pick me up; the driver knew where he was to take me. We would not communicate with each other but I was sure he knew his job. As soon as I arrived at Tokyo University, a young lady named Yori met me and served as my afternoon interpreter.

Me with scientists and staff of Tokyo University, 1969

Three specific and surprising events happened during the 45 days that I spent in Tokyo. The first event occurred at 10 am on a Friday while I was visiting the main school health care network system. My interpreter told me I had a telephone call from the Iranian Embassy. I grabbed the phone and greeted the person on the line. He said he was Ambassador Kiya and the reason he called personally was to correct an oversight - my name had accidentally been omitted from the guest list of that night's party arranged in honor of Prince Gholam Reza (the Shah's brother); he expected my presence in the embassy main hall at 8 pm that night. I responded with pleasure - I would be there. For a while I was speechless, then I explained the situation to my interpreter Midori - I had no formal dress with me; how could I go to the party? She suggested that we go shopping at lunchtime. We went to Ginza Street. She took me to three boutiques with beautiful Japanese-style dresses but none of them fit me. Time was limited; I had to be back in time for the afternoon driver to pick me up. I hurried home and made myself ready for the afternoon visit to Tokyo University. On my way I thought I would be better off if I bought at least a handbag for that evening. When I arrived at the University I asked my interpreter for help. She told me that in such a short period of time it was not possible to buy a formal dress. But I must go to the hair salon before 5 pm because they didn't accept anyone after 5 pm. She offered her help to take me there. At 4 pm we went to the beauty salon and she explained everything to them. She gave me a written note in Japanese for the taxi driver to take me from my hotel to the Iranian Embassy. I had to wait a long time because I was a walk-in customer. They did a nice job with my hair but when I came out of the salon the handbag shops were closed.

My interpreter, Yori, and me saying goodbye

So I went to the party in a very regular not formal dress. Among the one hundred guests at the party, four of them including myself were single; forty-eight women had on long formal gowns. I stood out so that everyone was interested to see who I was and how I got in to such a very formal party with such an every-day dress using my eyeglass case as a handbag. The presence of such an odd person tweaked everyone's curiosity, including that of Prince Gholam Reza. So most of the guests, especially the women, came and talked to me. One Japanese lady with a fantastic set of real diamonds and a beautiful Japanese outfit stood by me and kept questioning me about life in Iran. Meanwhile a gentleman, her husband, joined us and introduced himself as "Reza," an Iranian who came to Tokyo in 1928 with his parents. While we were talking a cocktail waiter came forward and asked for my choice of drink. I didn't know what to order. I had never been a drinker. Suddenly my mind became completely blocked. I couldn't remember any fancy drink except Cinzano that I had never tasted in my life. So I told him, "Cinzano." He asked me, "On the rocks?" and I said, "Yes, please." Reza kept talking to me without any reaction or impression that he realized how much I didn't know what I had ordered. When the waiter returned with the tray of drinks and stopped in front of us, I raised my hand to take my glass. Reza grabbed my wrist and ordered a glass of ginger ale for me. He then told me, "With all due respect, I am sure you wouldn't be able to drink Cinzano." He advised me to always order ginger ale because it looks like whisky. At that moment, I recalled the night that I was in Ann Arbor, Michigan and was invited to a party. I had a sip of sherry and forgot about the location of my country when they asked me. Since then, I learned how to order a drink to still be in fashion and not to make me drunk. I must admit that I gained a lot of knowledge about the attitudes and culture of people of other nations that night. It was a very enjoyable party despite the fact that I was so different than the other sophisticated guests. I was the one that Prince Gholam and Ambassador Kiya talked to more than anyone else at the party.

The second surprising event was an unexpected interview with a Japanese Professor of Pathology. The subject was "How did you find medical technology in Japan?" Professor Wada told me, "The University driver will pick you up and drive you to the interview." I thought he would take me to a radio or TV station but after 45 minutes driving on a very narrow, long, winding road, he stopped in front of a restaurant. He opened the car door for me and signaled with his hand that I was to go up the stairs; I assumed it was to an office because I was not able to read Japanese writing although I learned to speak a few words for my daily use. I went up about 15 or more very narrow stairs and entered a night restaurant where I saw only a single Japanese man. Neither of us could talk to each other, although in Japanese custom, he bowed several times to welcome me and directed me to a chair. Then the professor who was to interview me arrived. He sat in a chair across the table and started talking and questioning me.

The Japanese Professor of Pathology and me during an interview in a Tokyo restaurant, 1969

I saw nothing on the table except a round glass the same size and shape as a beaker. It was sitting on the table loosely, with no wire, no attachment or anything. After about two hours of talking, the restaurant manager brought us two beautiful round boxes, one for him and the other for me. He took the lid off and I did too. Inside the box were two whole octopi, two clams, two snails, two beautiful shiny raw fish and a few species of seaweed. It was my first time seeing sushi. As I looked at it, I got very red-faced. The professor immediately put the lid on top of my box and asked the waiter to bring me an egg sandwich. He said this was one of the most famous seafood restaurants in Tokyo that served only at night. The meeting was arranged at this restaurant so that I could be entertained in a highly respected manner. I will always remember that sushi box - I never saw one like it before, either in Michigan or any other place that I visited. When our interview and lunch was over, the professor handed me an envelope containing a thank you card and one hundred thousand Japanese yen equivalent to $55 at that time. I returned to my hotel at 4 pm by the same car.

The third surprising event happened on the same Saturday night that the Japanese Secretary of Education invited me for dinner and an evening of entertainment at a very famous theater. At 6:30 pm, he came to pick me up without his wife. I became curious because the invitation card was from Mr. and Mrs. Uguen Egami. I thought she would join us either directly from her job or their house. He took me to a tempura restaurant where the food was fried in front of each table. The food was a combination of fish, chicken and beef. When we entered the restaurant, he told me his wife had an excuse that night because his daughter was getting ready for the University entrance examination and his wife had to take care of her. After dinner, he took me to the Kabuki Theater. It was one of their famous plays. The first surprising thing was that I could not understand a word of it but I could understand it visually. The second thing was that 99% of the women were sitting in the periphery of the theater, which was huge in size and round in shape. All the men and a few foreign women like me were scattered in the rectangular area on very comfortable chairs by themselves or with their host. At the intermission when the lights came on, I looked around the theater and asked the secretary who the women were and why they were seated in the periphery and not in the middle of the theater hall. He told me that Japanese customs are very different. It would be very hard for the Japanese to follow western style; they are not used to sitting with their wives in the theater or walking behind them. While those ladies came to the theater tonight, their husbands might have been the night before or might go the next night.

During the last five days in Japan I was on my own. I bought a tour ticket and visited the local parts of Tokyo. I walked through the area around the shopping center and wondered about the area as I walked. I found so many Japanese old men sitting on little pillows that were placed on a rug or blanket covered with a rectangular while sheet and a lot of strips of paper that had some written words on it. A pair of horoscopes were used to predict the future for young girls that went to them and paid a chunk of money to see whether their star was going to match with the young boy star who they loved. They strongly believed in astrology.

About 5 or 6 months after I left Tokyo, I received a package from Japan by registered mail. I opened the package and found a medical technology journal that had my photograph on a certain page along with the professor who interviewed me on that unforgettable Saturday. The text is in Japanese except for my name and my identity, which was written in English.

College of School Nursing

I came back from Japan with a handful of higher educational information. I was very happy because I felt successful in providing health, welfare and higher education to so many of the younger generation, something I had always dreamed of doing. The Japanese school of nursing science program was adapted for Iranian students and submitted to the Ministry of Higher Education.

The two-year program was approved quickly. It was an easy task because the Ministry of Education had enough budget as well as land to build the school in the near future. In addition, the Office of Teachers' Health and Welfare had a group of physicians who always wanted to teach in the higher education division because it created great prestige for them. But the bureaucratic University system generally did not accept part-time personnel of any kind. Therefore the establishment of such a collage developed a great achievement for the Ministry of Education and the physicians who served and taught in student health services all over the country. On the other hand this was the first time that the Ministry of Education moved to the higher education program. The technical schools that were developed in Tehran many years earlier were only at the high school diploma level because the ninth grade students had been admitted for three years and their programs were mostly vocational. School nursing programs were at college level; applicants were high school graduates and had to successfully pass the entrance examination barrier. Their degree was an associate diploma and they were obligated to work in the school healthcare network system for two years before they could continue their education after passing yet another entrance examination to meet the requirements. In general the plan for the school nurse program was unique, especially for high school graduate girls; a decentralized program so the demands were great because the Ministry of Education instantly hired everyone who was admitted to the program. They received two years of free education in addition to the full salary after graduation when they started work. The demand was beyond our expectations. The Ministry of Education had planned to admit 1050 students while more than 12,000 girls applied. The top best one hundred were elected for the Tehran school and 950 for the other 19 schools in the cities that admitted 30-50 girls. All schools started on September 10, 1971. That September 1971 presented a landmark in the history of the Ministry of Education for the establishment of such a program in Iran under the supervision of two women, Dr. Farokhroo Parsay, Secretary of Education and me, Dr. Massoum Montakhab, as Director General for Teachers' Heath and Welfare. Although the critics and complaints about the development of such a program were whispered continuously in the ears of the Secretary of Education it didn't change my status. Later on it proved to be a very unique program, especially after the onset of the revolution and development of the Iran-Iraq war and the number of casualties in the hospitals. Because the graduates of that program were a great help after only six weeks of hospital training, it helped overcome the shortage of nurses in such a miserable period of war.

Dr. Parsay, Secretary of Education, and me at the opening of the College of School Nurses, 1971

CHAPTER 9

Institute of Paramedical Sciences

In contrast, the establishment of the Institute of Paramedical Sciences took over two years to formulate and become approved. After I returned from Tokyo in the fall of 1969 I also began to design a very strong program to present to the Ministry of Sciences and Higher Education. I consulted with a group of three scientists who were my colleagues at the National University of Iran. These scientists were experts in mathematics, chemistry and physics. They became highly interested in joining me to develop the curriculum for each subject and invest some money to become a shareholder. They were the most perfect partners for me. I arranged to meet twice a week after work to discuss the curriculum, the budget and the amount of investment. It took us six or seven months to formulate six different programs of study presentable to the Ministry of Science and Higher Education. We tried very hard to make a perfect program and a well-developed curriculum in hopes that the Ministry of Science and Higher Education would not refuse any part of it; otherwise, it would take years before we would be allowed to present it again. Although the curriculum presented was more than adequate, complete, neat, and flawless and we felt sure there was no chance of rejection, it took two years before it was approved because it was a Bachelor of Science program of four years duration and required the approval of many single specialists, numerous qualified professors, as well as qualified and approved hospitals and laboratories to practice in. In addition, the budget, the space, equipment and classroom furniture were other important points. I applied to establish a private institution of higher education, which required a basic investment of more than a million dollars. In those days that was a considerable amount of money. I had to convince the Ministry of Science and Higher Education that I was capable of handling such a big organization and providing all the necessary space, teaching materials, equipment, etc. I also had to select members of the Board of Trustees and educational committees and submit their written acceptances to the Ministry of Science and Higher Education. In other words, I was the only one to provide every single point that the Ministry asked for. It took us two years of constant planning, going back and forth, facing a lot of disagreements and disappointments, trying to convince those old-fashioned professors and bureaucrats to whom I personally had to present my complete plan of branches of study, to defend my ideas and to beg for their approval. The Ministry of Science and Higher Education and its committee also resisted the approval because some of the branches (like the medical secretary, radiation therapy and public health undergraduate programs) were completely brand new; so was the idea of accepting male applicants for the Bachelor of Science degree in the nursing program. All the nursing schools in the country offered an equivalent degree; therefore none of the nursing graduates could go on for further study. They believed that the shortage of nurses and medical technicians necessitated a shorter program rather than a longer one with a higher cost. I tried to defend my idea that every single individual has a right to study further or stop their education at whatever level they wanted.

Today when I think about my efforts 40 years ago, I wonder how I did it. It wasn't a simple, easy task to make an appointment with different professors, talk to them, defend my ideas, present my plan, and listen to their criticisms (such as "How can you open a school right beside Tehran University? Don't waste your time and effort. You have no idea and not enough experience to compete with University attorneys. It's a conflict of interest.")

No matter how strong you are and what perfect ideas you have, it's easy to feel shaky when people talk down to you and advise you not to do something. I tried to be calm and polite, to agree with their ideas first, then start to explain the reasons I wanted to establish the institute of higher education. I always told them, "Today I came to you for help and a great favor for young boys and girls starving for further education. And for those patients who need more help while in the hospital." The answer usually was, "This is the duty of a strong and more experienced man, not a delicate lady like you." These compliments or comments were like a sharp needle in my heart. I wondered if it would ever be possible to be successful. I told myself to try harder. "If you fail, you will be dead forever. So don't be disappointed and stand still; go forward." I did and became a most successful person when the submitted plan was completely approved and the permit letter was issued on May 10, 1972.

From May to September after the approval, I had to take many different actions simultaneously. Unfortunately my three friends from the National University who spent countless hours in curriculum development, budgets, equipment and teaching supplements collectively denied their participation. Their reasons were well understood because during these two years for some reason their interests and schedules changed. Therefore I had to (1) find a group of investors including myself, two of my sons-in-law and some of my friends, totaling twelve scientists and physicians; (2) set up and organize a 12-member Board of Trustees, including one member who represented the investors and one appointed by the Secretary of Science and Higher Education; (3) form a committee to arrange and hire staff and finalize all the curricula; and (4) find a proper building for such an institution, with a certain amount of open area and enough rooms for classes, laboratories, equipment, machinery and a training center. Fortunately one of the established institutions of higher education was moving to their private building at the same time and I could lease the structure for ten years before it was completely vacant. Therefore all the laboratory equipment, machinery and classroom furniture was ordered at once.

I was fortunate enough to have a group of young, honest, well-educated and trained people with me to form all the basic requirements, especially the educational program, for the privately-funded Institute of Paramedical Sciences. Three people in this group were my daughters. Minoo had a BSc degree in nursing and midwifery from the Royal College of London and a Master of Science degree in nursing education from the National University of Iran, Tehran. She was elected as supervisor in charge of the nursing and medical secretary programs as well as responsible for their training in various hospitals. Nikou had a doctoral degree in Veterinary Medicine from Tehran University with a specialty in Clinical Microbiology, a Master of Science degree in Medical Microbiology and Public Health and a certificate in Medical Mycology from Michigan State University. She was elected Associate Dean, in charge of all curricula. Nikrou had a Bachelor of Science degree in general education from the Tehran Girls' College and a practical training certificate in Architectural Engineering from Detroit Institute of Technology in Michigan. She was placed in charge of all examination programs that had to be well prepared and guarded. This was extremely important to maintain the Institute's reputation and prestige. The fourth person was my great-nephew Akbar Ladjevardi, a British-educated young man specializing in accounting and money management.

My unique team in establishment of IPS.
Left to right:: Me, Minoo, Nikou, Akbar and Nikrou

With non-stop help from this primary group, the place, the date
and time for the entrance examination was announced in two of
the popular evening newspapers and the next day registration
started. The demand was so great - fifteen thousand young men
and women applicants registered; we could only accept four hundred juniors. Therefore only the best were accepted. The quality
of teaching, the educational level of teachers, lab assistants, laboratory equipment and affiliate hospitals' laboratories and other
training centers associated with the Institute of Paramedical
Sciences resulted in a greater demand as well as fame for the
school and satisfaction for the students and staff.

Left to right: Nikou, me, Mr. Kamarei, Dr. Parsay, and Dr. Nellor, among the students and staff of IPS, 1972

Dr. John Nellor speaking while I translate in IPS, 1972

The Institute opened on September 12, 1972, with hours from 7 am to 8 pm according to the student and teacher schedules because 80% of the professors came from Tehran University and/or National University. Those professors preferred classes scheduled after 5 pm. Also, many students were working in hospital laboratories or other places and preferred afternoon and evening classes as well. In general all of the new

Institute's laboratories and training centers were active in the morning, with lecture classes in the afternoon. I was still working in the Ministry of Education at the same office (Teachers' Health and Welfare) and also taught at National University from 5-9 pm two nights a week.

The first Board of Trustees met on September 18th at 10 am and I was elected Dean, as had been approved by the Secretary of Science and Higher Education. Therefore I had to resign from my position at the Ministry and concentrate all my activities in the Institute of Paramedical Sciences. My employment status was Academic Advisor to the Secretary of Education but my salary was paid from the Institute's budget.

It didn't take long until my challenges started. Around December or January of that first year, I discovered there were things cooking against me. Even though I was elected by the Board of Trustees and was approved by the Secretary of Science and Higher Education, the pediatrician who was elected as representative of investors on the Board of Trustees decided to replace me with the wife of one of his friends who worked as a full time consultant in the Ministry of Science and Higher Education. She had a BS degree in English and her husband was a Member of Parliament.

To this day I cannot fathom how he convinced one of my assistants, a shareholder himself, to ask me to resign voluntarily. It wasn't easy for me to accept this horribly unfair, awful, shameful plot from the two of them. I felt I had to fight for my rights - none of them had been involved in the establishment of the Institute. When my three friends denied their participation I had had to round up a total of 12 investors; so out of desperation I included several about whom I had little or no personal knowledge. One of them was this French-educated pediatrician, the son-in-law of a banker who was one of the twelve investors.

I felt I had to strike out and put an end to his favoritism and interfering attitude. I called for a Board meeting immediately, explained the situation and offered my verbal resignation. All members of the Board except the pediatrician voted in my favor and the Secretary of Science and Higher Education again approved their decision.

This man's failure to do whatever he had in mind and his attempt to replace me as Dean resulted in a student strike. Later I found out that the same woman who was to assume the Dean's position started the sabotage by telling one student, "They fooled you by getting your money; there is no approval and no permit." That innocent student told his friends; the news spread like wind in the Sahara and a strike started with a few male nursing students refusing to go to class and also preventing the girls from attending their classes. The next day, other groups joined them one after the other. On the third day, the students started breaking the brand new classroom chairs, laboratory equipment, typewriters, microscopes, etc. They threw eggs and tomatoes at the staff and lab assistants and other office workers. After a series of investigations, the Secretary of Science and Higher Education notified me to shut down the Institute for the time being and we did.

After almost two months registration started again and the situation returned to normal, except for a budget shortage due to the damages incurred during the strike. Replacement of equipment cost almost the equivalent of one-fourth of the tuition collected from all 400 students. Whenever the accounting department reported the estimated deficit to me, I tried to convince them that one of our shareholders was the owner of the same bank we were dealing with; surely, he would give us an overdraft when we needed it. After spending more than three million dollars in less than a year and at least double that amount projected for the next year, the bank refused our request for an overdraft payment. So I called the CEO of the bank who was one of our shareholders. Although I expected his refusal because he was the father-in-law of the pediatrician who tried to replace me, I was still hopeful. I never expected his strange act. After two days of waiting for him to return my call, his answer was that it was out of his hands; the bank was not able to do so.

But it should have been a normal process in banks for a

customer with a great backbone (i.e. flow of student registration fees). Thank goodness a friend of mine introduced me to the CEO of another bank who offered unlimited overdraft protection if we dealt with his bank. Opening a new account and closing the old one took place on the same day ($3.5 million was approved). Surprisingly, our shareholder (the CEO of the first bank) called me personally and asked why we had closed the account. I replied politely, "It wouldn't be an easy task to be Dean of such an organization without enough power to act quickly." His response was, "Doctor, you have taught me a great lesson."

In the meantime, two incidents happened resulting in a considerable increase in the Institute's budget. The first was a two-month summer in-service training program each year for science teachers sponsored by the Ministry of Education. The Institute admitted 400 applicants to the program. The second was the flow of medical technology technician applications from graduates with associate diplomas from Tehran University from five or more years prior to the establishment of the Institute. About 1500 applicants were eligible for the "sandwich" program (two years of study, two years of full time work in the field, then two years of study) resulting in a B.Sc degree. But first they had to register and pass a special entrance exam. Out of the 1500 technicians who applied, 40 students were admitted each year to complete the program.

Today I can proudly state that the technicians that graduated from the program, came to the States for further education and received their PhD degrees have established their own clinical laboratories. And those graduates from Nursing and Public Health became hospital administrators, psychologists and successful representatives in who-knows-what other fields.

Although after the onset of the Revolution the Institute was broken into pieces and affiliated with other institutions of higher education, as far as I know the Public Health division remained intact. The Nursing and Medical Technology programs became affiliated with the National University of Iran as the College of Shaheed (martyr) Beheshty, named for one of the political opponents who had lived in Germany for many years and returned to Iran during the Revolution. The first bombing explosion that resulted in 150 deaths during the revolutionary assembly in the summer of 1981 had killed him.

I bring up Beheshty's name from an unexplained sense of ego and the injustice of the situation by wiping out the progress that occurred before the Revolution. Those students who graduated before the Revolution and remained in Iran were a great help to the revolutionary people, especially during the 8 years of the Iran-Iraq war. I'm sure the majority of them remain loyal to us, but when I met some of them in the Ministry of Health when I later visited Iran, I didn't recognize them - the girl's face was covered with a scarf and chadoor and the boy's face with ample hair.

The second school year started; the entrance examination for twenty five thousand new applicants was completed with great success and continued smoothly without the shareholders interfering. In one of the shareholder meetings I suggested buying a piece of land for a proper building in the near future. It was approved by a majority vote and one of my assistants was nominated to find the land. Shortly afterwards, he found a good piece of land; it was brought before the shareholders at the next meeting. The price of the land was approved and paid for but government payment of the approved loan was dependant upon approval of the floor plans and all the related procedures.

In less than four years the Institute gained enough fame that the Board of Trustees had the honor of meeting with the Shah of Iran. This was a unique event and had never before happened to any private school of higher education.

I am reporting to the Shah at the University official ceremony in the Golestan Palace, 1973

In the middle of the third year I faced a problem with my right eye. I was hospitalized for four days and was given so many contradictory diagnoses that one of the Iranian eye specialists referred me to a famous eye center in London, England. The diagnosis was retinal detachment and I was treated immediately. The surgeon recommended that I return to the center quarterly for follow-up visits. He also warned me that the same incident might happen to my left eye in the near future. Indeed, it happened in less than six months. Therefore, I kept going to London three times a year for check-ups. Today I must thank God that it never happened to me again with all the microscopic work that I have done since I left Iran after the revolution.

Transformation

It was September of 1976, exactly four years after the opening of the Institute of Paramedical Sciences that the Prime Minister suddenly decided to change the status of all private institutions of higher education to state-owned. During this reorganization, I was in London for my eye check-up. As soon as I arrived in Tehran, Nikou told me what had happened during my absence. I immediately called a shareholders' meeting and reported the situation to them. I also had to inform the Board because the school was no longer private. It was the State that now would dictate what to do; it was no longer for me and the committee to decide independently. The Minister of Science and Higher Education became responsible to apply the orders of the Prime Minister. So every institution of higher education became affiliated to a ministry based on the demand for graduates of that institution. The Institute of Paramedical Sciences became affiliated with the Ministry of Health since demand for its graduates was so great. The process of transformation from private to state took almost four months. During this period the status of all educational programs remained unchanged. But in actuality, the Dean's position had been suspended and I had to act as Temporary Dean until the Board met. Since the status of the institute changed, a group of accountants from the Ministry of Science and Higher Education as well as a group of accountants from the Ministry of Health came to audit our books and budget to see how the money was being spent and to check on the possibility that the accounting department was guilty of misuse of funds. After two months of each group auditing independently, they could not find anything wrong to put their finger on.

As the news of the changes from private to state spread, some people found it to be a good time to put their surreptitious plans into action. At this point I can only tell what happened to me, how hard they tried to get rid of me, how much nonsense they told and how often they brainwashed the staff of the Ministry of Science and Higher Education about me.

Two physicians were involved. One worked for the Ministry of Labor and taught Industrial Health; the other worked at the Health Department and taught Public Health at the Institute. They prepared themselves for new positions as soon as the

Ministry of Health (the new owner of the school) replaced me with one of them; the other would act as his right-hand assistant. In order to show their capabilities and interest in such a position, they made a plan to present to both the Ministry of Health and the Ministry of Higher Education. Their plan was to eliminate both the Public Health branches (school and industrial health), reduce the period of study from four to two years for nursing and medical technology students (offering an Associate Diploma instead of a Bachelor of Science degree), reduce radiology and radiotherapy to a six month course of study and offering a Certificate of Authenticity after one year of study for a medical secretary. They proposed a budget equivalent to one-fifth the previous budget to convince the "Powers That Be" of my lack of knowledge and that I was an enthusiastic capitalist. Every time I heard about their proposed plan I wondered how they could think it would work. They were making a mess. It would be easy to upgrade but down grading has never been and never would be acceptable what-so-ever except perhaps during a period of war when things would be out of control for everyone. Their plan would be mental torture for students, their professors and their parents as well.

One day I received an invitation from the Ministry of Health, Division of Laboratories and Research Affairs. I arrived on time but didn't know the purpose of the meeting. There were eight doctors specializing in clinical laboratory present including two reformist doctors; the chairperson was Undersecretary of Health. Before the meeting started I asked the chairperson why I had been invited to attend this meeting. He replied, "Mr. Secretary, Dr. Shaik is interested in your opinion." The meeting started with a brief explanation of every single item and the reasons for the changes. I tried to be as silent as possible as the "Imaginative Dean" was reading his list of changes. Some of the attendees agreed with each phrase; others were silent. When he finished reading his step-by-step list and the minutes were completed and ready to sign, it was the most uncomfortable moment of my life. I tried not to argue by defending my ideas; I didn't want to see a reaction from the male chauvinist attitudes.

When the minutes came to me for signature, I told the chairperson that I had some comments that I must first discuss with Mr. Secretary before I signed. Knowing that he was busy with other more pressing matters than the problems discussed today, I would like to share them with the chairman, but he must promise to tell the Secretary every single point. Then I would sign this page with great honor. They were all surprised; evidently they were expecting some reaction from me but not quite as such. I looked at the chairperson's eyes and classified my comments, trying not to lose my temper, not to be excited, not to say a word to insult the two reformists waiting for my reaction. It was very hard to control myself in front of my opponents. It was the hardest moment of my life to keep everything in order by swallowing my pride and my anger together. I started talking and comparing the formation of the Institute with making a building. I said to make a one bedroom house you need 3-4 certified engineers, at least 10 workers and so many different kinds of materials, a lump sum of money, a considerable amount of time and effort to finish this small house. But my main point was a very short phrase: you need only one person driving one bulldozer to break down the entire building in one hour. Then I said, "I thank you all for your attention to my words, I will sign the meeting minutes later on" and left the room.

Two weeks later the chairperson called me personally and asked me to attend a luncheon meeting with Mr. Secretary. First I accepted the invitation and then I tried to find out the agenda. He replied there would be monthly meetings with Mr. Secretary and all the Undersecretaries of the different divisions of the Ministry of Health. I arrived on time and sat in the designated chair next to the Secretary of Health who introduced me to all the Undersecretaries. He mentioned the previous meeting and the explanations of the two reformist doctors, then told me, "Please keep in mind that this Ministry will not change anything at the Institute - no reduction of the Public Health branch, no change in any degree or curriculum. Whatever you did was perfect and it will remain as such. The only thing that I want you to do is to develop a Masters' program with one of the American Universities. I am sure you know better than all of us." It was a very happy moment for me and very sad for the two reformist doctors whose plan was dismissed.

On January 10, 1977 a Board meeting took place and both the Secretary of Health and Secretary of Science were present. The agenda was the election of a new Dean and the establishment of a Masters' program to train the valedictorian and the second and third highest GPA graduates of each branch of the BSc program to enable them to teach and be full-time personnel of the Institute. I was elected as Dean again for four years and my employment status changed. I became the Academic Advisor to the Secretary of Health.

The Shah talking to me at the Noruz official visit at the Golestan Palace, 1977

IPS Graduation

The spring of 1977 was very exciting for everyone in the Institute of Paramedical Sciences in Tehran. It was like sunshine after a heavy rainstorm. The curriculum of the Master's Program, based on the cooperation of the University of Nevada-Reno (UNR) and the Institute, was approved by the Ministry of Science and Higher Education. Its main contract had been signed by UNR Chancellor Crowly; Dr. John Nellor, Graduate Dean; and Massoum Montakhab, Dean of the Institute; and had been approved by the Secretary of Health, Dr. Shaikh.

The first graduation ceremony had been postponed during the transformation from private to state and had been rescheduled for June 5th of the same year. All 1200 teenage high school graduates who started their higher education in September of 1972 in different branches of the Institute of Paramedical Sciences had become a group of well-educated, mature, independent and active people. The majority of them were in the military service; others planned to go for further education; and the rest were hired by the private or government sector, so the expectation for their graduation was very high. The management of the Institute was very busy getting ready.

About this time I was invited to a formal event. I can clearly remember every single moment of it, even the spot where the late Shah and his wife Shahbanoo Farah were standing. When I had a chance to speak with them, I requested the honor of their presence at the first graduation ceremony on June 5th. My request was accepted by Her Majesty Farah. I was extremely happy and proud of myself because now the graduation would be a unique event - like when the Board of Trustees of the Institute had the honor of meeting with the Shah in his Saad Abbad Palace in 1974. It was exciting news for the graduating students as well as for the committee responsible for the arrangements of the ceremony.

I had been informed that Dean John Nellor and Dr. George Smith, Dean of the Medical School of the University of Nevada, planned to be in Tehran by mid-May. The committee rearranged their schedule to arrive in Tehran on June 2nd and attend the ceremony on June 5th, then review the Master's program and its curriculum. As the Institute was under the wing of the Ministry of Health, the ceremony was held in the 5000-seat auditorium of the Ministry of Labor. The invitation letters and the graduation protocol were mailed to the 1200 graduates, their parents, and their husbands or wives. The Secretaries of Health, Science, Education and Labor were also invited, as well as their Undersecretaries, all shareholders, professors and their assistants and staff. Early on the morning of May 28th I was informed that Mrs. Farideh Diba, mother of Shahbanoo Farah, would represent her at the ceremony. Farah had been advised that if she attended one ceremony she would have to attend all to avoid the appearance of favoritism. At 2 am on June 2nd Dean Nellor and Dean Smith arrived at the Tehran airport. Mr. Hossain Shapoor, the Institute's master driver, took them from the airport to their hotel.

Nellor's suitcase hadn't arrived. The next day I met with them and Dr. Nellor mentioned that his suitcase had been left behind in the Frankfurt airport where they had changed planes. It was promised to be brought to him by June 7th, too late for the graduation, so he had to buy a formal suit for the ceremony. I promised to send someone to help him. Nasser, Nikou's husband, volunteered to go with John. They tried as many boutiques as they could but didn't find a single suit to fit him. The only suit he could wear was Nasser's. (This reminded me of the time in Tokyo that I was invited to the party held in the honor of Shah's brother at the Iranian embassy when I couldn't find an evening dress to wear.)

The 5th of June arrived and the ceremony started at 5 pm. A bouquet of flowers was handed to Mrs. Diba in the entrance of the auditorium by Shayma Kamarei, Minoo's youngest daughter and my granddaughter, who was seven years old at that time.

At the entrance of the auditorium (L to R): Shayma, Minoo, Me, Mrs. Diba, 1977

The ceremony started with the Iranian National Anthem. Then, as Dean of the Institute, I provided words of welcome followed by a short history of the Institute's establishment and its achievement.

My welcome speech at the first commencement of IPS, 1977

Next came the message from Shabanoo Farah delivered by her mother, Mrs. Diba, followed by the entrance of all the graduate nurses in their full yellow and white uniforms each holding a lighted candle singing the nursing anthem with wonderful piano music in the background provided by one of the public health graduates. The graduates entered from the back of the auditorium and came forward from both sides and gathered in front. It was the first candlelight ceremony in Iran, created by Minoo, and was so exciting and fascinating that it resulted in a standing ovation. The three top graduates with the highest scores in each branch came forward to receive their ceremonial diplomas with a sterling silver logo of the Institute for remembrance. Then each class of students was introduced as a group. The ceremony ended after three hours of excitement and joyful moments. At that time, no one realized what would happen to the Iranian nation two years from then; that many of the audience would be executed, in jail, or killed during the eight years of the Iran-Iraq war, or would leave the country for good.

The audience who attended the IPS graduation ceremony, 1977

After the onset of the revolution Mr. Hossain Shapoor the master driver of the institute was dismissed from his job and had to leave the institute after seven years of hard and honest work without any compensation because he was the Dean's (my) driver. He didn't have a chance to defend himself and to tell them that he was deprived of his job. And he wanted an explanation of who was going to be responsible for his four children of whom the oldest was seven at that time. Today, I am grateful to God that he has a much better life and his own business. Amongst forty five workers in the institute he was the only one who remained loyal to me and my family to this day.

Mr. Hossain Shapoor, IPS master driver

Transition Period

After I was elected Dean again for four years, every single part of the agenda was approved by a majority of votes. Although the political status of the Institute had changed, the Secretary of Higher Education explained the government's decision about repayment of the investors' money and payment of all expenses of the Institute from the budget of the Ministry of Health. The Government announced free education for everyone who could pass the barrier of the entrance examination. The Secretary of Health gave me *carte blanche* to spend whatever was required to upgrade the system of education and to establish the Master's program. The first two years were successful. The Educational Committee tried to develop and upgrade the curriculum of the

Master's program to attract some of the American Universities to cooperate with the Institute. The Universities who were established a century ago were not interested in such a little-known, newly formed institute of higher education in a country with a different basic language. Furthermore, from such a big and famous American University, someone should know you personally, believe in your abilities and trust you to pay attention to your letter and facilitate your request.

In this respect, I knew Dr. John Nellor, my professor at MSU and present Dean of the Graduate School at the University of Nevada-Reno (UNR). I wrote to him and asked for help in the formulation of a cooperative program for a Master's Degree to begin at the Institute and end at the University of Nevada. The Institute was a member of the Afro-Asian Affairs and World Health Organization. By constant corresponding with UNR, a group of three Americans who specialized in curriculum formation came to Iran and visited the Institute, then returned to the US. Life was going along smoothly; the students were happy and successful. All the graduate students found good jobs immediately and as a result the demand for applications increased. The proposal for the establishment of the Master's program was approved by the Ministry of Science and Higher Education and the government approved its budget.

On March 22, 1977, Nikou and I went to UNR to meet with the University Chancellor to sign the cooperative program agreement. We had a wonderful time getting acquainted with most of the professors and visiting all the labs and practical training centers. The Chancellor Joe Crowley, Dean Nellor and I signed the agreement; I also signed for Dr. Shaikh, the Secretary of Health. During the ten days in Reno, I spent enough time to find those related textbooks that we couldn't find in Iran. I placed an order and the bookstore promised to ship them to Tehran, to the Institute of Paramedical Sciences. I also bought a series of children's' encyclopedias for my grandchildren that I paid for and got a receipt, but the shipping company included in my order of books for the Institute. We returned to Iran after ten days in the US. It was the beginning of April.

According to our agreement with UNR, three people accepted the offer to come to Iran and teach English to the applicants of the Master's program as a proficiency course starting on June 1st. In order to house them, the Institute rented a three-story building next door. The first level was designated as a lecture room and audiovisual laboratory. The second floor was the office for the UNR faculty and the third floor was their living area. The reasoning behind housing the three Americans in the same building was to prevent them having to travel from the crowded town to the Institute. Furthermore the building was very large – every floor could be considered a 2,000 square foot room, furnished with all the modern facilities independent of the other floors. A total of 20 graduate students were registered and attended the English class.

It was unfortunate that about this time most of the regular students of the Institute started opposing whatever we called "rules and regulations." They gathered in the playground and started their prayers by noontime and refused to go to their classes or laboratories. They asked for free lunches and free room and board that was out of the Institute's ability to furnish. Day by day the students' expectations increased considerably. They became unreasonable and rough, tried to disturb everyone and kept asking for the money generated from the sale of oil. Almost all the girls who wore mini-skirts or open neck dresses and wore a lot of makeup changed their style of dress and reverted to covering themselves with black chadoors. The opposing group made serious discussion impossible, accosting their adversaries with boxing gloves, nailed sticks and other crushing equipment. Every day the students all over the country sent messages to each other and gave them the schedule of what they were supposed to do the next day. For example, one day all the students asked for a meeting with the Dean, no matter which school they belonged to. No one could ignore them because they kept insisting on their original demands.

In the meantime, it was fortunate that we rented the building next door for all the American teachers with living facilities in the same building as the classrooms. Undergraduate students were so busy with what was going on in the country that originated from the underground activities of Khomeini's followers that they didn't recognize the establishment of the Master's program and the presence of the American faculty next door. The Americans were kept invisible; they were safe and the Master's students had adequate time to be with them and attend their classes. By the end of the summer and the beginning of the fall semester, the situation worsened. The classrooms were closed, the students were in the playground, faculty was in their offices and the staff, assistants and others were waiting to see what was going to happen. The news was controversial and scary. The salaries, faculty fees for services and other dues including the rent for all of the buildings were paid by the Ministry of Health. Any time I heard that all the women had to wear full cover; I tried to leave the house at 6 am because I hated such attire. I had gone through these changes when I was very young and I didn't want to face them again. I didn't believe what I was going to see in the near future. I kept thinking that we had faced crises in this country so many other times, this time was nothing special - but it really was. During a short period of time, the Prime Minister changed 3-4 times and the Secretary of Health changed as well. As my government job was the Academic Advisor to the Secretary of Health, I had to go to the Ministry and hand in my letter of resignation personally to the each new Secretary of Health. If he disagreed with my request, he would write, "Your resignation is not acceptable; please continue your work as usual."

It was mid-August of 1978 that after thirteen years the Prime Minister changed. The new one decided to replace all the Secretaries with other qualified individuals. The first new Secretary of Health after Dr. Shaikh was Professor N. M. Mojdehi, one of the most prominent Iranian internists and ex-senator. He was the Dean of the Medical School of Tehran University when I resigned from the Pathology Department to accept a position as General Director for Teachers' Health and Welfare in the Ministry of Education. In speaking with him, I told him that I was tired of the stress related to the new situation and was ready to resign. But before I handed in my resignation letter, he told me, "You'd better continue your job; I don't accept your resignation. When I was appointed to this position I looked at the official chart and saw your name; I told myself this corner would cause me no problems. If you are tired, then take some time and go attend the International Symposium of Health Care Network held in Russia." He asked his assistant to facilitate my trip by replacing my name for someone whose entry visa was denied by the Russian embassy in Tehran. At that point in time, trips to Russia, especially to attend an International meeting, was one of the most prestigious trips of all.

I was among ten delegates from Iran. This trip helped me a lot. It was the most wonderful, exciting, very useful and perfect trip I ever had. I visited Moscow, Leningrad, Uzbekistan and Kazakhstan. The meeting was in Alma-Ata, the capitol of Kazakhstan. The magic effect of this trip occurred in September of 1981, when I applied for permanent residency in the United States Immigration Office in Detroit, Michigan. Upon proof of attendance at three international scientific meetings, I was classified as third preference, resulting in an immediate work permit; my alien number was issued sixty days after my arrival in the US. That, in turn, made great changes in my family life, in particular for Shaparak's and Shayma's residency status. We all are grateful to Professor M. Mojdeh for that meeting in Alma-Ata, Russia and to the late professor Takeo Wada for the invitation to the Tokyo International Symposium in Japan.

During those ten days at the meeting in Russia, many things happened in Tehran. The most important one was Black Friday. On that day, many innocent civilians and numerous young military men were killed in a matter of a few hours in a battle with the followers of Khomeini, mostly Palestinians placed on the roofs of tall buildings, invisible to the people on the ground. I watched the news on Russian TV, but I couldn't figure out in which part of town it was happening. Our mission in Moscow was accomplished and we had to return to Tehran, leaving from the Moscow airport at 8 pm. Nikou called me in the afternoon before we left and told me not to expect my driver at the airport because there was a curfew tonight. I should arrange to arrive after dawn. We had to leave the hotel on time; the bus was ready to take us all to the Moscow airport. There was no other choice. All ten Iranian members of the delegation had to spend the entire night in the airport. The Iran Air flight took off at 5 am and we arrived in Tehran safely at 6 am. Nikou picked me up at the airport and told me some of the stories. I became very worried about my three American colleagues. Although they were OK, I was sure they were desperate to return to the US. After that day, I didn't sleep well, not only worrying about them but worrying about my own family as well.

Student unrest came to a peak; no one was able to control things. The men started writing bad words on the surrounding walls. Surprisingly, the girls suddenly started disturbing the plants and flowers on the balcony adjacent to my office. They did it purposefully to make everyone afraid of the situation. No one could distinguish friends from enemies. Everyday the size of the student population increased in the courtyard as well as in the playground. The majority were strangers to us. Sometimes a huge crowd invaded the courtyard; after a while they would leave. I clearly remember those people were sitting on the ground in the praying position and whispering things to each other as I was watched them through my closed window.

In general the country was in chaos, irregular and disturbed. No one was exempt from the situation. Not only were food and gas rationed, money was as well. The major banks were closed; if they were open no exchanges were available. Salaries were paid directly to the bank and employees had to spend hours waiting in a long line to receive their money. Surely this was done to slow the movement of the country; it was the same everywhere. Almost all the farmers left their farms and came to Tehran to join the pro-revolutionary movement. It was no longer a challenge; it was a matter of life or death. People who claimed to be your friends became your enemies overnight and tried to terrify you by telling you if you didn't obey orders you would be in the hands of the revolutionaries. The situation became worse day after day. All the institutes of higher educa-tion including all universities were open. The students were present as well as the faculty, staff and others but no education-al activities what-so-ever were occurring except for the nursing and medical technology students who were willing to work for their practical training purposes. The English program for the Master's program was also still on as well. Every day students demanded things, which were not possible to provide them. They asked for free, well-prepared lunches not for themselves but for a minimum of one thousand others per day. They demanded special praying dresses for women and vast areas for all to pray together. Looking back, after the passage of more than a quarter of a century, it is difficult to imagine the situation and the state of my mind in those days. Not only was the BBC news terrible; every night the voice of "Allah-Akhbar" com-bined with the shortage of electricity and sporadic shooting sounds made our lives miserable. No one could go to sleep in peace. Those pro-Khomeini tried to brainwash the ordinary people as much as they could by convincing them to look at the full moon to see Khomeini's face, open the Koran to page so and so to see his hair. It was unbelievable how skillfully they accom-plished their job. For a long time they distributed free Korans to everyone who entered the mosque. No one realized this holy book carried a big lie. During that period of unrest the Institute was not exempt from the insurrection. Instead of educational activities there were sounds of revolutionary slogans being yelled and serious uprising against the government. One day I found the courtyard, playground and all the balconies were full of unknown individuals. Speakers came one after the other, talking about the necessities of the reform – by changing the government according to Islamic law written by Imam Khomeini. They kept asking for unity and co-existence. I wasn't brave enough to go out among them, especially since I was totally against their ideas. The crowds were very active, shouting, insulting and yelling bad words about the dynasty and to those who worked for the government saying they were either Secret Service (Savac) or the FBI. Anything that I describe in this manuscript is only one thousandth of what actually occurred in those days. How such a sad situation was created, I don't know. I can only say that none of the hardest tornadoes, earthquakes or sudden volcanic eruptions could make the country in such an upside down state. At this time the last government of the Shah's reign came to power. The Prime Minister Bakhtiar, who was later assassinated by Khomeini's followers in his Paris residence, was elected by the Parliament. A cardiologist, Dr. Razmara, who was against the Shah's system, replaced the Secretary of Health. I later had to go to Dr. Razmara's office and hand him my resignation. Because of a favor that I did for him two years before, he talked to me in a very friendly and polite manner while he used a lot of nonsense and irrelevant words to one of the previous Undersecretaries in my presence. She became embarrassed and left the room. Then he started talking to me and said, "I know you well. I have a tape recorder and asked everyone who was unhappy about their jobs to report their problems with enough reasons, so that by that tape recording I can decide how I will handle the problems of this office." I began to wonder, "Is he talking to me? If so, what does he mean?" In a few seconds his assistant entered the room (somehow he must have called him, but I couldn't figure out how). Dr. Razmara told me, "Lady, one of the tapes that I mentioned is about you. If you want to continue your work, you should tell your three daughters to resign immediately. Someone from your accounting department reported in my tape that whatever budget proceeds were available, you divided between yourself and your three daughters." I replied, "Doctor, I am sure you are right, that you heard this message; but first my three well-edu-cated, well-trained, well-known daughters and I will resign immediately. My resignation letter is already on your desk and their resignations will be sent to you today. But do you believe that a seven-year-old school with a considerable amount of income, either from the government or the private sector, has no accounting books, no balance sheets and no cancelled checks?" Then I stood up to say goodbye and he asked me, "Why are you in such a rush? Your strong voice convinced me that this report couldn't be correct and it has already been proven to me that the report is nothing but animosity toward you and your family. Please forgive me; go and continue your work." When I left his office, his assistant came out with me. He invited me to his office and told me not to worry because he knew me before I went to the US. The life of this Secretary would be very short.

I went back to the Institute. On my way I found so many car tires piled on the streets; the road situation wasn't normal. Most of the alley was covered with a white powder. I asked the driver, "The town looks strange to me, how do you feel about it?" He told me that the white powder was flammable and the situation was getting worse day by day. He took me to the back door. When I got to my office I found the courtyard covered with stu-dents sitting on the ground in a praying position. All of a sud-den I heard the sound of an Army tank moving in the street, adjacent to the main entrance to the Institute; it was part of a show of strength by the military. Then I heard my name called over the loudspeaker, telling me to come outside, they needed to talk to me. As I went out to talk to them, I was very shaky, uncomfortable and fearful. I faced the Commander-in-Chief and asked him what I could do for him. Before he answered, the students started shouting, "Our chests are ready for your bul-lets, Officer, please try it." I was unable to quiet them down. I could only plead with the Commander to leave right away to prevent further uprising by the students. I stood there until all the tanks left. The Commander never did say why he needed to talk to me. I went back to my office, half dead. I was so agitated, weak and pale in color that when one of my American colleagues came to sympathize with me, she couldn't talk for a while. Then she told me that they had been watching the Commander and me from the third floor apartment. She said they felt unsafe and wished to return to the US as soon as I could let them go. Her proposal was a great relief for me. I told her, "You all should get ready as soon as you can. I will take you out of this building and let you stay somewhere else until your airplane tickets are ready." I waited for them until all the students and staff left. It was almost dark when I took them in my car to my daughter's house far from the Institute. I had to take a short cut in order to leave the area as soon as possible. The fear of someone stopping the car to search it made me very nervous. Fortunately, none of us had any thoughts of a hostage situation at that time. It was my responsibility to take them to a safe place until they could leave Iran and return to the United States. Even thinking about it now, thirty years later, I still feel agitated and frightened. I can't explain everything that passed through my mind while I was driving. The revolutionary guard had made so many changes in all directions that I couldn't analyze them all. They closed all shortcuts - they placed DO NOT ENTER signs at both ends of the streets. So, you had to drive all the way south to a dead end until it would direct you to the north. They made it so confusing; regardless of the hour, you had to wait in long lines at the gas station because gas was rationed. I didn't want my driver Mr. Hossain Shapoor to help me because I had no idea about his political position although he was the only person who remained loyal to my family at that time. As we arrived at my daughter's I told the Americans, "This is Minoo's house, please stay here until you can leave Tehran." Minoo and her husband were in the US and their children were at my house. I am grateful to my son-in-law, Ali, whose office facilitated their return to the US, with the schedule arranged by the US Embassy in Tehran. Although they returned to their homes safely, it was a great misfortune for the Master's program, which was terminated without any successful results.

The Onset of Islamic Revolution

In 1979, the Shah, suffering from cancer, left the country. Shortly after Khomeini arrived in Tehran from Paris. Mehdi Bazargan became Prime Minister and almost all members of the government were replaced by a group of revolutionaries. They were tough and wild with no heart to feel and no brain to think. Almost 80% of the high-ranking Army officers were executed the first night of the revolution. Five percent of them escaped the country either during the Shah's time or walked across the border after the onset of the revolution. The rest were hiding in some unknown place or, if captured, they were executed or were sent to jail if they proved to be innocent. At that point in time, not only my life but the lives of all the members of my family became miserable. None of us could think of the future. Today I feel I was brain dead at the time. I walked with no hope and no plan but I had to keep my face strong, to stand like steel as much as possible. The revolutionary Secretary of Health who was a psychiatrist came to the office and I had to meet with him and turn in my letter of resignation. It was 8 am when I entered his conference room. He was surrounded by a group of revolutionaries that I had never met before. He called my name and introduced me to those around him. Then he told me, "Please go back to your work and continue your duties as you did before. Be assured that nothing will change the status of the institute; I have known you since the Institute was founded and I know how you tried to establish this Institute of Higher Education, also how your three daughters worked hard to prepare the training and teaching schedule." I went back to the Institute. As my car came close to the entrance door, one of the laboratory assistants was waiting for me and told the driver loudly, "Pull the car to the left side and give me the car keys." The driver was in shock and didn't know what to do. I told him, "Do whatever he asked; give him the car keys and go home and bring my own car." I got out of the car and went to my office. The laboratory assistant followed me to show me his letter of appointment as Dean of the Institute signed by the new Secretary of Health. For a while I thought I was dreaming. How could this be happening? Less than an hour before, I had left the Secretary's office. How could he say such a big lie in front of his colleagues? He was admiring my efforts in establishing such an institution of higher education, laboratories and the other health related organizations. It was unimaginable how a psychiatrist could say and pretend such. Did he forget what he signed? So I decided to leave the office before any other ugly work was done. Meanwhile the staff and faculty understood the situation. They gathered together and came to my office. Among them, one of the typists was crying very hard; she couldn't control the constant drops of tears from her eyes; all of us were surprised that she was crying so hard. It took me twenty-three years to discover the answer to the puzzle. This lady that I personally helped a lot during the eight years at the Institute had typed the letter of appointment for him the night before. He took it to the Secretary's home at 6 am and got his signature. Another point which really broke my heart and I couldn't forget and therefore forgave him after so many years was that one of my students from the National University of Iran who was now faculty of the Institute joined the new Dean waiting for me to leave the office. Although he became remorseful shortly afterward, I did not expect such actions from him after so many years of close working relations. Whatever happened that day has been over for more than a quarter of a century, but the wound caused by the actions of so many people including our maid and babysitter is still present as I write these memoirs. Some individuals remained loyal to my family and me; others did not. I couldn't blame them; they believed all the promises of free land, housing, electricity, water, gas and all other life requirements from a man who claimed to be the most capable person in the world. I had to leave whatever I had achieved, challenged and struggled for. I had been well known, famous and successful.

It was November of 1978 and the last day of my work in such a prestigious Institute of Higher Education, known to the world Health Organization, Japan, and the University of Nevada-Reno. I went home very sad, exhausted, depressed and desperate. I left the Institute with great memories and a simple pamphlet that to this day, after 34 years was proof of the countless hours that we all (my three daughters and I) spent and the immeasurable amount of energy that had been wasted until such organization of higher education developed and become functional.

I was not the only one to deal with the new government; all my family had some kind of problems with the revolutionary people. There was mass hysteria; everyone was afraid of those who worked under him or her. People started stealing small but precious objects. I assumed the revolutionaries taught them to do so because it started with the women students at the Institute, then the girl who had been working for me at home for so many years with honesty. First I caught her taking my unopened perfume boxes; the second time I found the freezer was empty and then the refrigerator. When I asked her, "Why do we have nothing left?" She told me, "I gave it to the needy people; you'd better go and buy for yourself. Don't you know this is Islamic reform?" Anarchy was running rampant all over the country. Revolutionary people as young as 9 or 10 invaded the streets and alleys with Kalashnikovs on their shoulders. Everyone was afraid of everyone; they might end up in jail or be killed for no reason.

Unfortunately my brother-in-law was one of them. He spent three months in jail and paid a considerable amount of money before they let him free with a written document of apology. We all knew him well and were sure he had done nothing wrong in his life, but after he became a captive we all became fearful. In addition, Minoo, who was in charge of the nursing school affiliated with the hospital and the nursing department in the hos-

THE INSTITUTE OF PARAMEDICAL SCIENCES

Address: 35, Arak Street, Villa Avenue
Tehran — Iran
Tel. 894767 — 897895

THE GOALS OF THE INSTITUTE

THE HISTORY OF THE INSTITUTE

THE PRESENT STATUS

FACULTY AND INTERNATIONAL COOPERATION

ADMISSION AND STUDENT ENROLLMENT

The IPS pamphlet, 1976

pital where the Queen gave birth to her youngest child, was under the surveillance of the revolutionary group inspecting that hospital.

The Shah and Queen Farah visiting the hospital where their youngest child was born. Minoo on right introducing the different wards. 1970 General (Dr.) Guran under the clock

Her boss who was living on the hospital campus was forced to evacuate the building in a matter of a few hours notice. It was not possible to find a place to rent in a short period of time, so the contents of his house were sent to storage. I had to move to Nikou's house and he and his family came to my apartment. They lived in my house for two months while I stayed with Nikou. We all were busy day and night because there was no help available. My son-in-law, Ali, had a high-ranking position in the government and his wife Nikrou was extremely fearful and agitated about her husband's life. She lost more than 50 pounds in one month. Today when I recall the situation, I am surprised at how strong I was and how I could suffer so much and still appear calm and "in control." No one, not even I myself, knows how I was able to withstand that much. In those days everything was uncertain and nothing we decided was definite. We had only one way to go - forward, to do whatever came first, and then clear the road. What would be easiest? First, we had to get rid of any belongings we had collected throughout the years before the revolutionaries confiscated them. We had to find a way to apply for entry visas to the US (during the Shah's time, we were allowed 4 years multiple entry). It was not easy to do this; the US Embassy was crowded; people slept on the street at night to get in early in the morning. Around the Embassy you could see two groups of people, those who received a visa were happy and those who were refused were crying. In addition, you needed an invitation letter or student forms to apply for a visa, not easy to get quickly. Fortunately the Dean of the UNR graduate school extended his hand to help me and my family by sending I-20 forms for Nikou and Nikrou and a sabbatical invitation for me. Both of my daughters with their two boys Hessam 7 and Adib 9 years old went to the London US Embassy and received their visas and then went back to Tehran. Ali, Minoo and I got our visas from the Tehran office.

When Nikrou came back from London she and Ali decided to sell their furniture, rent their house and come to my apartment temporarily. We all honored their decision. The most modern, precious, and beautiful furniture and the rest of her household goods were liquidated in less than six hours, with no auctioneer. When Adib's bedroom set was moved out he went to my sister's house next door and angrily told her, "This is the fault of your sister, who is my grandmother. She made us homeless." He refused to come to my apartment and join his parents. He went to Minoo's house to stay with his cousins. I was so preoccupied that I forgot about what was cooking against me at the Institute and the Ministry of

Health. I decided to apply for my retirement and went to the department to apply for it. On my way I met one of the faculty of the Institute who was also one of the staff of the Ministry and knew what was going on. He asked me what I was doing there; I told him I was going to the retirement division. He told me, "You had better turn around and go clear your name about the thirty thousand dollars you paid in the US for the children's encyclopedias." In order to keep my face as strong as possible, I told him it would be three-hundred thousand not thirty thousand. He told me to be careful and think about what I was going to say, the past period is dead. "They are savage and brutal and they will try to find a needle in a hay stack against you." I didn't know what to do; I couldn't talk to the Secretary of Health because I was no longer the Dean; I thought I had better write a letter and send it to him. I went to the library and started writing. "Dr. Saami, I am so glad you are a psychiatrist and can judge the people better than any other professional. Could you please let me come to your office for ten minutes?" Then I took the letter to his office to hand to his secretary. I was fortunate that day; he came to his office and saw me. I personally gave him my letter and he invited me into his office. Before I explained anything he told me, "I had asked for the book list to see for myself," then I talked to him after I saw the list. I came home and told my story to my family. Ten days later, on a Thursday at 2 pm, my phone rang; it was the Office of Health. The guy told me to hold the line for Dr. Saami, the Secretary of Health. He was on the line with great regards; he asked me if I was still an academic advisor to the Secretary of Health rather than the Dean of the Institute of Paramedical Sciences? I replied, "I believe so." Then again he asked me, "Why did you not come to my office?" For a moment I paused, then he said, "See you at 8 am tomorrow" and hung up. In the afternoon we all got together to decide what I should do. Accept the offer or insist on retirement? Because of the family situation, I decided to cooperate with him and forget about the retirement for now. I went to his office at 8 am. He was behind his conference table with piles of folders, books, papers and many other things. He pointed to all the files of different activities and told me, "You have been freed of all accusations. I went through the secret file page by page. I didn't find any students' names introduced to Secret Service, although I am aware of the trouble they made for you during their strike. I carefully went through the book lists and found them all related to the teaching subjects. I also looked through the children's books one by one and fortunately I found this receipt, paid by American Express not by the Institute's check. I have a copy of it for your future reference." Then he told me, "You must start working with me to transfer all the graduates of the school health system from the Ministry of Education to this office. We need all of them. I appointed Dr. Z to help you." I told him, "Dr. Saami, do you know that since the Institute was established, every year I met with the Shah on four separate occasions? This fact might cause problems for you." He said, "Don't worry, I have consulted with the revolutionary main office; you were accepted by majority vote for this position." I realized it would be a very difficult position, but I didn't believe how intolerable it would be. Dr. Saami told me that, "Due to the present situation in this office and in the entire country, everyone is responsible. You will have to work very hard, no matter where and when, probably day and night. Therefore, I made an agreement with the Secretary of Education to transfer all the physicians, nurses and school health graduates to this ministry and you were selected for the job. So you and Dr. Z are to get started as soon as possible. Your headquarters will be in the main office of Teachers' Health and Welfare in the Ministry of Education." The next day, I met with Dr. Z who was a new person to me. I had never seen him before and I didn't know anything about his attitude. It was the most dreadful and ugly part of my working life. Most of the doctors started shouting at me that I was the guiltiest person because I didn't facilitate their transfer from other cities to Tehran. All the nurses as well as the school health graduates told me that according to Islamic law they had to obey their husbands' orders, so they all refused my offers. As much as I tried to convince them, Dr. Z agreed with them. Therefore, by the end of every work day, I only carried a bag of disappointment and exhaustion home with me. There was no acceptance from them and no success for me. The Ministry of Education and the present Director General for Teachers' Health and Welfare were mad and disappointed with the situation and always complained. Why did we have to work in his office? To me, he was completely right. Everyday when I made myself ready to leave the house, I was almost in tears. I felt miserable, I was greatly surprised at how such nice, kind and polite people could become so wild, shouting, using bad words and showing a bad attitude. I felt like a sheep going to the slaughterhouse every morning. I was so naïve, fearful and powerless; it was difficult to perform my duties. I lived in this hellhole for three months. Finally one day the office of the Secretary of Health called and told me to meet with Dr. Saami at 8 am the next day. I went to his office and he told me, "With all due respect, I must say someone sent me this photo." It was one of the best photos of the Shah and Queen while I was talking to the Shah. I told him, "Doctor, do you remember that I told you I met with the Shah four times a year? This is one of those times. The picture was stolen from my office by the man who was the housekeeper who lived in the Institute with his family from the time of establishment." Then I asked for his favor, "Let me apply for my retirement." He told me he would agree to it. I asked for one more favor - to agree to my exit visa - and he did. But when I asked him with great caution, "Can I have the photo back?" he answered "No" with a strong voice. "Don't you know that burning the Shah's photo is one of the most religious obligations?" I must thank him today for all he did for me, for saving my name as well as my life. He was assassinated a few months later while I lived in London. When I came out of his office I felt so light, flying in the sky, happy, relieved and relaxed.

Separation of the Family

After two weeks Nikou and Nikrou and their two sons Adib and Hessam left Iran for the United States. Nikrou's husband Ali and her Pilipino maid were living with me in my apartment. The situation was so unsafe, even walking in alleys was dangerous and getting out of your car to reach the entrance of your house wasn't safe. The day we came back from the airport, my handbag was grabbed from my arm in front of my house. The guy was hiding and I didn't see him but he was waiting for me. I called the police and they told me to call the revolutionary committee. I called them and they told me they couldn't do anything; I should be careful, there were numerous hungry people in town. About at 3 pm, someone called from a pharmacy, mentioned my name, told me that my handbag was in the mosque and that I should go there and pick it up. I called Minoo and told her the story. We went to the mosque together. The mullah explained that he had found it and from my business card he asked the pharmacist to call me. My handbag had contained a considerable amount of cash, most of which belonged to Nikou that I had planned to give to her at the airport and I had forgotten – it was all gone forever. We all were happy that he didn't harm me as it was common in those days for them to strike a person on the head and grab whatever the victim was carrying.

Two months after my children were in the United States we found a way for Ali to walk across the Iranian border to Turkey and from Turkey proceed to the United States. He was fortunate to receive his US visa in Tehran. Therefore, Ali, Nasser, and I went by car to the city of Bazargon close to the Turkish border. There, Ali was met by a retired police agent. After Ali managed to bribe him with a big chunk of money he facilitated his passage from the Iranian border to Turkey. Then Nasser and I returned to Tehran and for five days I had no news about Ali whatsoever. I had no way to follow what had happened to him. Did the revolutionary guard at the border capture him or was he in jail? How could I find out? It is hard to explain my train of my thought during those five days. None of us was aware that there was no telephone line from Turkey to Iran. Finally Ali called from Germany on his way to the US; it was a great relief for me.

When I returned to Tehran from Bazargon, I felt strange at home and afraid of Pilipino girls because anytime I left the house, even for less than two hours, my apartment was invaded by girls who were former maids to those families that were executed or had left the country leaving their maids behind. Those girls had no jobs and were wandering all around the area. I wondered how they contacted each other to get together. My apartment was heaven for them because no one was in the building except Nikrou's maid, Natima, and me. One night around 7:30 or 8 pm, when I opened the front door I couldn't believe my eyes. I saw more than 15 girls around the dining room table in two rows chatting, laughing loudly and eating the meal that Natima made for them out of food in the house - and for me if there was any left.. They paid no attention to me, made no apology for being in my house without my knowledge. it wasn't just once or twice; they invaded my home any time they wanted to. I was afraid of the crowd and tried to be nice to them but when I asked Natima why she didn't tell me, she replied, "You are not my boss." At that point I decided to go to the Iranian immigration office to terminate her contract by paying off the remaining time and her return ticket to her country even though Nikrou and Ali had asked me to keep her up to the end of her contract. It was not an easy task. She tried to stay by telling me I was not the one who signed the contract. I was fortunate enough that the gentleman in charge was a part-time English teacher in the Institute who knew me well although I had never met him before. This process took me 10 days to complete and to take her to the airport and make sure she left. During that period Nikou's husband Nasser came to my apartment every night to prevent their gathering time after time that resulted in my exhaustion and fear. As soon as Natima was gone, I decided to apply for a pilgrimage to Mecca accompanied by Minoo and my sister Azam. That year, more than a million Iranians went to Mecca for Hajj, among them more than 200,000 were young boys and girls ranging in age from 18 to 20. They all traveled under the new government's budget as Khomeini's messengers to export the Islamic Revolution to other Muslim nations by distributing the Islamic guidelines translated in so many different languages.

About that time, the revolutionary students invaded the American Embassy and held 150 Americans hostage in Tehran. The duration of this trip was supposed to be 21 days but we spent 31 days instead due to a shortage of aircraft to return us to Iran – because the neighboring countries would not lease their aircraft to revolutionized Iran. Political relations between Iran and America were jeopardized. The situation worsened. Day by day, there was no safe life anywhere especially for lonely people at night with the overwhelming noise of bullets from guns. In spite of the loneliness, I was worried for my daughter Nikrou all the time. Although her husband Ali joined them in the US, I was feeling more and more lonely and frustrated, wishing to see all of them again. Finally, I decided to terminate my wariness and go to the US and visit them. At that point in time, I had a multiple entry visa to the US for four years.

Trip to Reno, Nevada (London Visa)

I left Tehran on November 25th 1979 to London, where I spent two nights with my cousin and childhood friend, then went on to Reno, Nevada where my family was. I found all of them well. The boys Adib and Hessam were going to school; Nikou and Nikrou were registered in college. Ali kept reviewing his electrical subjects and waiting for a job. I spent forty days with them free of all hardship, relaxing and happy for the kids and praying for their parents' future to find proper jobs, despite the evening news and wondering what would happen next in Iran. All my American friends who had visited the Institute in Tehran, especially the Dean of the Graduate School and the staff who spent the recent four months in Iran, advised me not to leave the US. I didn't understand what they meant. I tried to convince them I left a great deal of unfinished work behind. Besides, how could I leave Minoo and her two girls, Shaparak and Shayma, behind in such an unstable situation?

Shayma and Shaparak, Minoo's two daughters, Tehran

On December 28, I returned to London and spent one week with my cousin who was living outside of London. Early every morning I went to the underground station that was rather far from her house. I took the train to the central part of London, then from there by London bus to the US embassy to obtain student visas for my two granddaughters (Shaparak and Shayma). The first day, after standing in line for a rather long time, I obtained two visa application forms. I completed them and had to hand them to an African-American gentleman. At first glance, he mentioned that I should let the Iranian fellow, who was an expert in completing the visa applications and was helping everyone like me, help me. I wondered what was wrong; then I asked him where I could find the gentleman and what his name was. He told me to go to the cafeteria across the street and wait there until I found him - that I couldn't miss him. I went to the cafeteria and waited for a man I had no notion about. After almost 1? hours, the same person whom I met in the US embassy waiting room showed up and came to my table and politely asked if he might have a chair. I replied, "Yes, please." We both were silent for about 45 seconds or so. Then the waitress came and asked for our orders (she had done that 3 or 4 times before and I told her that I wasn't ready yet and was waiting for someone. Besides that, I was worried. I didn't have any appetite. Above all, I didn't want to spend any money for enjoyment at this disastrous time. The man ordered black coffee and I asked for a glass of ice water. He started asking the same questions about my children, my own education, my last job, my future plans and so on. He spoke to me very smoothly. He seemed very kind and very nice and supported my idea of taking the children out of such an unstable country. Then he looked at his wristwatch and told me that break time was over and he had to go back. He told me to stay there until the Iranian guy came back. After about 10 to 20 minutes a young modern Iranian came to me; we greeted each other. He said, "I am at your service, what do you need?" I told him the story of my meeting with the African-American gentleman who introduced him to me; then I asked him his name. He said, "You can call me Hass and the guy Tom, but these are not our real names; we have to keep them secret." I told him I didn't mind but I needed to get the student visas for my two girls. Hass told me, "It is almost 3:30 pm and you have to go a long way and me too. The US embassy closed at 3 pm. Give me their passports and application forms, then come back tomorrow to see me here in the cafeteria." When I handed the passports and application forms to him, he told me they were not the real ones and he would have to go and get special ones for me. I said, "The US embassy is closed," and he replied, "Never mind, I can enter." I must confess, at this point, if I had today's wisdom, I would never have done it. Just thinking about it and writing about it makes me feel shaky again.

I left the cafeteria and returned by the same route to my cousin's house. In spite of all rough waves and unclear future in front of me, it was very pleasant to reminisce about our childhood and sometimes our teenage lives. However, I was very tired from walking a long way on the street, the underground stairs up and down and traveling from one point to another. The next day, according to Mr. Hass, I had to be in the cafeteria at 9 am. I arrived on time but he didn't show up until 9:45 with two passports and the same application forms that I completed the day before. He apologized for his delay and asked me to stay there until he came back to see me again.

Can you imagine, for such an active person like me, the amount of hours I had to sit in one spot waiting for someone to help? I started thinking it might be a trick. I tried to think otherwise; I kept telling myself not to be stupid, to calm down and wait for him. He came back after 2 pm and asked me if I had had my lunch. I said, "No, I have no appetite because I am so worried. I didn't know what I should do." He said, "Order a sandwich and we will split it." We ate our half sandwich and while we were eating he told me, "Today is Tom's day off and I didn't know it; come back tomorrow and I will see you here." He then left in a rush.

Once again my anxiety kicked in and I kept thinking who I could consult. I needed a wise man to guide me as to whether I should tell Hass to forget about it and to give me back the passports or what else could I do?. I didn't want to spend one more day in the cafeteria. All of the above was repeatedly passing through my brain on my way back to my cousin's house. When I arrived there, they were watching the news. It was about the Army aircraft or helicopter accident while trying to free the American hostages. They had failed and all the American soldiers were killed in Iran. The news changed my mind. I told the story to my cousin and her husband. They told me not to rush, that I could stay in their house as long as I wanted. But that was not the point. I said, "I have no idea what Mr. Hass has on his mind." My cousin advised me to go and try to see Tom himself.

The fourth day passed the same as the other days with no success except the long conversation between Hass and me. I told him that if I needed to pay some money, please tell me; I had a limited time to be in London. He promised to make everything clear for me by the next day. He told me not to come in the early morning but to come late in the afternoon and he gave me written directions to a nearby hotel. With great surprise I asked him, "Hass, why should I go to the hotel? What do you mean? Please tell me straight out; this seems to be a game rather than a way to obtain the student visas." Hass tried to convince me that the process was for all Iranian visa applicants and not to worry and to be on time. I had no choice because I had to get the two passports back.

It was Friday afternoon about 4:30 that I arrived in the hotel lobby. Hass was waiting for me. After greeting he told me Mr. Tom, the consul, bought a nice house in Spain and all Iranian visa applicants should pay for part of it. I said, "Hass, what do you mean?" He told me, "I have talked to Tom many times; he decided not to charge you a lot but the minimum for you is $5,000 for both, otherwise you can have their passports back." For a while I was speechless after I received the two passports. Then I thanked him and Tom both, sending my regards to him and left the hotel and went back to my cousin's house. Then I left London via Iran Air to Tehran carrying a big bag of experience about student visas that I returned without in January 1980.

CHAPTER 10

Minoo's Family Trip to the U.S.

After I arrived back in Tehran, Minoo came to see me to convince me to move from the vacant apartment building to her house, which was rather far from the center of the action, the US embassy. She told me, "If something happened to you, how would I be know about it?" She was right and I accepted her offer. I decided to sell all the furniture and most of my household goods after Natima's friends took as much as they could. Finally, I moved to Minoo's house and shared a bedroom with Shaparak who was then 11 years old. At that time we all were jobless, sitting in that house. Neither of us was used to lying down and watching TV and pretending to relax. The news was terrible and disgusting. The number of men and women in jail was unbelievable.

Meanwhile Minoo received an invitation letter from a nursing school in Reno, Nevada. She decided to go there with her two daughters for an interview. Her husband accompanied them to London where they spent one week together; then he came back to Tehran and they went on to the United States. In those days, England's gates were open to all Iranians (no visa was required). Minoo and her two girls had one passport together with multiple visitor visa entries to the US. They left Tehran on January 20th at 5 am local time to London via Iran Air. After a 2-hour flight, her husband showed signs of internal bleeding. From the air, Minoo called a London clinic and made an emergency reservation as well as arranged for an ambulance to be ready to pick them up from Heathrow airport to take them to the clinic. As soon as they arrived they went directly to the emergency room and from there he was sent to ICU. It was 5 pm when I called their hotel to make sure they arrived alright. The receptionist told me they had cancelled their room almost an hour ago. I was shocked and wondered what had happened this time. I called Mrs. Watts, a longtime friend and Minoo's landlady during her student days in London. Shaparak answered the phone and told me the story of their flight, the time on the aircraft and about the London clinic. She told me that her father was going to have surgery the next day at 8 am. Her mom cancelled the hotel, brought them there and went to buy dinner for them. As soon as she got back Shaparak would tell her to call me. An hour later I called again. Minoo talked to me and explained the situation and the doctor's idea about the surgery. She said she cancelled the hotel because she couldn't live there alone. I asked her if she wanted me to come and stay with them. She said, "No, you might be needed in Tehran to take care of so many other things and any unexpected items." The day after the surgery I called and talked to Mohsen. I asked him if he wanted me to come to London; he said, "Not at all. Stay in Tehran; we may need you there." At the same time, whenever I called Mrs. Watt's house and talked to Shaparak and Shayma, they sounded unhappy. I called them 2-3 times a day because I was sure Minoo was staying in the hospital during the day and coming home at night. The girls couldn't communicate with Mrs. Watts if they needed something. On Thursday morning I left Tehran to go to London and from the airport I went directly to Mrs. Watts' house. When they found me at the door, they were jumping up and down surprised to see me. It was 5 pm and Minoo was still at the hospital. After greeting Mrs. Watts, she asked me what I wanted to do with the kids. I told her I wanted to get a pass from the Iranian embassy and take them home. She said it was a perfect idea. So far she was trapped and did not know how to handle them. As soon as Minoo came home and found me, she was so surprised and kept asking me why and how

I did it. She said, "They came with one passport, how can you take them back?" I told her to give me half a day, the passport and the directions to the Iranian embassy. I would let her know how I would take them back to Iran. Early the next morning, Shaparak, Shayma and I went to the embassy. I spoke with one of the consuls and explained the situation and asked for passes. He directed me to a nearby photo shop to take their instant photos for the passes. He also called the London clinic to get a verbal permit from their parents. Then he gave me their passes and the address of a travel agency to buy their return tickets. In the afternoon we went to the hospital for a visit with their father; then we went to Mrs. Watts' to collect their belongings. We returned to Tehran at 3 pm on Tuesday, January 27, 1980 after 72 hours in London for me and seven days for them. The day I arrived in Tehran, one of my closest friends and colleagues at the Institute called me and asked me to join a party that was to be held at her house the next day. I accepted and went there. I met with Dr. F. Parsay who was the Secretary of Education during the period I was the Director General for Teachers' Health and Welfare; she became my colleague and taught children's diseases at the Institute of Paramedical Sciences. She was happy and told me we should go to the Secretary of Foreign Affairs and ask him for recognition of University Graduate Women's Association. I was surprised; no one knew what would happen tomorrow. Did she believe in this wild government? If so, why was she absent for a year or so? I asked her, "Doctor, are you sure we should do this?" She replied, "Not now, let's wait for a few more months, but we have to do it anyway." She was not aware of such a savaged revolutionary government that announced, "We found Dr. Parsay innocent and therefore removed the ban from her bank account" while the accounts of all high ranking officials were banned completely. Since they couldn't find her anywhere they tricked her to appear in public, then grabbed her five days later when she went to her son's house for lunch.

I was at home day after day doing needlepoint. Every morning I took the two girls to their school and brought them back at 3 pm. Sometimes I visited my sister Azam and her family in their house, which was close by; other times they would come and visit the kids and me. Minoo's nanny who was the only remaining loyal person to all of us was at home with me. Minoo and her husband came back from England on February 28, 1980. He was still in the convalescent stage so Minoo sent a letter in response to the nursing school invitation in Reno and explained what had happened and asked them to postpone her appointment. Meanwhile the situation in Tehran got worse every day. Different political groups were active and tried to brainwash the children and attract them to demonstrations, even the students at the primary school level. One day at 6 am, devastating news was announced that all visa entries to the US were voided by order of President Jimmy Carter. Everyone who had their families, especially their children in the US called each other. I was so shocked; I started crying and wondered how I could see my daughters and my grandchildren. I became entirely hopeless and thought for my age that it would not be possible to see them again. It was a very harsh situation. No one knew what their fate would be for the next day or so. We had to keep our eyes on the children, seriously preventing them from getting into the crowds. School was rather close, but not within walking distance; so every morning one of us gave them a ride to school and waited until they were under the supervision of the school staff; in the afternoon one of us would be there before they were out on the street. A week after Minoo's arrival from London, she received a dated appointment letter for a job interview from a London clinic. She decided to accept the job if it would be able to facilitate her children's education. We planned for the time she would be in London. I promised her I would do whatever was best for the girls and would take them with me to London after the school year was over. Iranians needed no entry visa to England. In those days, we went to London as Americans go from state to state and were relaxed in this respect. Meanwhile, I was planning to sell Nikrou and Ali's house that had been rented for a year with an option to buy and it was time to act. I had Power of Attorney from them; but it was not easy to do in those days. Everybody tried to accuse you of wrong doing, to trap you in the hands of the revolutionaries and confiscate your house or whatever they could grab. So I tried to be soft and kind to the tenants who were trying to make me a fool for the price of the house and the way of their payment particularly when they found out that the owners were in the US. Therefore I had to try as hard as possible and I was very involved with the process.

Evin Prison

One day while Dr. Parsay was in Evin Prison and Minoo and I were out of the house, someone called and the nanny answered the phone. The caller asked for me and the nanny told him I was not home. He said he wanted to leave a message for me. The nanny promised to tell me. He insisted that the nanny remember my official name that she had never called me. The message was for Dr. Massoum. Montakhab must be at Evin Prison's front desk at 9 am, Tuesday, April 10th. It was Saturday, April 7th and Minoo planned to leave Tehran for London on April 15th. Looking back, it's difficult to imagine how fearful and deteriorating those days were. I asked the nanny, "How did you remember it?" She said, "He asked me to repeat it more than 10 times until I learned and could repeat it correctly." I called Minoo's husband and asked for his advice. He said that he believed it would be in connection with the Institute. Then I called Nikou's husband who was working with the government. He told me, "I will ask my secretary to find out who the person was that called." To my surprise, none of them offered any help, although I always helped them in so many respects. I had no other person to talk to and had to keep it a secret from my own sister and her husband, who had recently been freed from jail and had very bad memories of it; I didn't want to remind him. So, Minoo and I started thinking and preparing my thoughts to answer questions as well as collecting documents they might request. At that time, no one believed the revolutionary government would execute a woman. So, on Tuesday at 9 am I was at the front desk, a half-opened window. I had on a light green German-made dress with sheer sleeves and a French-made scarf. A young revolutionary man was behind the open window and a group of modern ladies and gentlemen who had someone in that jail were waiting in line around the building. I introduced myself to the young man and told him, "You wanted me?" He replied, "No one wants you." I said, "You called my house." He said again, "No we did not." Then I told him to please call the main office to make sure. While I was bargaining with the guy, Minoo was trying to get me to leave but I didn't pay any attention to her wishes. She couldn't change my mind. She asked the gentleman standing behind me for help. Then all of a sudden I felt a warm hand grab my neck collar and tell me, "Lady, you are out of your mind. Go away from this area as soon as possible; you don't understand how dangerous it may be." I neither knew him before nor met him after that day but I am grateful for his quick action. The reason I insisted was that with Minoo's upcoming trip to London, if they called me again I would have no one to help me either mentally or physically. The second part of my repeated request was about Minoo herself. I wanted her to be sure about my whereabouts while she was gone. So we went back home and concluded that someone was just trying to disturb my family and me. Early on the morning of April 15th, Minoo left Tehran to go to London. Two days later, she called and told me she had accepted the job but planned to stay at Mrs. Watts' house because she was afraid to live alone by herself until we got there and could find a place together. Time was so limited for me to finish the process of selling Nikrou's house and transferring the proceeds to them.

There was a black market for dollars, pounds or any other type of currency, but that wasn't the only problem. You couldn't buy more than a certain amount of money ($2,500 US dollars or $1,250 sterling per person) at the time. Therefore you had to go to the black market, either merchants or students' parents who lived in Tehran. The government sold the currency to the students. They made an agreement with those who needed to transfer their money to the country where they recently resided and held no job. Therefore it was sold and bought according to the black market value of the day. It wasn't an easy process and if the government found out either the seller or the buyer, they took them to jail and discontinued their permit to buy currency. That was another reason for all the turmoil in my life in those days.

I was also going back and forth trying to finalize the sale process but the tenant tried to broadcast that the owner lived in the US and tried to sabotage as much as they could to make me afraid of the situation so they could buy the house as cheaply as possible. There was no contest because they occupied the house; there was a constant debate between us over the value of the property. It was more nerve-racking than heart-breaking in those days. They tried to make me weak, exhausted and fearful in hopes that I would give up. On the other hand, I tried very hard to keep myself strong and to show no fear and anxiety. I was in the middle of the battle when we finally made an agreement for the price with the payment of one-fifth up front by check on May 10th, 1980 and the rest at the escrow office 30 days later. It was Saturday, May 4th at 4:30 pm that the sale was finalized. Meanwhile I gave a Power of Attorney to my son-in-law. In case something happened to me, he could take over and send the money to Nikrou and Ali.

The Moment of Misery

On May 8th, around 6:30 pm, Minoo called from London crying very hard and asking me to leave Tehran as soon as possible, even tomorrow. I didn't understand why she was crying so hard and why she wanted me to leave. I asked her if I came, what about her two daughters? She was repeating herself and begging me to come and said, "My children can stay with their father and nanny." I promised her I would do my best and asked her to make an appointment with my eye specialist for my usual check-up. I had to get an airline ticket and also, according to the new government rule, my passport should be sent to the airport for further investigation. So I needed a minimum of 5 days to be able to travel. At 8:30 pm Nikou called from the US and told me, "They killed your friend. We need you; please do not resist. Leave tomorrow." I got nervous and told Nikou that I hadn't heard any such news. I was watching the news in Tehran every moment and there had been no such news; this must be an exaggeration of the foreign press. That night passed and in the morning I took the kids to school. On my way back I heard the voice of a newspaper seller. Dr. Parsay, ex-Secretary of Education was executed at midnight last night. I started trembling; I couldn't drive and I didn't know what to do. I went home crying and was so sad and so surprised at what had happened. It was unbelievable for everybody. I wasn't brave enough to call any of my friends and relatives but the phone rang continuously as the day progressed and the news spread around town. All my friends, colleagues and relatives called and begged me to go to their houses and hide somewhere. I was so upset I couldn't stop crying, especially when they told me not to go in public and not to go to the memorial service for my friend - although an executed person shouldn't have a public service - in other words, the revolutionary government didn't allow any service or a designated grave for them. That was Thursday and my son-in-law usually went to his mother's house with all of his siblings for lunch and would come home late in the afternoon. But on that day he came home right after his lunch to sympathize with me and to tell me that no one could have prevented what had happened. He advised me to prepare myself and leave as soon as I could. I asked him, "Do I take the kids?" In spite of the situation, he had told me before that he was not planning on sending his children abroad no matter what. I couldn't convince him otherwise. He always told me that out of ten million students in the country, only two of them were his; why would he send them out of Iran? I kept telling him that I wouldn't allow myself to leave those two behind; either they would come with me or I would stay there regardless of what would happen to me. He said that they were in the middle of a school year and if we took them out right then so close to finals, they might lose a year. I told him I would never leave without them. I was insistent; he tried to ignore my comments but he couldn't change my mind. Then he told me that we'd better leave it in Shaparak's hand; she was 11? years old at that time. I agreed because I had talked to her about the schools in other countries and the joy of learning some other language, people's customs, education, religions and beliefs both moral and spiritual. She always listened to me and followed me all the time, even from the age of six when she tried to come to my house and help me when I had friends gathering. She would keep reminding me about the date of the gathering three or four days in advance and would never miss a gathering.

It was Friday morning and the weekend. Shaparak had a long talk with her father before coming to the breakfast table. She started talking and told me that she and Shayma had been in school almost a whole year and now that they were close to finals they shouldn't go anywhere but that I could go if I wanted. This kind of talk was not the usual type of talk from Shaparak; I always felt she was a friend of mine. I was sure someone had instructed her in what to say. I told her that I would never try to go anywhere without the two of them; I would wait for them. There was no further conversation because a telephone call came from Nikrou's tenant, a retired teacher. She came to visit me and sympathize with me, indirectly ignoring Dr. Parsay's name but at the same time appreciating the work she had done during the period that she acted as the Secretary of Education. The phone was ringing again and again and I had no tears left to shed and no string in my body to stand still, with a broken heart, fearful and gravely upset. I could not think of anything except why my son-in-law insisted on keeping the girls in Tehran while the Secretary of Higher Education announced that the government was planning to close all the schools for five years as the Chinese did. I felt it wasn't safe to leave the 11?

and 10? year old girls in the hands of the nanny and their father who was working with the government. Besides, the British government was to impose entry visa requirements in a matter of two weeks from that day. I kept telling him either I go with my two grandchildren or I stay in this country with them. Once again he tried to convince me to go alone; time was running out for me and he said he would bring them after their finals. I wouldn't accept any of his promises and kept my word. Meanwhile, Nikou's husband came to the house, sympathized with me and advised me to decide a better way for myself. He said I might be in trouble; this government would have no mercy for anyone. I was exhausted and left the room to go to the kitchen; it was lunchtime and I wanted to help the nanny set the table. I tried to stop the tears falling from my eyes in front of the children; Shaparak came to me, gave me a very happy kiss and said, "My father has agreed to let us come with you." "Are you sure?" I asked. She said, "I was in the room when Uncle Nasser spoke with my father and he kept telling him that he'd better let the children go with you; otherwise, if something happened to you everyone would blame him. Nikou called him last night and told him if he didn't facilitate you getting out of Iran she would leave their child in the US and come to Iran to rescue her mother herself. Then my father agreed with him and told me that Shayma and I would go with you to London to join Mom." She was jumping up and down. It was Friday (our "Sabbath") and everything was closed. So I had to wait for Saturday to send all 3 passports to the Iran Air ticket counter at the airport for investigation and exit stamps. I bought a ticket for myself; the girls had had their own tickets since January. I decided to leave very quietly, with no goodbyes to anyone. I called and spoke to my close relatives and friends but didn't mention my trip. From Friday to Tuesday when we left Tehran, I didn't sleep more than two hours a night. I kept working to select my personnel belongings for immediate needs, to store some of them in a suitcase ready to be mailed or sent and the rest made ready for donation. I thought if I took two suitcases for myself and two for the kids it would be easier to pass the customs office; I didn't want them to think that we were leaving for good. When I was preparing my suitcases I placed the 3,000 pounds sterling that I bought from the black market when I sold my own car in the lining of my suitcase. I thought it would help to pay for a few months rent and act as a safety deposit. I had no choice because each adult could only take 2,500 pounds per adult and 1,250 pounds for each child. They had a system of body searches - even inside the shoes. Therefore everybody tried to "steal" his or her own belongings from the government. In the meantime I asked the kids to write their names on the labels of their suitcases so they could be recognized quickly.

CHAPTER II

Trip from Tehran to London

At 5:30 am on May 13, 1980 my son-in-law took us to the airport. He dropped us off at 6:30 because he had to be at work at 7:30. He couldn't wait until we passed all the barriers that existed in those days. At the ticket counter, a young revolutionary person in charge kept asking me the reason for our trip. I showed him my file and told him I needed to go for an eye checkup. Then he asked why I was taking the two girls with me. I replied that their school was closed and I had no one to let them stay with. Then he told me that "Shayma's ticket isn't good; you didn't tell the truth when you bought it." I didn't want to tell him I didn't buy the ticket but I didn't understand what was wrong with it. I asked him politely, "Please let me see the ticket." He shouted at me, "Mother, don't you know what the problem is?" Once again I repeated, "Please let me see the ticket." He threw it toward me. "See. Look at her age." Then I looked at her birth date, which was February and it was now May. In other words, she was ten years old in February; therefore, the price of her ticket was short 1,000 tooman. I didn't have any Iranian currency on me and I didn't want to give them US dollars. I asked him to give me the solution. He said, "Either pay 1,000 tooman or don't go, or I will send you to the airport police." Instead I went to the police desk myself. The man was so kind and asked me how he could help me. I introduced myself and showed him my Tehran University ID card. I explained the situation and asked him if he would let me call someone to bring the 1,000 tooman later on if

he would let me catch my plane now. He accepted my request and let me call my sister's house. I spoke with my nephew about the situation. I gave him the name of the police officer and the location of his desk for their father to bring the money and pick up my ID card. The police officer himself guided me to the ticket counter and told the agent that he would accept the responsibility for the money and to let us board the aircraft; there was only 15 minutes before take off. I thanked him and prayed for him as we ran toward the aircraft as fast as we could. We finally boarded the airplane and took our designated seats.

As I write this, I feel like I am in the Tehran airport, first facing that young revolutionary then a real gentleman police officer; what a difference!. If he had not facilitated our departure that day, I don't know what our fate would have been the next day. I am grateful to him wherever he is. I want everyone in my family and the children of these two young teenage girls in particular to know that that man is still in my prayers when I remember those terrible moments on May 13, 1980. As we sat on the plane, I was feeling very upset - fearful, depressed and nervous, trying to hold myself together and not break down and cry. I had to pretend I was happy in order to keep the children cheerful and happy. But my heart was beating vigorously, my hands were trembling, my face was red and I stuttered as I spoke. I thought I'd better stop talking to them, so I closed my eyes even though the motion of the plane made me dizzy and sleepy, especially after four consecutive nights of little sleep. I remembered all the stories I had heard about how, if they decided that a passenger was not to leave Iran, they would order the aircraft to land in some other Iranian city and capture that particular passenger and take him for special punishment. It was not a joke; nor was it easy to stop thinking that at any moment they might receive the order to land and capture someone. Until the aircraft passed the Iranian border I couldn't sleep; then I slept for about two hours until they started to serve lunch. After that I could talk better and I was no longer trembling. I asked the girls if they remembered what they had written on the labels of their suitcases and both of them said, "Yes." Then I told them that it was their duty to take their own suitcases from the carousel and carry them themselves; otherwise the suitcases might get lost very quickly. As the aircraft got closer to London, they distributed a customs declaration which asked your name, passport number, your job, your place of origin, the purpose of the trip and the address of the place you were planning to stay while in London. To answer the questions in the job column, I wrote University Professor. These two words became the focal point of all other questions.

London Immigration

The aircraft landed at Heathrow airport. We got off and walked toward the immigration desk. When it was our turn, they looked at me and told me to go and sit on the bench. All three of us were sitting on the bench and waiting for Minoo to show up and bring my doctor's appointment slip and her children's permits to enter. We saw that some people had been selected from the line and sent with a supervisor downstairs. They came back by the same route with their luggage and then went in different directions. Shaparak asked me "Who are those people?" I told her that they had been in the immigration office and were being deported. She asked me why and I told her I didn't know; I had no clue. When the line of foreign visitors was finished, they asked Shaparak and Shayma to go forward. Minoo was standing on the other side and they saw each other, so I felt they were OK. A young woman came toward me, read my name and took me downstairs to the carousel. All the suitcases were gone except for four on the side; she asked me which were mine. Then I pointed to the one that had no money in and had me take it upstairs by the same route the other people went before. She asked me to open it. Inside the case were my mink coat, a lamb coat, two pairs of shoes and two handbags, one of which was crocodile. She asked me why I brought all of this; I told her they were my daughter's things. "She has started working here;

you met and spoke with her." Then again she asked me why I had two coats; I told her that one coat, one pair of shoes and one handbag belonged to my other daughter who was in the US. Then she asked me about myself, I replied that I would go back to Iran after I saw my doctor, which would be in less than a week, so I didn't bring anything with me. She asked me about underwear and I asked her if Mark and Spencer were closed? She said, "No" and I told her that was where I would go the next day to buy my underwear and other things. She asked me to open my handbag and I did, she searched as much as she could. Then she wanted me to hand her my briefcase and asked me what I had in the case. I told her the files of my eye surgery; I didn't remember what else. She kept the briefcase that was really a conference case and then guided me to the branch of the home office in the airport. I entered the room with my suitcase and without the conference case. A young woman officer started questioning me for three hours. She told me, "I am sure that you escaped from Khomeini, as they executed the Secretary of Education; so you came to this country seeking a haven to rest and get money from the government. We cannot accept you; you must return to Iran on the next flight which leaves late this afternoon." It was almost 1 or 2 pm - can you imagine how I felt? I kept telling her, "Madam, I have been coming to this country 4–5 times a year for my eye check-ups. This time is not any different from my other trips before." She asked me to show her the evidence. I had none in hand because the other woman had taken my folder with the briefcase. Then she asked me about my daughter and her children that came with me to London and she kept asking why I didn't stay with the kids in Tehran. I replied, "Lady, since I had my surgery I have lived with my daughter who has been a nurse since 1974. I was not able to stay alone." Once again she asked me if I was dependent on her. I said I was. Then she shouted at me, "Did you forget what you wrote on your declaration form?" I started thinking about the question about my job - I had written University Professor. She asked, "If so, how are you dependent on your daughter?" I replied, "I am not dependent on her for money; to be sure, I have more than enough money; I am dependent on her health-wise." Then she started asking me about my education, my degree, etc. Then she asked me, "Don't you have multiple visas for a year for the US?" I replied, "Yes I do." Then she asked me why I didn't go there instead of England? I said, "Madam, I had my eye surgery in your country because Tehran to London is only a 7-hour flight, while Tehran to Detroit, Michigan is 24-26 hours and if you consider the layover it would be about 36 hours. How could a patient tolerate such a long flight?" Then she asked about a bank account in London. I told her I had none. The next question was, "How much do you have on you?" I answered, "$2,500," (at that time dollars and pounds had equal value). "Furthermore, I am going to stay with my daughter, so I don't have to pay rent for a week or so." Believe me, during that three hours, I felt I was sitting on a hot plate; I was burning from the inside- I was sweating like mad the entire time. I had no way to escape from any of her questions and I had to be very careful to answer in the right way. I pleaded with her so many times to allow me to prove that I had a doctor's appointment. She kept asking me the date. I didn't know the exact date, but I knew that Minoo arranged it for me while I was in Tehran. Can you imagine how long those three hours felt? To me it was more than three consecutive days with no food, no drink and no sleep. It's impossible to adequately describe just how completely exhausted I was. I had a pounding headache and asked her, "Can you please let me know what my fate is going to be after all? Otherwise, I believe I am going to die in this room. I am unable to tolerate any more." She saw the way I was sweating and how red-faced I was and said she would have to talk to my daughter alone. I told her, "Please make up your mind for whatever you would like to do. But please let me go wash my face and drink some cold water and then I may feel better to answer the rest of your questions." She agreed to let me out and to talk to Minoo who had been standing behind the door for the 3 hours; in fact, she forgot all about her children who were waiting in the area next to the carousel. The woman showed me to the restroom and then let Minoo in. When I saw Minoo I only said "74" in Farsi and then went on past her.

The woman questioned Minoo; she wanted to make sure that everything I had told her was correct with no controversy. When I came back to the room, Minoo was still there and the woman had my medical folder on her desk. She told me, "The airport physician will examine your eyes." I told her, "With pleasure I will go to him." So another woman on her staff followed me to the other side of the airport to the doctor's office. When I went in he was very kind and understanding. I told him the story of my eye surgery and showed him my file as well as my appointment, which was for Friday, May 16, 1980 at 10 am. He told me there was no need for him to examine my eyes. He called the woman and signed the paper that was brought to him by the officer's staff. She took me back to the other room to get my entry stamp on my passport and told me she would give me 40 days to stay in London. If I didn't leave London in 40 days she would personally come and ship me out of England. My reply was, "Thank you, officer, I assure you I will leave London before the end of the week, which would be Sunday, May 17th. Finally I left that hole; the time was 5:30 pm, May 13, 1980, with the time difference it was fifteen hours since I had left Tehran. I was constantly thinking of a way to find a place to live, a job to apply for, and many many other things. Minoo was carrying my suitcase and I had my handbag as well as my conference case in my hand.

We went down the stairs; the crowds were gone and the carousel was vacant except for the two little girls (11? and 10?) who were sitting on the bench with their two suitcases. They hadn't had anything to eat or drink and were worried about me. Because Shaparak was always with me, she had a very red face and a lot of blisters around her lips which had developed during the 3–4 hours; she was nervous and exhausted. Shayma was very anxious to know what would happen next. She was nervous and kept asking where we were going to sleep that night. Minoo said, "In the Finchley Hotel; but first we are going to Mrs. Watts'. She is preparing dinner and I'm sure her dinner time has passed." Then Shaparak said, "Mom, don't worry, I called her and told her we were going to be late because Grandma was still being detained." We left the luggage claim area and caught a taxi to go to London. We weren't far from the airport when I started counting the number of suitcases and found 3 not 4. I was so shocked that I was speechless for a while. I grabbed Minoo's arm and tried to tell her what had happened. I wasn't able to say it so I pointed back toward the airport. She told the driver to turn and go back to the airport luggage claim. As we got closer I was able to talk and I told her that we had only 3 suitcases and we should have 4! I went inside and looked around to find the airport police. I saw a suitcase similar to mine standing next to the carousel. I went closer, saw my name on it and I took it. Then an Iranian young man wearing an airline uniform came to me and told me to open it. I immediately opened it and told him, "Sir, you can dump it out on the floor and look at it piece by piece; all the contents are lady's personal belongings. But if you are going to do it, please do it quickly because my two girls and I are exhausted as we just arrived today. Then with a big surprise he said, "Are you the lady that was trapped in the Home Office?" I asked him how he knew. He said, "When I saw the two girls and a suitcase with no one to pick it up, I thought something had happened so I tried to watch them as well as this suitcase." I thanked him and carried it to the taxi.

When I became sure everyone plus all our belongings were in the taxi, I told them the story of the money placed in the lining of my suitcase. By this time, the roads were dark, the rain was pouring from the sky and we all were in a state of exhausted relaxation in the taxicab. As we arrived at Mrs. Watts' apartment door, the driver helped us bring in our luggage. She opened the door and told me, "You'd better call Nikou in the US before doing any other thing; she is very worried." So I called Nikou and told her I was in Mrs. Watts' apartment safe and sound but that I couldn't talk to her right then. She insisted that I tell her what the actual problem was and where it was. I replied it was a political issue in the London Home Office - they wanted to return me to Iran; we all should thank God at this moment. So we sat at the dinner table; Mrs. Watts had made up a nice, tasty English dinner. We all felt very tired after dinner. We went to the Finchley Hotel and the receptionist told me that one of my daughters was very worried about me and to please call her; she had called from the US more than 10 times since 1 o'clock. I thanked her and told her that I had already called her and she knew we were safely in London. Minoo called her husband and gave him our current phone number. Then we went to our rooms to shower and change but we realized we left everything at Mrs. Watts' apartment. It was too late to go back there; besides we were so tired and frustrated that in no time we were dead to the world until 10 am the next day. Minoo had gone to work. Shaparak and Shayma asked me to go to Mrs. Watts' and get our suitcases but I didn't know the address to tell the taxi driver. So I told them, "We will have to suffer and stay in the rooms and wait for your Mom to come to help us or we can just accept the situation, wear the same dresses and go down to the breakfast room and eat; no one will recognize you. After we eat we can go for a walk until Minoo comes home; then we can go and collect our suitcases." When Minoo came back from work, we all went to Mrs. Watts' to collect our suitcases.

When we arrived, Mrs. Watts brought me a bunch of sterling bills and told me, "These were wrinkled badly so I ironed them for you." With great surprise, I realized she had opened my suitcase and found the money in the lining. She had taken it out and repaired the torn lining where the glue had given way. She suggested that we take whatever we needed immediately and leave the cases in her apartment until we found a place to live.

It was Thursday morning when I found a realtor in the Swiss Cottage area. Shaparak, Shayma and I went to the office and a young lady named Susan took us to a very modern apartment building located within walking distance of a grocery store, butchery and the underground station. We all liked the first floor apartment, which had two bedrooms, two baths, a living room, dining room and a very small kitchen. The rent was 500 pounds a month and another 500 for the deposit. In front of the living room was a small porch adjacent to a rather large lawn that made a pleasant view. I told Susan, "When my daughter comes to see and approve it, what time can we move in?" She told me, "As soon as you pay the first month's rent plus the deposit." I told her we would see her that afternoon. This was a positive point for all of us because I had 5 months' rent and the deposit in hand, no matter what. Thank God, we were not homeless! The address of the place we rented was Flat #2 Imperial Tower, Netherland Gardens, Finchley Rd. NW3 5RT, London. As soon as Minoo came back from work, we rushed to the office. Susan was waiting for us and we all went to see the apartment again. Minoo told her that she would sign the contract if it were ready. Susan said she would bring it to us the next day if we paid now. I paid and went back to the hotel, then to the nearby grocery store to buy sandwiches for dinner.

Back to front (L to R): Shaparak, Minoo, Shayma and me, March 20, 1981, London

That night we took our sandwiches to our room in the hotel and after a rather long period of worrying, we enjoyed our dinner together. We had found a place to live, but I still had to find a way to get around the Home Office problem. Once again, I didn't know what to do and what my fate would be in the very near future. Minoo told me that she made an appointment for me on Tuesday, May 20th at 9:30 am with the ex-Dean of Westminster Medical School who was now Head of the Pathology Department at the London clinic. Also, that I was to see the eye doctor on Friday the 16th at 10 am. I told her we should be settled in by the weekend and move in the next afternoon. But the girls reminded me that we had no sheets, no pillows and no blankets. I told them not to worry; we could go and buy whatever we needed in the morning. Minoo told me which bus I should take and at what store (Mark and Spencer) I should buy them. The girls and I followed Minoo's directions and bought whatever we needed. Once again I bought items for lunch and dinner, then went back to our new home and organized everything.

The next day, Friday morning at 10 am, Minoo and I were in the doctor's office. He examined my eyes as usual and asked about my status in Iran. I told him the stories and he kindly told me two things. First he said he would try hard to find me a job; although it was a very bad time; he would tell all his friends and see what the outcome would be. The second thing was that he promised me if I developed any problems as a result of working in the laboratory, he would take care of it free of charge. (He meant microscopic work, which had been forbidden after my eye surgery.) I don't know what happened to this man; I am sure he has retired, but I would like to thank him a great deal because of the way he treated me, talked to me, supported me and gave me a great deal of courage.

Over the weekend Minoo tried to show me the entire area and gave me directions to the bus stop, the bus routes, etc. I couldn't stop thinking about the future of our lives, now that everybody was out of the country and safe and sound. On

Tuesday, May 20th, Minoo gave me directions to the London Clinic to see Professor Lacy at 9:30 am. She had to go to work so I went by myself. I left the house at 8 am and I was in his office 45 minutes ahead of time. He came in wearing a white coat, with white hair, pale face, blue eyes under glasses and a big smile on his face. He received me with great compassion and kindness. He told me not to be bashful and to tell him the stories of what we had all been through and the process of leaving everything behind. Then he asked me to tell him what he could do for me. For a while I couldn't talk and tried to stop the tears from dropping from my eyes. He started talking to me and kept asking me about my education, my family, my belongings, etc. I explained to him about the immigration and finally I told him, "Professor, after all these tragic stories, I request only a very small area the size of a chair space for research to keep my brain alive." He told me that he was willing to introduce me to the present Dean of Westminster Medical School, Professor Sidney Selwyn. "As for what you requested, if he doesn't have the space and facilities for your research, I can give you a job in this department; but because of budget limitations I couldn't offer any money." I told him, "Professor, that is the one thing I don't need." He looked at me with great surprise and asked me, "Then what do you need?" I told him, "I will work either place with great pleasure if you or Professor Selwyn would write a letter to the Home Office saying that you need me, so they will extend my permit to stay in this country longer than forty days." Once again he promised to do whatever was necessary to help me stay in London and advised me not to go back to Iran until all the government changed and became stabilized.

The memory of those moments in the London Clinic talking to Professor Lacy is still so vivid to me after 27 years. I have never forgotten his help, his compassion and his kindness. The next day I followed the written directions that his secretary had given me, taking two different underground trains and a long walk to the 10 am appointment with the Dean.

I woke up at 5:30 and made myself ready by 6 am. Minoo told me, "This is too early; you will only need one hour to reach the Medical School. If you leave at 8 am you will be there by 9." I said that might be true if I was familiar with the route and could go direct, but I had no idea about the road. Finally she convinced me not to leave the house until 7 am. I arrived at the Dean's office at two minutes to 9 am, so I walked around the area until 9:30 and then presented myself to his secretary. She told he was teaching but would be in his office by 10. While I was waiting for him in the secretary's office, a young man with a heavy mustache came in and then immediately left the room. He appeared to be an Iranian. The secretary asked me if I knew him and I said, "No." She said he was Dr. Bakhtiar, a PhD candidate working under Professor Selwyn. He was a pharmacist and was working on antibiotics.

Right at 10 am, Professor Selwyn entered and invited me into his office. He was in a white coat and spoke very fast. He told his secretary to call Mohammed (Dr. Bakhtiar). He came to his office and the Professor asked him to show me around the laboratory. We left and Dr. Bakhtiar showed me around all 7 floors, explaining the research on every floor; his office was on the 7th floor.

We went back down to Professor Selwyn's secretary's office to see him again. When the secretary announced us, he opened his door and gave me the letter he had written to the Home Office. No words can describe today how valuable that letter was and how happy I became at that point in time. I felt like I was flying. I talked to Dr. Bakhtiar for a while and asked about the location of the Home Office and his program of research. He told me microbiology was available and a clinical laboratory was located on the second floor. I had never been a student in England and didn't know their system so I decided to stay under the wing of Dr. Bakhtiar to learn what I needed to do. By 3 pm I left the Medical School and went home by the same route.

Professor Selwyn and me, September 24, 1981, London

Because Minoo had a half-day off, Shaparak and Shayma had been registered at Quinton Kinston School in St. John's Wood. It was located close to our home and within easy walking distance. The next morning we all left the house together. Minoo usually left at 7, Shaparak and Shayma and I at 8. We went together to the train station where we separated; they continued to school, I went to the underground. On the 23rd of May 1980, Minoo gave me directions and I went to the Home Office. I became so shaky when I recalled the moment at the airport when the immigration officer was questioning me; how hard it had been, how unfair and what an injustice it was. I told myself to be strong; in this world you can find justice; don't be shaky; pray to God and ask him for help. I said some prayer words while I was in the main Home Office waiting room. I repeated the words "God is great" (Allah Akhbar) one hundred times. You might say, I tried to hypnotize myself.

At last, I was called in and a middle-aged woman received me. I handed Professor Selwyn's letter to her. She asked for my passport and stamped it for three years' residency in England. She welcomed me and wished me a better life at the medical school. We shook hands and I wished her a good life and left. I can't describe my happiness that day. It was a great slam in the face of the airport immigration officer who had grilled me so harshly for three hours at the airport. In addition, I had been told that if I wanted to stay in London, I must present a minimum of 50,000 pounds in an account under my own name. I was unable to do that; I had money in Iran but it wasn't transferable. Many mothers and/or sisters had accepted the risk but they were in jail because they tried to send currency to their children or relatives. Now I didn't have to worry about the money. I considered it a blessing from God who had accepted my prayers in the Home Office waiting room.

The residency permit gave me much courage and was a tremendous joy for my entire family, especially the girls who had silently worried about my deportation while they were sitting on the bench in the airport. I had explained to them the process of deportation with no notion that it might happen to me shortly afterwards. That day I went home and enthusiastically started working to arrange the home and prepare dinner. Shaparak and Shayma came home from school and asked me what happened. I told them that I had very good news; I got a three-year residency permit. They were so happy they were jumping up and down. They said they wanted to give this good news to their mom themselves. So we sat in the lobby until she opened the door and we saluted her with the news.

As Minoo came and they gave her the news she was very happy and asked if she could call Mrs. Watts who was also worried for me. She had called her son and asked him to go and see the Senator. She said that he might come to see me that night and I told her to invite Mrs. Watts for dinner; it would be ready soon. She called her but before Mrs. Watts arrived, her son Leslie arrived and told me he had tried to make an appointment with their district senator but his secretary was sick; she would be back in on Monday. I thanked him for his efforts and told him that I would be a good guest during this three year residency. In the meantime, Mrs. Watts arrived; she was so happy when she heard the story. We all had a cheerful meal that night and kept giving thanks to God.

The next day I woke up early as usual; Minoo left at 7 am and the girls and I left the house at 8. They went to school. I went to the medical school and arrived exactly at 9. Dr. Bakhtiar wasn't there yet. I sat in the secretary's office waiting for either Professor Selwyn or Dr. Bakhtiar, to tell them about my residency. It was about 9:20 when the Professor entered and his secretary told him I was waiting. He invited me into his office and I thanked him for his help and explained how happy everyone was the night before. He told me he was happy as well and was glad he had made it possible for me. He told me to enjoy my life and started to shake my hand. I told him I did not want to go home; I wanted to stay and work for him. He replied, "You are welcome to stay and work **with** me, not **for** me. I am sure you understand about our budget problems." I said, "As I mentioned to Professor Lacy, I want to keep my brain alive before my body dies; please let me start some research. If you would allow me, I can start right away."

Dr. Bakhtiar came looking for me to find out what happened at the Home Office. Professor Selwyn said, "Mohammad, help your friend find an interesting subject other than antibiotics to start her research." Dr. Bakhtiar asked him what the most desirable subject today would be rather than antibiotics? Professor Selwyn said, "I am in favor of nosocomial infections." Once again, I thanked him personally and sent an appreciation card to Professor Lacy. Although it was volunteer work, the goal was much greater than money; I started on May 27, 1980.

Mohammad Bakhtiar, MD, whose great concern has always been appreciated, London, 1981

Westminster Medical School

Everyday, I started and finished work at the same times just like the rest of the personnel of the department. While the educated British received me with high respect, it was not easy to work with ordinary British people who were very prejudiced. They believed that Iranians were Arabs living in the Sahara desert, not in houses or apartments. They tried to give me a hard time, especially when they saw me working, going to the Dean's office to talk to him, etc. For example, one of the technicians came to me at lunchtime and said, "Doctor, all your friends are gathered in front of the Superior Court (located across from the medical school); don't you want to join them?" I said, "Why should I be with them? What do you mean?" He told me, "Khomeini is offering free gas, electricity and other necessities of life. Since London is very expensive, I believe you'd be lucky if you went there." Another day someone came in and said, "Don't you know that Khomeini ordered free education, free land and free housing; and here you are paying a lot of rent; why aren't you taking advantage of it instead of staying here and becoming a burden for the British system? It would seem Iranians are not appreciative at all." It was very hard for me to be silent and not to respond.

Sometimes I became very mad and nervous; my face became so red that the doctors sitting around the next table would come over and start talking to me and disrupt the others from focusing on me. They comforted me by apologizing for the actions of the others. Finally, as the days passed little by little, I got used to their attitudes and they got more and more friendly.

One day Professor Selwyn called me and told me that I should go to the Society of Apothecaries of London and become a member. Dr. Bakhtiar explained it to me and gave me directions. The Society met once a month, there were a lot of activities and entertainment from pharmaceutical companies. By attending that society, I found an announcement that the History of Medicine course registration date would be September 10 and the classes were to start Saturday from 8 am to 4 pm. I asked Dr. Bakhtiar about this class. He said, "This would be a year of course work and a very useful subject. You would write a thesis and a written and oral exam would be held the first Monday of November next year. They accept only 15 applications from those graduated from medical, dental, pharmacology or basic medical sciences."

I decided to attend this course to keep myself busy enough that I wouldn't have time to think of anything else. But I was thinking of tuition and didn't ask him about it. The next day I filled out an application and gave it to Professor Selwyn's secretary for his signature. By the time I got to my office, the secretary called me and told me the Professor wanted to see me. He said, "I signed your application and waved the tuition for you." I was so grateful to Professor Selwyn because I could not possibly have paid 5,000 pounds tuition at that point in time. I had been lucky to have a 6-year scholarship from the government of Iran while I was studying in the US and Tehran University was free for those who could pass the entrance examination.

On Saturday morning, I began attending the class as a student after 15 years away from the student routine. All attendees were about the same age, some a little older or a few years younger than I was. The subject was very interesting and after all the years of pure science, it was very different and attractive. It pulled me away from the state of depression that I felt I was on the borderline of. Working during the week on my research, going back and forth by the underground and walking a long distance from the station to school was great exercise for me. Although it was very hard and tiring the first two weeks, I got used to it and enjoyed it, especially when I found a seat in the train and could read about the history of medicine or some paper about my research. If necessary, I would shop along the way when walking.

Minoo advised me not to go too close to the Iranian consulate office and I tried not to do so because none of us knew what might happen to me later on. At the same time, I needed money so I had to find a way around it to bring my own money from Iran. At that time, the government ordered the bank to sell currency only for the students abroad and only if they presented some University evidence and the Iranian consulate office approved it.

Tuition and Living Expenses

My hard work, being on time every day, helping the clinic to read the slides for immediate diagnostics of fresh smears in the absence of Dr. Bakhtiar who was in charge of the lab, drew Professor Selwyn's attention to me. One day when he asked me about the financial status of my family and life in London, I grabbed the opportunity to ask him for some help. I requested a formal letter regarding my registration from the History of Medicine class and the payment of the tuition. He told me he would do it with pleasure and that he wanted me to be happy but asked who would take care of it in Iran? I told him my niece would. He kindly wrote the letter the way I requested.

I showed it to Dr. Bakhtiar who advised me not to go too close to the Iranian consulate office. I told him I had no other choice; not only was I desperate for money but if I could get an approval stamp from the consulate office, the currency price would be one-fourth of the black market rate. Dr. Bakhtiar repeated himself and promised to find some Iranian students who wanted to sell their currencies. I am very grateful to him; he bought as much currency as I could pay its value in Iran from students that I never met.

Finally after a week of debating with myself, I decided to accept the risk of whatever might be my fate. It was 3 pm on Friday when I went to the consulate office, nervous and trembling. As I entered, a young man was sitting behind a desk. I said hello and he stood up with respect and asked me what he could do for me. I handed him the statement letter. He looked at my name then at my face and wrote on the top of the letter "The subject of her study is very much required for the country" and stamped it. He also told me that my monthly expenses would be covered as well. I was quiet and tried not to say anything except to tell him thank you. However, when he asked me what had happened to the Institute of Paramedical Sciences, I was greatly relieved and explained very briefly. I asked him how he knew me and he said he was one of my students at the National University of Iran long ago. I asked his name, he replied, "Please don't ask." He respectfully followed me to the door. I wished him the best and thanked him. He said, "Doctor, if you need anything please come to me and ask for brother #2 and no one else." Today I still do not know his name and I didn't recognize his face at that time because a beard covered it. However, I am so grateful to him and wish him the best of the best wherever he is.

I went back home very cheerful, happy and with no more trembling. It was 5:20 pm and Minoo was home preparing dinner. I told her I had very good news. She asked me, "Is it that you registered in another subject?" I said, "No, my dear, I found a chunk of money." "From where," she said, "in the train?" I said, "Not in the underground train, not on the street." "Then from where, tell me please." "From the government of Iran!" I showed her the letter and with great surprise she asked me if I went to High Street, Kensington where the consulate office was. I said, "Yes, I did it and I would do it again if necessary; the young man was one of my students, his name is brother #2. I wanted to go to the kids' school and ask for a change in Shaparak's status. Today I heard the bank sells currency to the O level students as well." Then Minoo said that I did not understand the system; Shaparak had to be 16. Then Shaparak became unhappy; she said that if she went to O level, she would lose her friends. Minoo tried to convince her that I did not understand the system of education in London but that she should let me try it and Shaparak accepted the idea. The next day I went to the principal's office at the school. I introduced myself and explained our situation. He was a very understanding person and very helpful. He told me O level students had to be 15-16. I think Shaparak was only 12? at the time. I asked him to please help and he promised to find a way, if Shaparak was an exceptional student. He would need a month to test her, then he would let me know if it was possible to accept my request or not. When I told Minoo that it depended on Shaparak's test results, Shaparak started crying and saying she was not ready for the tests and was not going to sit for it. I told her not to worry; there was no pressure behind it. Three weeks later when I came home she ran to me and handed me two letters, one for the consulate office and one for me congratulating the parents that their daughter passed the test, was considered an exceptional student and would be moved to the O level. The consulate letter was testament that she was an O-level student. I took the letter to brother #2 in the Iranian consulate office and he kindly stamped it. We thus became eligible to buy 10,000 pounds from the bank in Tehran. This was the way that we survived those days with no pay for me at my job and only Minoo's salary. We had to bring our money out of Iran; we had to pay a heavy rent, plus all the other routine daily expenses including transportation fees to go to work every day. Therefore, I sent my evidence to my niece, Firoozeh, via a passenger going to Tehran. It was common in those days for passengers to accept envelopes only if it had one or a maximum of two pages and oral permission to read it to be sure it belonged only to students. It was not safe to send those kinds of letters by mail - the possibility of being lost or not delivered was very high.

Life was going on, no matter what. I was busy with my early Saturday morning class and weekday research. Every day I had to go to the basement of the medical school to pick up supplies, the ready-made plates or to ask them to make a microbiology plate of different kind of additive. On my way I tried to read all the information that was posted on the boards in the halls. One of them, which drew my attention, was about the International Symposium of Gnotobiology in Tokyo, Japan in July 1981. At present, it was November 1980. I wished I could participate but how could I? With only a temporary job without pay and no money of my own. I told myself it could be my dream from now on to wish for such a long and expensive trip. I told myself again and again that those days were gone with the wind; no wishful thinking anymore unless you find a permanent job or a handful of money to spend. Meanwhile, Dr. Bakhtiar told me he had some news for me. He said, "It is very important but you should be prepared to hear about the serious puzzle." I asked him to shoot because I was ready for it. He mentioned the name of the Assistant Dean of the Medical School, Mr. Forest, who accepted the 5,000 pounds check under my name, which was received by the accounting department of the medical school from the Iranian bank in London.

I immediately called his office and asked for an appointment. His secretary told me he was busy this week and that I had to wait to see him next week. I asked her to please tell him my name; that it was urgent and I was desperate because my apartment rent was long past due. She called me at 1:30 pm to talk to Mr. Forest. I told her I had to see him personally, that I couldn't talk to him on the phone because of my broken accent. Finally I went to his office. He was a gentleman with a strong voice and British accent sitting behind his desk. I introduced myself and explained my status. He told me that no matter what, the money belonged to Khomeini not me, so he had to return the check to the Iranian bank. I told him, "Mr. Forest, the money belongs to me. If you would read the accompanying letter you would see that my niece Firoozeh was the sender and I was the receiver.

He said unfortunately the receiver of the check was not I but the Westminster Medical School. I very politely tried to convince him and once again explained my family status. Finally he told me it was impossible to do anything with this check except to send it back to the government of Iran. I was really desperate; I couldn't convince him to believe that the money was my own. He kept asking me so many questions. I don't remember all of them but I recall he kept insisting that the money belonged to the government. This bothered me more and more because another 10,000 living expenses were on the way; if he returned this check to the bank, the others would go automatically. I asked him to let me go to the bank and talk to the bank manager to find out a good solution. He accepted reluctantly. I went immediately to the downtown bank; it was almost 4:30 pm when I asked for the bank manager. An Iranian gentleman came forward and asked me what he could do for me. I explained the situation and he asked if I brought the check with me; I told him I did not. Then he wrote to Mr. Forest on the bank letterhead asking him to write on the back of the check "transfer to the account of Dr. Massoum Montakhab," then sign it and return it to him. I went home.

The next day at 1:30 I had an appointment with Mr. Forest. I handed the bank letter to him and he wrote exactly what the bank manager instructed him to write and handed the check back to me. Finally, after three days of discussion and confusion I was able to prove that the money belonged to me personally and that I was not making it up. I am grateful to the bank manager who helped me in this respect.

Life was going on. I received the tuition as well as the monthly expenses, so I had a total of 15,000 pounds in my hands. At first I wasn't brave enough to spend it lavishly for the trip; but I couldn't forget about the international symposium, especially when someone told me if I could present three pieces of evidence of attendance at international meetings to the US immigration, they would classify me as a third preference - scientist and offer me permanent residency. So, I couldn't stop thinking about it.

Finally, I decided to give it a try and write an abstract and send it to the symposium. I tried to speed up and finish it as soon as I could but Professor Selwyn was on a trip and I could not send it without his consent. When he returned, I took the abstract to him. He told me that it would be past due when it arrived in Tokyo and he was sure it would be rejected. I asked him to allow me to go to the airport and send it with a passenger. He laughed and said the Japanese people are not as flexible as Iranians are, so forget about it this time. I told him that if they accepted it we would celebrate and if they rejected it I promised I wouldn't cry. Again, I asked him to please let me send it and wait for the celebration. He said, "Montakhab, I surrender, go and send it." I mailed the abstract to Tokyo hopelessly and continued to work on the literature review for preparing my thesis. Ten days later, I received a letter from Professor Takeo Wada, Dean of Sapporo Medical School and one of the reviewers on the symposium committee. He wrote that he was very happy to find me safe in London and that he had sent me numerous letters without either response or the return of the letters. Therefore, he had been worried about my family and me. He said, "The good news is that your abstract was accepted but only for the poster session because it was received after the deadline." I was torn between my enthusiasm for being accepted and the sense of the need to avoid spending money on unnecessary items. At the same time, because of the American hostage situation in Tehran, I doubted the US would consider permanent residency for me. Finally I received an invitation letter from Professor Wada who informed me that the University of Hokkaido Sapporo Medical School would sponsor all expenses including the airfare and the hotel. I would receive the airline ticket from Japan Air directly. When Professor Selwyn saw the letter he called Dr. Bakhtiar and asked him about my background, my relationship with Wada's family and the reason for such a VIP invitation. Dr. Bakhtiar explained it to him.

My schedule became very tight because I had to finish the results of my research as well as write the thesis, which itself was not an easy task. All the references were located in the Welcome Library and no books were allowed to be removed. Therefore, I had to spend a great deal of time in the library to use them. At the same time I prepared everything for my trip to Tokyo.

My Trip to Japan

I traveled by Japan Air. I didn't know how many of the passengers were going to the symposium until a group of six including me gathered in the hostess' cabin to take a photo over the North Pole. I was a stranger among five British men. One started asking me about my origin, my background, my work and my position in the Westminster Medical School. I explained to them and tried to convince them that I did not receive any funds from the school. The aircraft landed in Anchorage, then after 2–3 hours, we flew on to Tokyo. The airport bus took all the passengers to the air terminal except me. Professor Wada and his wife Yuriko were standing next to the bus and took me in their car to the hotel where the symposium was to be held.

Professor Takeo Wada and me
at the Tokyo Symposium

Mrs. Yuriko Wada and me at
the Symposium, 1981

The opening ceremony in Japanese style was as beautiful as the closing one and the scientific presentations from different nations of subjects related to cancer were very attractive and informative. The third day Professor Wada, his wife and I flew to Sapporo where I gave a lecture, which was translated into

Japanese simultaneously, about the revolution, which resulted in me and my family leaving my country and going to London and my scientific research in London.

Sapporo Medical School.
My speech was being translated by a professor. 1981

The first night Wada's family and I had dinner at the same hotel that I was staying in and the second night a Japanese-style party was prepared by Sapporo Medical School and four of the medical Professors were invited but I did not see their wives. On the second day of my stay, Mrs. Wada and her daughter Dr. Sato Honma took me to some important parts of town and the third day I left Sapporo accompanied by the Professor and his wife and returned to the symposium to attend the rest of the meeting and to prepare for the return to London. Meanwhile Professor Wada handed me an envelope containing $1,000 cash as a fee for the lecture at the Sapporo Medical School.

The closing ceremony or Sayonara party was unique and fascinating. Then the group of London scientists including myself went to the Hakozaki terminal by bus and from there to the Tokyo airport (Nariti). During the meeting, I had become acquainted with other British scientists that were curious about my presence and my 2-day absence accompanied by a VIP Japanese couple. They started questioning me about my origin, my work and my life in London, especially during the flight since we had nothing to do but have time to talk. One of the scientists asked me how I decided to go to London, since I had been educated in the US and how I knew the Japanese couple. I explained that the first question was exactly the same one the immigration officer kept asking me for three hours in her office when she tried to deport me at the time of my arrival at Heathrow. Thank God, it was over and with the help Professors Selwyn and Lacy I had a three-year residency in London.

I explained that I was introduced to Professor Wada and his wife way back in 1969 at the Tehran University while they were visiting Iran by invitation of the Medical School. The couple including their daughter came to Iran five times and I treated them as VIPs. This time they invited me and treated me as a VIP in return and paid all my expenses including the registration fee. The aircraft landed at Heathrow and we all got off the plane. The British gentleman who was talking to me during the flight talked to his friends and told them they should go through the citizen line and that I had to go through the foreigner line. They didn't go directly through the citizen line but stayed next to the foreigner line. They told me not to worry; the five of them were going to stand there and support me and take me with them if immigration became difficult. I was very tired, with a very swollen foot and had an aircraft slipper on when we got to the check point. I handed my passport to a young British man who was standing behind the desk, he looked at me and asked me if I had spent all of Khomeini's money in Japan. I said, "No, sir, but tell me what you mean." He replied that he was wondering how much I could smuggle from Iran and spend in Japan. I told him, "None" and showed him Professor Wada's letter as well as the Westminster Medical School's statement of my status. It was not enough in his eyes. He told me his supervisor was going to come and see me. At that time my heartbeat increased and my hands started trembling as his supervisor and all five of the British scientists came forward. They started talking to the supervisor. I didn't understand what they were talking about but he immediately handed me my passport and said, "Welcome to London." Today, I must say without the support of those five scientists, I could not imagine how long I would have had to stand there and how many more questions I would have had to answer. I am grateful to all of them wherever they are.

After all that, with no shoes on, I got my suitcase and went home by taxi. It was 1 pm when I arrived. I took a warm shower and went to bed until late afternoon. When Shaparak and Shayma came home from school they both came to me. Shayma told me she was glad I was back home and that while I was gone her Mom had received a letter about a job interview from one of Nevada's nursing schools. She took the letter and applied for a visa at the US Embassy, but it was rejected. They were very sad because they couldn't see their cousins anymore. I told them we would try again and not to worry. Meanwhile, my daughter Nikrou called and told me her husband Ali had talked to the Senator of Michigan about Minoo and me and that it was time to apply for a visa. Two days later, I called Mr. Freedman, the gentleman that the Senator mentioned, and made an appointment for the following Monday at 10 am. Minoo and I went to the Embassy and entered from the back door as Mr. Freedman instructed us to do. We went to his office and he took us to another room where a handsome gentleman was standing. He received us very kindly and talked to us, stamped Minoo's passport and included Shaparak's and Shayma's names on her passport visa page. I told him how grateful we were. He told me, "As the American consul, I assure you we judge people individually." Then he asked me if I needed a visa. Unfortunately I didn't have my passport with me. I wanted to finish my History of Medicine class as well as my thesis exam, which was in November. I was not planning to go to the US at that time because I had some unfinished business, including the transfer of some additional money from Iran via registration again to get my tuition as well as a year's living expenses. I must emphasize again that the money I received from Iran was not government money; I just wanted to get the benefit of the value of exchange.

CHAPTER 12

Minoo's Trip to the U.S.

Minoo and her two children were preparing themselves to go to the States for good. I decided to stay in the same apartment by myself until I was sure they didn't want to return to London. It was the girls' first trip to the US, although Minoo had been to the US two or three times before with her husband on business. She wasn't used to the US system of living. By the end of July 1981, Minoo and her two daughters had left for the US, first to Los Angeles, then on to Reno, Nevada, where they finished high school and went to college.

I was living alone, which caused a lot of worry for my family in the US because I was the only one in the UK and was busy the whole time. I found ample time to study and wrap up the results of my research and prepare for the final review of my thesis and oral and written exams in November. I was also eager to take advantage of my student status and to receive tuition and living expenses on the basis of the government currency value, in other words, to buy currency from the bank rather than the black market.

During this time, I received a letter from Michigan State University, Department of Endocrine Research, the laboratory where I did all my Master's and PhD work. It was the 25th anniversary of the Endocrine Research Unit and all the former graduates were invited. This was the best and most effective reason to apply for a visitor visa to the US. It was very hard to let go of everything I had worked on during 16 months, with no results. But I couldn't ignore this opportunity to get a visa and join the family that I was desperate to see after two years. I couldn't even close my eyes for the entire night. I decided to go to the US Embassy first to see what would be the fate of my visa and then think about the rest. I received the letter on Friday so I had to wait until Tuesday because Monday was American Labor Day. I decided not to tell anyone that I received the invitation letter until I knew the fate of my visitor visa.

On Monday morning I met with Dr. Bakhtiar and talked about the History of Medicine exam in general. I asked him what would happen if someone was unable to attend the exam. He told me that it could be deferred once for the next year at the same time. I was relieved because the currency value that I bought from the government bank was special for students only. I felt I should have the results of my study to present to them if it became necessary or I might be accused of taking advantage of the government. Although the Society of Apothecaries did not charge me the tuition for the History of Medicine course, I had benefited from the Society, not the government of Iran.

At 10 am I was present at the US Embassy with my invitation letter and passport. It didn't take more than 45 minutes before my name was called and my passport handed to me with the visa entry stamp. I went back to the Medical School as cheerful as could be. I told Dr. Bakhtiar and then Professor Selwyn. I showed them the invitation letter and discussed the pressure of time limitations. Dr. Selwyn kindly told me there was nothing to worry about. I should go and enjoy my family; I could come back for the exam in November of 1982. He also told me that if I needed any immediate assistance to let him know or if I needed a letter of recommendation to the Iranian government or any other institution he would be glad to prepare one. I promised to continue my research and give all the collected data to his secretary by September 25, which would be my last day in London. I would probably return to the UK for the exam.

My Trip to the United States

On September 26, 1981, I left London via British Airways to Detroit, Michigan where my daughter Nikrou and her family were living in Birmingham, Michigan. After a week of rest, Nikrou took me to Michigan State University in East Lansing where my old friends were waiting for me.

Reunion at ERU (R to L): Gail, Shirley and me. 1981

Some of them wondered if I was still in one piece, no matter how much weight I had lost and how many more wrinkles had appeared on my face. I had a wonderful time during the reunion. When I arrived at the Endocrine Research Unit laboratory, Dr. Dukelow who was in charge of the unit welcomed me back to the Unit and then took me to the main lab.

L to R: John Nellor, Mrs. Dukelow,
me and Dr. Dukelow, ERU, 1981

He said that it had been 14 years since he had heard my name but he saw my sign every day. He showed me the board - written on the first line was Monta, symbol of hard and continuous work, followed by the other graduates names. Since they could not pronounce my entire name, Monta became my nickname. I wondered about my sign and asked him about it. He took my arm and guided me to the center of the main lab next to four completely colorless tiles and said, "it was a good and permanent Monta signature of your continuous work written on the board." The spot was the results of my work at 3 am when I found that not only was the xylene jar empty but the backup stock xylene bottle was empty also. That night I promised myself to finish staining of all the slides collected for my subject thesis. Therefore, I did not stop and decided to pick up the full metal container of xylene, use a funnel in the glass bottle and transfer some xylene. Because of the heavy weight of the container, I lost the slow-pouring motion balance and the xylene splashed out of the funnel onto the tile. I tried to wipe if off immediately but was not successful. The next morning at 10 am, I went to the ERU and found Dr. John Nellor, my major professor who was in charge of the Unit. He was standing at the door of the main lab. I was sure that everyone was laughing at me. I said, "Good morning, Dr. Nellor, I did it last night." He said, "Yes ma'am; I'm glad you didn't catch the lab on fire." In reply I told him I was willing to pay for it. He smiled first, then looked at my eyes and told me, "Monta, are you stupid?" The word stupid was very heavy and intolerable for me; I tried to escape and avoid looking at him. I went to Joan who was his first hand assistant and asked, "Joan, how can I pay for the tiles?" She also laughed and said never mind Monta." In the afternoon, I went to Mary his secretary and asked the same question. She told me to take it easy, accidents happen, do not worry. For two or three days I tried to hide myself in the corner of the microscope room, reading the slides with no breaks and no coffee except at lunch time when I was sure he was at lunch or at a meeting. Finally, after a week we met and he very kindly said,

"No one believed you were negligent; it was the ignorance of the person who was in charge, not you."

United States Immigration

The 25th anniversary of the Unit was accomplished perfectly and I had the great opportunity to meet with so many people who worked at the Unit and also my University Professors of different areas of study. Everyone was very kind to me and offered their help. On the recommendation of Dr. Nellor, the graduate Dean at the University of Nevada-Reno at the time, Dr. Dukelow offered me a job and wrote to the Immigration and Naturalization Service. I will always be grateful to him. I enjoyed spending three days and nights with my old friends, especially John and Barbara Nellor, Fred How and his wife Lillian who hosted us, and Shirley Johnson who worked at the ERU while I was there. They arranged an evening party and we also had a luncheon meeting. My daughter Nikrou and her husband Ali invited all of them for dinner at their home in Bloomfield Hills, Michigan.

L to R: Ali, Mrs. Seegers, me, Nikrou, Dr. Seegers, Nikrou's home, Michigan, 1981

The next day Dr. Nellor and his wife flew to Reno. I remained in their house because my immigration file was there since I spent eight years in Michigan. In order to get an alien number and a work permit, I had to be the first-degree relative of an American citizen or I had to have proof of eligibility for a third preference internationally-known scientist, including a job offer. In fact, I was lucky enough to have the job offer available but had no evidence of attendance at three international scientific meetings except one from the recent event in Tokyo, Japan. I had attended more than three others, but I had no proof of them; I left all the documentation behind in Iran. After all the difficulties and unrest that I had endured, I couldn't recollect any of them except the international symposium of the health care network held in Alma Ata, USSR in September 1977. I remembered that because it was associated with Black Friday in Iran.

After 14 years of being away from the area, there were so many changes in the town, I was unable to get to the library to find the information about the international meetings. The Wayne State Medical School and its library had moved from the area that I used to know. I had no car and no driver's license to go anywhere by myself. My daughter and her husband didn't want me to do everything by myself. I couldn't understand why they were so worried and kept telling me not to go alone. They told me they would help but I really didn't want to be a burden to them or interfere with their routine schedule.

I decided to go to the Wayne State Medical School and meet with Dr. Seegers, the head of the Department of Physiology and Pharmacology while I was working on my post-doctoral research. I believe it was Monday at 8 am when I entered Dr. Seegers' office. As usual, he was so kind and offered me his genuine help and told me he could give me a written job offer. He also advised me not to leave the US until my status was settled. I explained that I was desperate to find out the international meeting I attended and couldn't recollect the time and the place of it. He was really kind and very much concerned about me. He called his secretary and asked her to search the medical library for international meetings. In less than a half an hour, she called back and said, "How about the Canadian Symposium in 1967 where Montakhab presented her doctoral thesis data?" I became so excited and cheerful. Dr. Seegers asked her to provide the evidence of my attendance plus a strong letter of recommendation regarding my past research related to the present job offer. Dr. Seegers then invited me for lunch.

During lunch he asked me about the situation in Iran and the fate of the Institute of Paramedical Sciences. He encouraged me a lot and gave me many examples of people like me after their country's revolution and their present status. We went back to his office where I received the evidence of the two symposiums, one in Alma Ata in September of 1977 and the other in Canada in 1967 as well as a copy of the letter of recommendation to the Immigration Office.

It was 4 pm when my son-in-law came to pick me up. At that point in time, no one in my family had received their green card (alien registration card) yet, even though they had come to the US in 1979. They had been waiting for almost two years. I was worried for my own because I applied in Michigan and I wanted to join the larger part of my family in Reno (my two daughters and the three grandchildren, Shaparak, Shayma and the youngest one, Hessam were all in Reno. The only other grandchild, Adib, was living in Detroit). I had to have patience and wait for my interview with the immigration officer. I prayed day and night asking God to make it happen faster.

After 15 days, I received a letter about my interview with Ms. Lisa in the main Immigration Office. Nikrou took me there. After about an hour of waiting (a rather short time) I was called and guided toward the stairs. I met with a beautiful, young, well-educated woman who asked me so many scientific questions, especially about EDTA that I used as anticoagulant for *in vitro* platelet-leukocyte aggregations and microclot formation resulting in myocardial infarction *in vivo*. She was so knowledgeable; I later found out she had degrees in both physics and chemistry. After about a full hour of discussion, she told me I had a very clear file. In addition to the two job offers, my good letter of recommendation and the evidence of the international meetings, the most important of which was the one in Japan because of the invitation letter and the VIP treatment, were impressive.

She stamped the work authorization in my passport and told me I was classified as a third preference internationally-known scientist. She told me, "I'm sure there is no need for a labor certificate, so you can start your work as soon as tomorrow morning." I would like to send my great appreciation and gratitude to all those individuals who stretched out their hands to take mine and helped, not only me, but also my two grandchildren, both of whom I am very proud today. I went home with my daughter, Nikrou, who waited for me while I was with Lisa. In the middle of the road on Woodward Street, I saw the airline ticket office and asked her to stop and let me buy my ticket to Reno. Although she wasn't happy about my departure, she followed my instructions.

Family photo (L to R, back to front): Nikrou, Minoo, Adib on my lap, Hessam, Shaparak, Nikou and Shayma

I realized that I had spent such a long time in Detroit to fix my status that it wasn't possible to return to London for the November exam. I wrote to Professor Selwyn and asked him for an extension until November of the next year. It was approved. I left Detroit five days after my interview and flew to Reno. All my family had been calling me one after the other from Reno, telling me they wanted to see me and celebrate my entry to the US. I wanted to join them as soon as I could. Shaparak and Shayma had been with me since September 1979 when I moved into their house and then we went to London, living in the same apartment since May 13, 1980. Hessam was the youngest of all. In Tehran, he lived close to my house and I always spent time with him. Adib, my other grandchild, had lived farthest from me in Iran and we visited him every Friday.

All my family came to the airport to welcome me. I found that Hessam forced his mother Nikou to buy a bottle of champagne and to bring an opener to the airport. As soon as I entered the hallway they were going to open the champagne and offer it to everyone who came close to him or me. To be honest he tried hard, but his hand was not strong enough to open the champagne on time, so he was a bit disappointed. When I entered the hallway and understood what happened I kissed him a lot and hugged him and told him not to cry, we would open it at home and serve it there. He was a little sweet 8? year old boy at that time. We all went home happily together once again and enjoyed our life, no matter what we had left behind.

To celebrate my arrival the family decided to go to Disneyland during Christmas time 1982. We went by car; Nikou's husband was the driver of a big rental American Chevrolet. The three kids enjoyed Disneyland. And Minoo also took them to Sea World and the Wild Animal Park on a one day tour to San Diego

Life in Reno, Nevada

Before I arrived in Reno, Minoo and Nikou decided to change apartments and move closer to Reno High School where Shaparak and Shayma were enrolled. As Nikou explained to me, their enrollment wasn't easy because the school wouldn't accept both of them under one person's sponsorship. Minoo only had a visitor visa so she wasn't eligible. I was still in London at the time of enrollment. Therefore, Shayma came under Nikou's visa and Dr. Pacita Manalo, a Professor of Pathology at the Reno Medical School and Nikou's mentor, volunteered to be Shaparak's sponsor. So they were enrolled at the Reno High School. I am extremely grateful to Dr. Manalo for her strong generosity and her continued friendship.

Shaparak was accepted in the 11th grade and Shayma the 9th. They had had to change schools in different countries twice, but it was to their benefit because they went forward and didn't lose any time. After their move, Nikou's apartment was on the first floor and ours was on the second. There was no comparison to our London apartment, which had been much larger and had a better floor plan. But the Truckee River passed the apartment complex from east to west and we had a beautiful view of the river with the bushes and trees around it. Reno High School was just across the street so it was within walking distance for the girls but Hessam had been enrolled in Roygom Primary School, which was rather far from our apartment. Since he didn't reside in the proper district, he couldn't use the school bus; so Nikou had to give him a ride every day. Minoo was very concerned about their piano lessons and had found a teacher for Shayma and Hessam. Shaparak had to have advanced lessons because she had a certificate from the Royal College of Music in London. Therefore, she required a more advanced piano teacher than the one for Shayma and Hessam. They went to piano class individually. In other words, Shayma had to be in the piano teacher's house by herself then the same for Hessam. Either Nikou or I took one of them to the piano teacher and returned home then took the other one and brought the first one back. Anytime they had a piano lesson we had to travel 5 times between the teacher's house and our home. I took Shaparak to her piano lesson myself and waited in the car for an hour then took her back home. This continued until Shayma became 16 years old and got a driver's license and her own car. Then she started to complain about her teacher and wanted to collect her $50 teacher fee for herself. She was the first one to quit piano lessons. As soon as Shaparak was accepted into medical school, she quit also. When Adib in Michigan found out Shayma had quit he also quit. The last one was Hessam. When we moved to San Diego, he quit automatically.

Back to front (L to R): Adib, Nikrou, Nikou and Hessam, March 20, 1981, Reno

It wasn't long before I was called by the Department of Physiology and Pharmacology in the Reno Medical School, based on the recommendation of Dr. Nellor. The project was on Hirschsprung's Disease. It was not an easy task because the project involved infusion and an active rate of absorption of radioactive material from the intestinal wall of 15-gram mice.

Minoo Returned to Iran

Minoo decided to leave the girls with me and return to Iran and join her husband. We decided to buy a house, it didn't matter where in town, the most basic of structures, to be able to have enough room for each of us to move around more freely. At that time I didn't know where the majority of Iranians lived in Reno even though in 1980 when I went to visit Nikou and Nikrou and their two sons Adib and Hessam I had gotten acquainted with some but not all of them. Nikou's neighbors, Mr. and Mrs. Kavoosi had become our close friends and they recommended an area, which was under construction. We all visited the area; the model homes were 2, 3 or 4 bedrooms. The three-bedroom house with a very good floor plan was priced at $80,000. The seller explained to us that if we paid $2000 now, we could have the house and move in by June 1982. The company would lend us $50,000 with no interest if we could provide $30,000 at escrow and pay $1000 a month for 5 years.

No one could find a better deal, especially for us, as we didn't have any income at that time. Minoo told me it was a good deal but we didn't have enough money in our hands and she couldn't talk to her husband because he was working and it might have caused a big problem. Shaparak was insisting that we buy the house and said I couldn't go to work after school and was begging constantly. Finally I told Minoo I would pay the initial $2,000 right away. She tried to stop me and kept telling me that I could lose the $2,000 if I couldn't provide the $30,000 on time. I said, "This is a gambling city and I am willing to gamble this way no matter what."

At this point I must say although it was three years after the revolution and Iran was involved in a war with Iraq, people still weren't safe talking about money on the phone. They were also cautious in even talking to their children or their wives living abroad. I paid the $2,000 with a check and the seller told me I had 90 days to decide, otherwise I would lose it. We went back to our two-bedroom apartment and Minoo and I agreed to buy the house and pay 50% each. She said when she got home and talked to her husband she would call me and let me know if she could buy half or if I should cancel. Minoo left Reno in February 1982 and went directly to Tehran and joined her husband. They sent their OK to me by phone. Her husband Mohsen had been working for an Iranian oil and gas company in a high ranking position since they got married in 1963. After the revolution he had been demoted to a low level job and had very limited or no authority so he was discouraged about staying in Iran.

When Minoo returned to Iran after three years, she received a job offer from the Tehran Clinic, as general manager of the hospital. She accepted the job primarily because of the numerous war casualties that were brought to the clinic every day. In the meantime, Shaparak, Shayma and I were preparing to move into the new house. Shayma had always been very close to her parents and had never been without both of them for long. She started having tantrums and kicked Shaparak out of their room (the master bedroom). Therefore, Shaparak and I shared the small second bedroom that had two twin beds and a very narrow space between them. Since I started working at the University Medical School where Nikou was already working, we went together in the morning but I came home earlier and picked Hessam up from Roygam at 3 pm. Shaparak and Shayma walked home at 4 pm. I tried to supervise all three in the afternoon and gave a ride to Nikou at 5 or 6 pm. We enjoyed living so close to each other; in particular Hessam didn't feel so lonely anymore since Nikrou and Adib had left Reno and gone to Michigan to join his father. Hessam's father had started working in Kuwait at that time and continued for a long period of time. At that point in time we all were happy. I tried to be very easy with Shaparak and Shayma, to accept whatever they demanded, especially with Shayma, because I didn't want them to feel the absence of their parents.

One afternoon when I came back from work I found both girls standing behind the entrance door with a gray and white kitten in Shayma's arms. We greeted each other as usual; then Shayma said that Shaparak brought the kitten, not her. They were trying to convince me that if we returned the kitten the owner would drown it. In such a small apartment I didn't see how we could manage with a kitten. I finally agreed to keep it but told them we couldn't keep it without the consent of the owner. Shaparak told me the kitten belonged to her math teacher and she would bring the consent tomorrow. Shayma gave me her weekly allowance and asked me to go with her to buy food and a litter box. I told Shayma to keep her money and that I would pay for it. But honestly, who was going to take care of it while we were not home? The cat would sleep during the day time and be active at night like our 4 cats in Iran. The answer was that we would leave the kitten with food, water and a litter box in Shayma's bathroom and close the door when we left for school and work.

The next day I came home at 4 pm and heard three kids, Shaparak, Shayma and Hessam standing behind the door giggling loudly. I knew Hessam had come home with his mom so I opened the entrance door and saw all three plus two kittens, the one from yesterday and another gray and white one from today that I myself was in love with. They were jumping up and down, saying, "They are sisters, please let us keep both of them, we are two and they should be two as well, not one." Now Hessam was convincing me by trying to tell me that it would be more economical to keep both together, you only pay once for both to buy food and litter and so on. I had no choice except to be agreeable with them because I loved the second one as well. That night they had a party for the two kittens; they cheered, they laughed and celebrated. That was not always the case every day. When we were home and we wanted to open the door to change the air or sometimes to enjoy the flow of the water in the river and its smooth noise, in a matter of a blink of an eye one kitten or the other would drop down from the balcony and our first level neighbor would bring them up the stairs and hand them back to us. Any time Shayma decided to have a tantrum she would lock her bathroom door and leave the litter box outside of our small bathroom. She wouldn't let us use hers; she was punishing us this way because she believed Shaparak and I were naughty. It was very uncomfortable to keep these two kittens in the apartment.

I kept telling them that we should look forward to our two new identical homes with a joint open back yard for them to play in as much as they wanted. At that time I was still working in the Physiology Department with a limited budget so I wasn't brave enough to spend money lavishly. I had no one like Dr. Bakhtiar to buy money for me from students. The girls still received money for their living expenses from a London bank every month. In the meantime, we were close to moving in June, as promised. Whenever Nikou and I planned to go and select our upgrade materials, Shayma complained about the location of the house. She said she saw many cows around and that we were taking them to a village not to the city. She either didn't come with us or didn't give us her ideas about what to select. We really didn't pay much attention to her claims because she was the youngest among us and we couldn't afford to buy a house in a better area farther from the airport. At that moment, the most important necessities for us were this house and a car.

The house was far from the Reno High School as well as the University. We had bought a house in the tail of the city while the kids' school and our daily workplace were located in the head part of the town - but there was no other choice. Although there was a high school located much closer to us, I didn't want to change their school and move them to a strange and unfamiliar environment while their parents weren't with them. So I would have to give them a ride every day. Fortunately Nikou bought a brand new Honda and I had the two-door Ford, so I became freer to manage our move.

I received the money to put the down payment on the house. As school finals neared, so did the date for our move. I notified our landlord by the first of June and started collecting and wrapping everything whenever I could. This was my first time to move by myself and I didn't know where I to start every afternoon. When I came home I tried to collect something with the help of the girls and take it to the car; the car was a two-door and I wasn't used to it. I would pack my car full and drive to the new house. Although the house wasn't completely finished yet, I had permission to move our things in. I moved all our dresses on hangers and all the pots and pans inside a suitcase. I left the

TV remote control inside my sewing machine. It wasn't found for at least 3 months until I wanted to sew something.

The last few days of our stay in the apartment were very busy, especially the last day that we had to move our large furniture. Every night when Nikou and I found a bit of time to talk to each other and plan for our move Nikou told me not to worry, that we would carry all the big stuff by U-Haul. I didn't know anything about U-Haul and Nikou wasn't really familiar with it. The day the telephone company went to the new house to connect the telephone line in both houses; Nikou left Shaparak and Hessam there to keep the door open for them. Shayma, the two kittens and I were in the apartment. Nikou went to the U-Haul office.

When the sun set and it became dark outside, in spite of all of the streetlights, the inside of the apartment became darker and darker as the night fell. The telephone in the apartment was disconnected as well as the electricity. I had no way to know why the U-Haul wasn't coming and I had no idea what happened to Shaparak and Hessam. I couldn't leave the apartment because I was expecting the U-Haul at any minute. I had to keep myself busy as much as I could so I wouldn't show how worried I was. No U-Haul, no Nikou and no news from Shaparak and Hessam. I couldn't do anything except pray and talk to myself. All of a sudden the light from the U-Haul made the area shiny and the driver came up to move the furniture to the truck. As soon as Nikou came up the stairs to tell them what to do, Shayma and I jumped out with the kittens and drove to the new house to see what happened to Shaparak and Hessam. Nikou told me that she would wait for the gentleman who drove the U-Haul and his helper while they carried our few pieces of furniture from the first and second floors to the truck and from the truck to our new house.

Nikou later explained to me why she was so late in arriving home with the U-Haul. We did not realize that U-Haul meant you do it by yourself. When she got to the U-Haul office, she had to arrange for someone to drive the truck and another person to help with the moving. After some discussion with the U-Haul staff, they agreed to supply people to help.

We arrived at the new house located at 1295 E. Huffaker Lane, Reno, Nevada, 89511. It was very comfortable and affordable. Shayma, Shaparak and I were very happy there. Nikou and Hessam lived on the left side of our house and Mr. and Mrs. Kavoosi on the right. Sometimes the noise of the airplanes was loud but we got used to it and it didn't bother us at all. We were very happy living so close to each other.

Shaparak decided to move to Nikou's house and live with her. One night Nikou suddenly developed a severe pain in her belly that caused her to faint and fall down in her bathtub. Shaparak knew about it but didn't come to tell me at the time of the incident or the next morning as she had promised Nikou not to. Nikou came to me the next afternoon and told me what had happened. She had gone to her gynecologist and he had scheduled her for exploratory surgery the next week. Can you imagine my feelings? I was alone with the two girls and Nikrou was in Michigan; she couldn't leave her husband and son by themselves. Minoo was in Iran and couldn't come to help. So I just had to accept what was going to happen. Nikou decided to send Hessam to Michigan and not tell him. She went in for surgery that ended up as a hysterectomy. Then she came home to rest and was on a leave of absence for two weeks. After a few days she decided to go to Michigan for the rest of her recovery. She took both girls with her; I was left at home with the two kittens because I was still working in the Physiology Department. I also was planning to go to London as part of my annual vacation for the History of Medicine exam.

In November 1982, I went to London for a week, presented my thesis and passed the written and oral exams, for which I received tuition and living expenses for two successive years. I must thank Professor Selwyn who introduced me as the Honorary Research Fellow to the Society of Apothecaries so that my tuition was waived.

Our life was moving on with no problems. We all were happy in our new home. Nikou and I were trying to furnish and decorate our houses and to take care of landscaping our front and back yards, something that neither of us had ever done before. Nikou was much more familiar with the town and the landscape contractor but we didn't have enough money to contract the entire job. We decided to take care of the front yard and contract the sprinkler placement and seeding the lawn on both sides of the houses. Every Saturday we went shopping and on Sunday we planted shrubs and trees. Shaparak and Shayma dug the ground and helped me to plant the flowers, trees, etc. One time after digging a hole, we found a big stone at the bottom of it. We were deliberating whether the tree should be planted or if we should dig another hole. I convinced them that the root has the ability to grow around the stone. That evergreen tree that the three of us planted in 1982 grew well and is still alive.

To *Massoum Montakhab*

We, the **Master, Wardens** and **Court of Assistants** of the **Society of Apothecaries of London** give you greeting. Having true information that you have made a special study of the **History of Medicine** and being informed by the trusty examiners appointed by us that you have proved to them that you possess special knowledge and skill in the subjects relative thereto, your name has accordingly been placed in the **Society's Register of Diplomates** in the **History of Medicine.**

Given under our hand and Seal this

30th day of November 1982

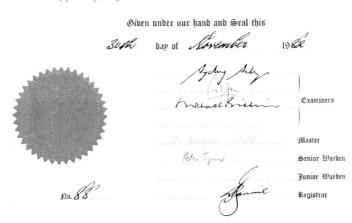

Examiners

Master
Senior Warden
Junior Warden
Registrar

No. 88

Post-Doctoral Diploma in History of Medicine, London, 1982

273

CHAPTER 13

In Vitro Fertilization

The grant and project that I was working on was terminated in February of 1983 and I was laid off. At the same time the Reno Women's Clinic announced the establishment of an *in vitro* fertilization and embryo transfer laboratory. They were looking for an embryologist. My daughter Nikou was working in the pathology department and introduced me to Dr. C. Stratton, who was a Professor at the University, a Mormon priest by religion, anatomist by education and probably a part owner of the *in-vitro* lab at the clinic. He was also a friend of Dr. Geff Sher and probably Dr. V. Knutzen, both South African gynecologists and founders of the clinic. They were among the pioneers of *in vitro* fertilization in the US. Dr. Stratton gave me an interview and then spoke with Dr. Helen Cook about my previous work in the Physiology Department. He later mentioned to me that he had received a good recommendation from Dr. Cook's.

Dr. Stratton told me the *in vitro* laboratory was not ready yet but that he wanted me to start working and practicing the development of an embryo in his own laboratory. I accepted the job offer with pleasure because it was my wish to use my knowledge of embryology after all. Two or three days later he brought me a contract and instructed me to sign and return to the clinic to meet with Dr. Sher, head of the clinic. I started to read the contract and noticed a phrase that appeared to be controversial with the modern law. It was written, "Dr. Massoum Montakhab agreed that if for any reason she were to quit working at the laboratory she would not practice embryology in a radius of 100 miles for a term of five successive years." I asked him what it meant. He replied that it was an old-fashioned rule and not to worry because he had signed the same contract with the clinic. It was lunch time and I was sitting alone in Dr. Stratton's lab debating to myself if I should sign the contract and start working or sit at home and wait for another job. I told myself that I was an immigrant and that I had to abide by their rules regardless of how unfair and unjust they might seem. Finally, I signed the contract as he had instructed.

The next morning I went to the clinic and met with Dr. Sher who personally gave me a tour of the clinic and introduced me as the embryologist of the group. I returned to Dr. Stratton's office in hopes of starting my practice in embryo development. But instead, he wanted me to copy a lot of subjects, none of which were related to *in vitro* procedures or developing an embryo. He also asked me to wash all of the dirty dishes and rearrange the laboratory. I tried not to refuse his demands but it was really hard on me. When I started taking care of those things I closed all of the windows, locked the main door and started washing/fixing, the lab because I felt terribly demoted, as I was hired as a scientist for the clinic and not an orderly for the basement of the university. I felt I was trapped in the net of a prejudiced person. I kept telling myself to be strong and not to lose my confidence and self-esteem. I wondered he did not like me to read the technical papers and why we weren't optimizing the equipment, the sterility of the medium, practicing the development of an embryo to make sure that everything was in a perfect state instead of rearranging his own lab that academically was very quiet and very inactive at that time. I spent five weeks of wandering around the lab – it seemed more like five months.

Meanwhile, Dr. Stratton and his family were about to leave for ten days vacation so I decided to spend a week at the endocrine research unit where I graduated that was involved *in vitro* fertilization of monkeys rather than humans. I spent five

working days in the lab and learned a lot because the entire procedure was a replicate of the human procedure. Dr. Stratton and
I returned to work and waited for the *in vitro* laboratory to be
completed at the clinic. Finally, one day he told me to go to the
lab next door and get a certain Petri dish from the incubator,
look at it under the microscope and tell him what I saw. I followed his instructions. I observed a few eggs and I asked him to
whom the eggs belonged and he said, "A cow; it's for developing an embryo." I told him that we should have sperm to mix
with the egg to make an embryo. The best way would be rat egg
and sperm. Dr. Stratton asked me to order it.

At 8 am the next day, rat eggs and sperm were mixed and
incubated at 37°C. At 4 pm the dish containing egg and sperm
was transferred from the incubator to the microscope. The
developing embryo was at the two-cell stage and clearly visible
because of the absence of the corona radiata in rat embryos, that
is present around a human egg and hard to see even under high
magnification until it is unveiled. I suggested taking the dish to
Dr. Sher; he agreed but said that Geff had left the clinic for the
day. "You should take it tomorrow because you are the one who
developed this embryo." I believed him and took the dish back
to the incubator and left for the day. The next day I took the
dish to the clinic to proudly show them. But they all politely
told me, "Today we see more cells than when Dr. Stratton
brought this dish to show us yesterday." You cannot imagine my
train of thought at that particular moment! How unfair and dishonest would it be if someone tried to introduce your work as
his or her own? I lost my confidence and self-esteem and my
trust toward him. Two weeks later, the *in vitro* laboratory was
completed and ready to use. I moved to the clinic.

Everything was going well with my family and I was very
happy and content with my new job and enjoyed working with
Dr. Sher at his clinic. Their first attempts, for a Canadian woman
and an African-American woman, were free of charge. Dr. Sher
and Dr. Knutzen performed the egg retrieval while we watched;
it was perfect. Using a hood, Dr. Stratton and I washed the eggs

and placed them in medium under sterile conditions and incubated them in a specific incubator at 37°C with a constant flow of oxygen and CO2 similar to the human body. Meanwhile, without Dr. Stratton, I received their husbands' sperm that was then processed and incubated in the same incubator for four hours. Eight hours later, the sperm of each husband was mixed with the eggs of their wives and incubated again for twelve hours. When I reported to Dr. Sher that everything was completed, he was suddenly concerned that the samples might have become mixed up (because one family was South African and the other Caucasian) and kept asking me how I had kept them separated. As the most responsible person, it was Dr. Sher's right to be worried. It was their first attempt and they didn't pay attention to the different races. They could have performed the procedures on two different days rather than one without any agony; but they didn't. I didn't blame him, because he wasn't familiar with the accuracy of my work and this was their first attempt. I was a stranger amongst them and new to this subject. Although I had a degree in embryology I had never worked in this area and never on human subjects. They had gone to London and learned the technique. Personally, I was 100% confident about the way I mixed the eggs and sperm. I told Dr. Sher I had no doubt that I correctly mixed them. I asked him if he could tell me about their uteruses and their ability to accept or reject the embryos. His answer was no. I said that we should go home and wait for the results before we start worrying. Those first two women showed signs of pregnancy after 10 days by their blood hormonal levels but unfortunately they later aborted under natural conditions.

As time passed, the number of *in-vitro* applicants increased, as did the rate of success. It exceeded the normal rate of 10-15 to 20-25% at that time. I have a vivid memory of a 40-year-old woman who came to the clinic for artificial insemination. Her ova were completely matured and ready to be fertilized but her husband had no sperm after three tests on three successive days. She came from Southern California because of the fame of the clinic; it was her fifth attempt - four times in another clinic.

Microscopically, I found that her husband had been sterile to begin with. After the husband and the wife signed the consent for the sperm bank, she went through capacitation, a different technique similar to artificial insemination, and became pregnant. About two weeks later I received a beautiful bouquet of orchids from the clinic in appreciation of my discovery. She used to come to the clinic and sit in the waiting room and talk to the new applicants. If by chance I appeared in the hallway she would tell everyone that I was the one who made her pregnant because I diagnosed the sterility of her husband.

The success and fame of the clinic spread all over the country; the religious people made a fuss about the new technique; they believed it was against God's will and began to protest. There was a big meeting in a church with several religious men and women and we were invited to attend and defend our position. The priest talked about the issue and the conflict with God's creation and his concerns about interfering with God's decisions. The Christian doctor was by the podium and had found a phrase in the Bible to support his work. The Jewish doctor was sitting among the audience silently; the third doctor and I as embryologists were standing at the corner of the podium. In response to the priest, the Christian doctor started reading from the Bible. Then the priest called on an embryologist to defend. Dr. Stratton spoke up, saying that he had seven children and all of them came to this world under natural conditions but every one of them had been suffering from a rare kind of disability. He sounded miserable and very naïve; I believe he messed up badly as he didn't say even one word about *in vitro* fertilization.

Then I was called to the podium; I was rather shaky, remembering the time twenty-two years ago while at the English Language Institute when I had been strongly rejected by a group of Christians when asked to speak and they found out I was a scientist rather than a religious person. This time I first apologized for my broken accent; then I introduced my religion as Muslim and the holy book, the Koran. I explained that as a Muslim and follower of God's path, I hoped I could convince them that it is

God's order to help your family first, then your neighbor. If yours was not a needy family, then your neighbor would be the first. I tried to tell them that God is the original Creator and there is no one else. This is the only God who created the basic units of creation (i.e., eggs in the female ovary and sperm in the male testis), the precursors of creation and finally the development of a child. Further, when God created us he gave us a more active brain, a delicate hand and sharp eyes, the ability to think well, to choose a more proper way of work and to utilize the most delicate techniques to imitate Nature's functions. *In vivo* can be accomplished by *in-vitro;* in other words, pregnancy either by Nature or by *in-vitro.* "Why should we forget the need of a person who comes forward and stretches out her hand to ask for help?" Today, I do not know how many of the words or phrases I spoke with such a broken accent the audience understood; I only know that they did not reject me and I was more accepted by both gynecologists after that day. Dr. Sher was very disappointed with what Dr. Stratton mentioned about his family in public but Stratton didn't care much. Almost two months later another meeting was held in the Medical School; the audience was mostly University staff and medical students. This time Dr. Sher was the sole speaker, but Dr. Stratton and I had to be there. I was sitting close to the podium; Dr. Stratton was sitting in the last row. The lecture took about three hours and there were many questions. During the lecture, Dr. Sher introduced me as a skilled embryologist and asked me to stand up. I have no idea today whether he didn't see Dr. Stratton or if he ignored him because of his last miserable speech at the church.

The next morning, I went to the lab happy and cheerful as usual. Dr. Stratton arrived at the lab at 9 am and started nagging and bothering me with lots of nonsense criticisms. He made my day a living hell; I had never had such a hard time. Today, thinking back, I feel the same as I did that day after the meeting - so shaky, frustrated, exhausted and depressed. I couldn't remember what made me cry. I just couldn't stop my tears from falling; all the nurses at the clinic were surprised. I believe

Sandy (Dr. Sher special nurse) called Charlene Sher (Dr. Sher's wife) who came to the clinic and took me out for lunch and spoke very kindly to me. Every time I think about that special day I thank God both gynecologists were out and there were no patients to see my misery.

After that incident, Dr. Stratton was obviously mad and tried to get rid of me. It wasn't easy for him because I was available any time they needed me and I didn't mind how many hours I spent at the clinic, while he was always busy with a death or marriage ceremony at church. Both the gynecologists were supportive of me although Dr. Sher was the most influential. Besides, I was the "resident expert" on the cytology of sex determination from amniotic fluid. When a Caesarean section was considered in a case of multiple pregnancies and the maturity of an infant's lungs was in question, it was I who provided the necessary information about the sex of each unborn child.

The work at the clinic was very pleasant and satisfying for me. I had no set working hours because of the nature of the work that often started at 5 am and ended at 10-11 pm. But when the work was done, I could leave the clinic and do my errands, take care of the girls or do other personal business matters. Every morning Nikou took her son and the girls to school and in the afternoons I brought them home. I had to pick up Hessam from Roygom at 3 pm, Shaparak and Shayma from their school a bit later, then go to the house and return to the clinic if I had to continue work until it was completed.

I remember one day I didn't have enough time to take the kids home and be back in time. When I picked them up from school I talked to them about the necessity of returning to the clinic, which was a rather long way from the house. I asked them if they would mind going to the clinic with me to finish my work before going home. They agreed so I took them to the clinic and asked them to stay out of the waiting room, to sit in the hallway and not to talk to anyone, even each other, until I came back. Once again they agreed. Eventually I became worried about Hessam (not the girls) making noise. I didn't know that the clinic had a hidden abortion room and that its back door opened to the same hallway. After about forty-five minutes, Dr. Sher came to the lab and said, "Your kids believe Geff is out of his mind." I gathered something had happened but I didn't know what it was. He told me, "When I came out from the abortion room and saw the kids sitting so quietly I thought their mother was the one who had undergone the surgery. I sat by them and tried to explain everything to them. They were very careful to listen to what had been done. Then the young boy said, 'Doctor, you did all that to my grandmother, Dr. Montakhab? So how can we go home today?' Now you'd better go talk to them and let them know you are not sick." I said never mind, I was almost done and we had a long way to go to reach home; they would tell me the story.

In spite of all the happy moments that resulted from the successful work that Dr. Sher was in charge of, Dr. Stratton was uncomfortable with me ever since that night at the medical school; but he couldn't complain about my work. Anytime I asked him about some extra material or if I said Dr. Sher planned to do this or that, his answer was, "You and Geff are both capitalists and enthusiastic, free from the actual world." It became clear to me so many times that Dr. Stratton tried to ignore or deny Dr. Sher's and Dr. Knutzen's support for me. The first time was when Dr. Sher lectured at the medical school; the second episode happened when the *in vitro* fertilization conference was held in San Francisco in 1983. Dr. Sher arranged for Dr. Knutzen, Dr. Stratton and me to attend the meeting at the expense of the clinic. Dr. Stratton told me that if I wanted to go I would have to pay for my own fare and accommodations. I accepted because I was eager to find out what other clinics were doing. Dr. Knutzen said his wife invited me to ride with them in their car but they were planning on staying longer in San Francisco and suggested that I could ride back with Dr. Stratton. I said if he didn't mind I would and he said no problem. In San Francisco I arranged to stay with my friend who lived far from the conference area; my friend would come and pick me up after the meeting at 8:30 pm.

We attended the first day of the meeting until 5 pm then Dr. Knutzen proposed a get-together at 6:30 in the hotel lobby. I joined them on time. All of a sudden Dr. Stratton asked me why I didn't go to my friend's house. His question hurt me so much that my answer was "yes, definitely" and I left them immediately and went to the other part of the hotel lobby where I waited by myself until 8:30. I told myself not to feel bad; I was an immigrant and would not always be accepted by some idiot individuals, no matter how educated and how well trained I was and how well I had lived in the past. I should just think of today and. best of all, consider tomorrow and the future. I should have enough patience to keep my brain strong and active until I could achieve my own goals.

Dr. Stratton generally arrived at the lab about 8:30 or 9 am during egg retrieval; the gynecologists started at 5 am and I had to be there by 6 am at the latest when the retrieved eggs were ready to come to the lab. Sometimes they booked three applicants one after the other at one-hour intervals. But if they faced problems with the first patient, egg retrieval for the 3rd person was not performed until 11-12 noon. I would then have to be in the lab until 9 or 10 pm to finish all the process since Dr. Stratton was resting at home – after all, he was the boss. When he came to the lab during the embryo transfer and we unveiled the embryo and determined the cell stage, I stood by him and realized that he often wasn't looking in the right area of the dish. When I told him that the embryo was at the edge of the dish, he told me that I had an eagle eye. I was not brave enough to tell anyone he had a vision problem. At one point, he tried to convince Dr. Sher that it was I who did not have good vision and if some applicants didn't get pregnant it was because of the dead transferred embryos – my fault. However, it later became obvious to everyone in the clinic; it wasn't more than a year until he was called for immediate corneal transplant. He had been on the waiting list to find a match, probably long before the clinic started its *in vitro* laboratory.

Whenever Dr. Stratton arranged for news reporters to come to the clinic, he came to the lab the day before and talked to me very nicely and kindly asked me to rest (stay home) the next day. "I am free tomorrow so it is a chance for you to be free." So I wouldn't go to the clinic. When I went to the lab the following day, all the nurses would come to me and with a great surprise ask me why I hadn't come to the clinic the day before - that the news reporters had been there. When I asked Dr. Stratton why I had to "rest" when the news reporters were coming, he said, "Believe me, they came unexpectedly. I could call them to come back and talk to you if you want." I was a poor immigrant and he was a priest, a university professor and probably a shareholder of the lab, with all the power.

After almost 10 months of working at the clinic the first two pregnant women came to term, both carrying twins. They had a big celebration at the clinic the night before the first Caesarean section. The next day during the surgery, numerous reporters and paparazzi came to the hospital. The mother, her husband, both gynecologists, the nurses, Dr. Stratton and I were in the room adjacent to the OR. When they started the Caesarean section, Dr. Stratton went into for the OR and told me not to go in there. Dr. Sher didn't like that so he called me and told me to go in. The other pregnant woman gave birth a few hours later in Las Vegas, Nevada. On the evening of the same day, Dr. Sher held a celebration party at his house; he called me himself and told me to bring my entire family with me. He said, "This is one of the most important nights for all of us, especially you as a stem cell of the family chain." The success of the clinic was broad cast and each member of the I.V.F group was introduced on national television. Since then, any time I appeared in public different people would ask "aren't you the baby maker?"

Out of the 153 women who came to the clinic during the period I was working as an embryologist, 26 live babies were born; 7 sets of twin births and 19 single children, all in very good health. The International Symposium for *In-vitro* Fertilization and Embryo Transfer was held in Helsinki, Finland in 1984. Dr. Sher and I attended. As usual, Nikrou joined me; my daughters would never let me go alone on a long trip. She came from Detroit, Michigan to Los Angeles. We met at LAX and flew to Helsinki. The conference was held for a week and then we returned home.

The following day I went to the clinic. Dr. Stratton asked me why I did not stay in Europe, spend time with my daughter and enjoy my trip. I replied that I believed I had accepted a responsibility at the clinic and should be back on time to carry out those responsibilities. Besides, I had traveled to most of Europe when I was in Iran. At the present time neither my budget nor my schedule allowed me that luxury.

Dr Sher, me and Nikrou at Helsinki IVF Congress, 1984

Nikrou and me, Helsinki, 1984

Meanwhile, I found two new people hanging around the lab. At first I thought they were visiting; then I found that Dr.

Stratton had hired them to replace me. They started working. I think the one who was a technician was trained to ignore all the safety regulations of the lab. She tried to leave her leftover coffee or coke on the sterile counter, under the hood or any other place that I had sterilized no more than ten minutes earlier. She kept doing it more than 4–5 times a day. Any time I told her to stop bringing her drink into the lab she would tell me to "take it easy, doctor." I tried to ignore her for two weeks but finally I decided to leave. I wrote my letter of resignation and left it on Dr. Sher's desk. It was the spring of 1985.

When I left the clinic, I went to work at the Café de Paris because its manager was on vacation. A week later, Dr. Sher sent his new partner's wife to talk to me and convince me to return. When the she asked me to come back to the clinic, my answer was "If I can make a baby, surely I am able to make bread." I promised myself I would never work with or for any American like Dr. Stratton ever again in my life. I was certain that his goal had been to get rid of me ever since that night at the Medical School. He understood that I was aware of his vision problem so he tried to bring someone in to specialize in the destruction of my work and my reputation. For these reasons, I would be better off if I continued to work at the Café and keep my friendship with Charline and Dr. Sher rather than go back to work and have the situation repeated.

Dr. Sher and his family remained my friends; they invited all of us to their house and treated us in a very high class manner, especially when Minoo came and Dr. Sher planned to hire her to run the gynecology clinic in the hospital in a British midwifery way. Her interview was set for September 15, 1985 but by that day she was gone forever.

I later learned that any time the status of the clinic was broadcast to so many people at the Medical School as well as the Physiology Department, I was told that they knew for sure who did it and that they were well familiar with the work of "that Mormon priest," Dr. Stratton. As I never look back no matter what, I never went back to the clinic, even when a

Persian applicant for *in vitro* fertilization came from Iran to the clinic. When she and her husband found I wasn't there they got my home phone and address to contact me. They came because they received advice from their physician or relatives who were either gynecologists or some other doctor who knew me personally or saw my name in the *in vitro* fertilization paper. They only wanted to have the procedure if I could be at the clinic. My answer was, "I am sorry I am retired from the *in-vitro* laboratory now."

After I left the clinic a few Iranian gynecologists who were planning to establish an *in vitro* clinic went to the clinic to talk to Dr. Sher who was among the first forerunners. When they found out I was no longer at the clinic, they tried to visit with me. When I talked to them they told me how surprised the nurses were when I left the clinic, especially when Dr. Stratton went for eye surgery. They told me everyone at the clinic spoke very highly of me and had many good words, they were told about my success and the meticulous work I performed and the very good results the clinic had. Dr. Mozayani, one of the famous Iranian gynecologists who was persistent in establishing an *in vitro* clinic, came to my house and spoke to me and invited me to his clinic to see his work. He specifically went to Reno and spoke with Dr. Sher and his special nurse and asked about me. According to Dr. Mozayani himself, I was a perfect catch for him but his clinic was in Los Angeles and I was planning to move to San Diego in the near future. In reality, I didn't want to be separated from my family and asked him to please accept my excuses.

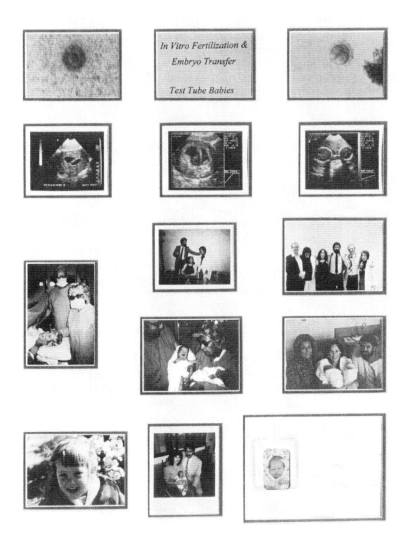

Summary of IVF/ET at the Reno Woman clinic, 1984

CHAPTER 14

Immigration and Adoption

The month of February 1982 was a lucky month for my two granddaughters, Shaparak and Shayma and me. I received my residency permit (green card) in mid-February. I immediately hired a young woman attorney to help me apply for the adoption of my granddaughters. She was very concerned about the status of the girls and gave me all the required paperwork that the biological parents had to sign and that had to be certified by the US Embassy located in the country of origin (Iran). Fortunately, Minoo was still in the US planning to return to Iran in a few days when I received the paperwork. Minoo took it with her to Iran (it was very difficult to send such documents by mail because of the random inspection of the mail). At the end of February or beginning of March I received a letter written to Minoo from the Immigration and Naturalization Service stating that her visitor visa had expired and that she and her daughters must leave the US within one week. I was shocked; Minoo had already left - but what about the girls? I talked to Nikou and kept the letter in secret from the girls; both Nikou and I agonized over what we should do. In those days, the immigration officers were not easy on Iranians; they were very tough and uncompromising due to the hostage crisis in Iran, no matter who was innocent or guilty.

First I called the attorney and asked her to file the adoption papers and set up the court date as soon as she could. Fortunately the paperwork was completed and certified and had been returned to me by a mutual friend. There were two important purposes for the adoption. The first was to obtain permanent residency and later on US citizenship for the girls. I had no desire whatsoever for them to obtain their citizenship through marriage. I always wanted them to be free from the world's obligations and dependency. The second one was the relief of sponsorship because after the adoption I would be the only one responsible for their status. However, while I was in London and they wanted to register for school; Nikou could only sponsor one of them, Shayma; Dr. Pacita Manalo had agreed to sponsor Shaparak.

The process of adoption wasn't easy for me. Shayma refused to participate in the adoption process. She kept asking us why she should leave her beautiful young parents to be adopted by her grandmother. She absolutely refused to be adopted. Whenever I tried to explain to her and convince her why I wanted to do it, she would become angry, refuse to discuss it and would reject my reasons. As the court date drew closer, Shayma appeared to be more and more frustrated. During the adoption procedure my heart was pounding - would she accept and say yes or refuse and say no? Fortunately, at the last moment she changed her mind (according to her) and her answer was "definitely." She used that same word seven years later when her fiancé asked her to marry him; her reply was "definitely."

Although the adoption process went well, it was not the end of the visa problem. Instead it was the beginning of deportation, which took me more than a year to get settled through to the immigration court in San Francisco. Everything else was going well for us, except for the frustrating and ugly section of the immigration letter that stated, "Do you want to send them back voluntarily or do you want the immigration police to come and take them to the airport?" There is no way that I can explain how I felt. Whenever I saw an immigration envelope, my hands would start trembling so badly that if someone saw me, they would wonder what was happening to me. I didn't receive just one or two letters; they came every other week because I wasn't able to answer their questions. My Iranian friends understood the problem and suggested I let the girls get married "temporarily" to a US citizen, but that was like a bullet to my heart. It was common for boys in those days but was NOT for my children or grandchildren; I had to find the right way around it. This type of suggestion, entirely against my idea, crushed my heart and my soul. I explained this to my American friends. They were so kind; they told me not to worry and suggested that I send the girls to the home of an American (the immigration officers weren't allowed to remove anyone from an American house unless the person was a criminal). The girls didn't know anything about it and didn't want to go to anyone's home. This process continued for almost a year or perhaps longer – it was such a miserable time for me that I can't remember it well. I tried hard to find a way around the problem but it was impossible unless we hired an attorney to handle the matter. Hiring an attorney required a good chunk of money, which I didn't have enough courage to spend in those days.

Finally one of the assistants to a Detroit senator who was aware of the situation sent me a message and instructed me to go to the Association of the US Immigration Attorneys in Sacramento, California to get help. I decided to follow his suggestion. One day Nikou and I applied for a one-day leave of absence and went to the Sacramento main office. On the way we agreed to listen carefully but not to accept any payment obligation. The young attorney was expecting me. I explained the situation to her; she told me she could solve the problem very quickly if I allowed her to search for a similar case in the law library. She said it might take 10–15 hours to find one and if she was lucky, she might find 2 or 3 similar cases; that would solve the problem quickly. I looked at Nikou; she suggested that we have lunch first then come back to the office. The attorney said she would be waiting for us at 2:30. It was 11:30 when we left her office and we had plenty of time to discuss the matter with each other. After lunch we returned to her office and paid $800 for 10 hours of library search. As is typical of any office I filled out some forms and answered all sorts of questions.

We returned to Reno and waited for a miracle to happen. Two months later the attorney called the University Medical School Physiology Department and asked for me. She told me she had not been able to find any related subject similar to my daughter's case and she had spent more than the 15 hours we agreed upon. She said at this point if I agreed to pay another $1200, her husband was going to New York and she could ask him to spend 10 hours to try to find what we needed. I asked her, "If you could not find any evidence in the law library in Sacramento, why are you so sure about the New York library?" She said that there was no comparison between the two towns and their educational materials. I replied, "With all due respect, I do not have that amount of money on me." She said, "You're working in such a nice, prestigious place, your attorney fees would be tax deductible." I replied that I had been laid off. She said, "You are still there." I told her I was collecting my stuff to take it home.

Immigration Court

After a year of suffering all these problems and waiting for the adoption results, I received a letter from the immigration court in San Francisco. I had to be there with both Shaparak and Shayma on a certain date. I wondered how I could do it alone. I decided to talk to the attorney and ask her to come to court with us. She said she could come and help us but not for free. She said I would have to pay $1000 in advance and also $100 for her transportation. I had no choice, so I sent the advance of $1100 as a cashier's check as she instructed. I told the girls we had to go to San Francisco and I wrote their school to get one day off for them. A close family friend of their father, Mr. Tehranchi, volunteered to come with us and drove my car. I had never driven to San Francisco and it seemed to be much safer to have a wise person in the car during a long trip. We met the attorney in the court lobby on the 10th floor. She arrived with her sandwich for lunch. I had all my evidence including my photo with the late Shah. The woman started eating her lunch and talking to me and asked me whether I had any evidence to show the judge. I told her I had whatever I could collect. She said she forgot to tell me to bring anything, so she was glad I was smart enough to do so. We were called into the court while she was still busy with her lunch.

Shaparak, Shayma and I entered the courtroom, which was about the size of a movie theater. The judge's desk was on the north side of the room and we entered from the south side door. No one was there; we sat on the last few benches. First the clerk of the court, then our attorney entered, then the clerk announced the grand entry of the judge. We stood up. The judge proceeded and asked Shaparak and Shayma to sit in the front row. The attorney and I were sitting in the last few rows, a considerable distance between me and the girls. The judge started asking them questions and Shaparak answered according to the instructions that she had been given. The judge mentioned the names of many countries around the world and kept questioning Shaparak and asking her if she and her sister were citizens of one of these countries rather than Iran. Her answer was only Iran. At the end, the attorney (who didn't provide the judge with the evidence) stood up to speak and the judge loudly told her to sit down. Then he asked me what kind of evidence I had. I said, "Your Honor, I have live evidence in my photo with the Shah of Iran." I handed the photo to him and told him, "As you can see, my two girls sitting in front of you are so young. They are as innocent as you feel, but if you refuse their status and I have to send them back, they will be the new and youngest hostages in the hands of the revolutionaries who may recognize their age and the level of their innocence but they will keep them, question them and torture them until I go and turn myself in to the them. By then I will have no idea whether they are alive or dead. I'm not sure whether they would ever let the girls free after they captured me and executed me as they did Dr. Parsay, an innocent physician and Secretary of Education of Iran."

I was standing far away from the judge and I couldn't see his face clearly. Shaparak told me that while I was speaking, his face became red and started sweating. After I finished talking the judge gave them political asylum for the time being; then it would be cleared from their file after the approval of their permanent residency two years from that day, according to the immigration law. We left the courtroom and the attorney said goodbye and left us. Later, Mr. Tehranchi, with his great sense of humor, started joking to make the girls laugh while he was driving from San Francisco to Reno. We have never forgotten his kindness that day; and we all value his family friendship, which is on-going. It was about four hours from San Francisco to Reno. Shayma didn't talk to us along the way because she was feeling carsick. But as soon as we got home she started her critique. "Did you pay this attorney?" "Yes." "Are you sure she is an attorney?" "Yes, Shayma, she was introduced to me as an attorney, not an ordinary person." Then she said, "Honest to God, tell me how much you paid her." I said, "$1100." Then she looked at me and said, "You paid her to come to the court lobby to eat her sandwich and ask our names and our nationality while her mouth was full. Then she went into the courtroom to be punished by the judge? Can't you ask her for a refund?" I said, "Shayma, I had to do that; otherwise we would have been in trouble. Thank God it is over now. If I hadn't gone to court, you would have had to pay out-of-state tuition, which would have cost a lot; in addition, you would not be able to become an American citizen and so many more things that you will see in your future life."

Today as I am writing this memoir, every single issue of those days comes to my mind, then to my eyes. I can see it clearly. I have no doubt that without the help and concern of the late Mr. Tehranchi who took us to San Francisco, the wisdom of the honorable judge that gave the girls political asylum until their status became resolved, the late Dean John Nellor and President Joe Crawly, Chancellor of the University who admitted them as Americans and not as out-of-state students, my two granddaughters might not be where they are today. I am most grateful to all of them wherever they may be physically living somewhere on the face of this earth or if their souls are flying around the infinite universe.

About Negar

In August 1986 my sister Azam came to the US to visit me and attend Minoo's first memorial service in September. She came with her daughter Firoozeh and her granddaughter Negar. Firoozeh and Negar had been in the US for their summer vacation in 1985 and unfortunately faced the grave tragedy of Minoo's death. Negar was another young female among our second generation that had to live with her parents in Iran during that terrible period of time (Revolution) due to the political turmoil in Iran and also the closeness of Iran-American relations. Although it was a very sad period of my life, I decided to assist my sister's family in return for their earlier constant and frequent visits to my two daughters Nikou and Nikrou who were living with their father (my ex-husband) and paternal grandmother after I left Iran for the US in 1959, despite the distance they had to travel to do so.

I decided to adopt Negar legally and let her be with her own biological parents in Iran until she finished high school. Negar, my grand-niece, was the third young woman I adopted in order to fix her immigration status before it was too late to do so. Due to the necessity of her biological parents' consent and also formal paperwork, the process of adoption was finalized in the court of law in Reno, Nevada a year later (1987). Negar and her mother used to come to the US every year and spend from May to September with me in my house. Negar was too young to be separated from her parents and both maternal and paternal grandparents all at once. And I preferred the schooling system of Iran, including her ability to learn English parallel to our native language Farsi in the country of her birth.

In 1991 I applied for Negar's alien registration number that, according to immigration and naturalization laws, should be initiated from a designated US embassy outside the United States; I selected London, England. In November of 1992 I went to Iran for the second time that year and planned to bring Negar back with me to finalize her residency status. Because of some rearrangement in the US embassy immigration division in London I received notice that her file had been transferred to the US embassy in Abu Dabi in the United Arab Emirate. So Negar, her father and I went to Abu Dabi for her interview with the American Consul. He asked for Negar's passport and I presented him her father's passport who himself had also applied for a visitor's visa into the US. The Consul refused to issue him a visa. I told him that under the new law, the Iranian passport office does not issue any independent passports to 13-year-old children. To my great surprise he said, "Negar, although I refused your father's visitor visa I marked your file so that you could enter the U.S. without an Iranian passport; this is an exceptional case." Although I had no chance to see him again and never knew his name, I appreciated his kindness and understanding. I am sure Negar has the same feelings today as I do. It was a great privilege to meet such a kind person. Two days after we returned from Abu Dabi to Tehran I realized that if I took Negar and her father with me to London they needed to apply for visa entry to the UK. So Negar, her father and I went to the British embassy in Tehran. He applied for a visa but it was denied immediately.

Therefore, I had only one choice - to apply for an independent passport for her - but according to Islamic rule that was impossible. I needed to find a way around the law. To do so I needed to know someone in the passport office. Meanwhile, I had to go to my apartment to pick up some papers that had been left there before. At that time Nikou's husband Nasser was living in my apartment temporarily. I called to let him know that I needed to go to the apartment. He welcomed me and told me about his friend who was coming to visit. I went to the apartment and met with a gentleman who was one of the revolutionary members of parliament. I arrived in the middle of their conversation about how Nasser could prove to the Islamic government in a very careful and honest way that he was one of them. This gentleman had been one of Nasser's colleagues before he went to the US, lived there for ten years and finally became an American citizen. Since he was a member of parliament, I asked him if he would help me by introducing me to someone in the passport office. He said he would gladly do it with pleasure but that it was not possible to do so in person. He mentioned the first name of a colonel and asked me not to tell anyone including the colonel who gave me his name. I promised and returned home.

Early the next day I went to the passport office. I gave the colonel's first name to the guard; he went in and came back to me and directed me to the colonel's office. I entered the room and greeted him. He stood up and asked me what he could do for me. I told him a "big lie" and said, "My great-niece who is 13 years old faces an internal woman's problem. I am her great-aunt living in the US. I came to take her with me to the US for medical diagnosis and treatment." He asked me if I had any evidence of her illness. I said yes, if it was necessary. The colonel very kindly and politely told me that if I could bring her medical certificate, he would issue her an independent passport but no later than tomorrow because he might not be in this position even this afternoon. I called my friend Dr. Syrous Farokh, a gynecologist, and asked him if he would be willing to write a medical certificate the way I would dictate to him. I told him it was for my great-niece, Negar. He wrote the certificate and I took it to the passport office the next day. Fortunately the colonel was there. I handed him the certificate and after an hour or so, I received her passport. I will be forever very grateful to that colonel. Also to the late Dr. Farokh. I am sorry that I never had a chance to see him again and express my gratitude for his assistance. In return for his great concern, immediate action and his friendship, I applied for permanent residency for his widow Mahshi, who is also a scientist, his daughter Samira and his son Sina. They are now living in the US, happy and successful.

Negar and I returned to the US on December 15, 1992. She received her residency card in 15 days and became an American citizen on the day I applied for her. I am most grateful to all those that facilitated her residency and citizenship. She is extremely happy living in the U.S. as a free woman working as a future scientist.

CHAPTER 15

The Bakery (Café De Paris)

At the beginning of 1982, Nikou's husband, Nasser, started working for an engineering firm in Kuwait and would come to Reno every few months. He told Nikou that his boss decided to apply for U.S. residency through investments. He also consulted me about a type of business and the way to establish it in Reno. I believed all immigrants were eager to develop their own businesses because it took such a long time to learn how to be accepted in American society; and if they were accepted they had to start with a job and work twice as hard as others to prove themselves, no matter how educated and how capable they were. Although "equal opportunity" was the law and everyone pretended to believe and apply it, you had to be an immigrant to understand the situation, even if you were the investor, the producer or the developer of the company. Those whom you hired expected each and every single point of law to be applied to them but still they didn't believe you and didn't like to accept you in their heart. For these reasons I had always wished to set up a business but I only knew about education and clinical laboratories. I didn't do it because I felt couldn't do it by myself and was much afraid of bringing in a stranger rather than my relatives as a partner. Nikou was the only one that could do it but she had no desire to be involved in private business ever since she had worked as an Assistant Dean with me in Iran. She was planning to study for a PhD degree and was about to start.

I had no knowledge of other businesses so I told Nasser that if he insisted I do it, I needed to do some research to find out about a business other Iranians had already developed in other states and the actual benefits of doing so. I heard that Dr. Ganji, ex-Secretary of Education in Iran, had moved to Texas and established a very successful French bakery shop. Dr. Ganji and I had known each other very well, so I called him and asked him about his establishment. He was very satisfied and happy. He advised me that no matter what the economy was like, people needed to enjoy themselves by eating different foods and so a French bakery was a new kind of business to develop, at least in Texas. I asked him how to develop a business like his, as none of us had any such knowledge or experience. He said, "As you know, I didn't have it either. Don't be afraid; if I did it, surely, you can do it also. If you don't know where to start, I will be glad to help you as much as I can." Then I asked him, "What about a good French chef? Where would I find one?" He told me there were many available to accept a job offer, especially for the purpose of immigration. They tried their best and if they succeeded and were satisfied with their salary and their job, they had no desire to move to another business. So, this appeared to me to be a very promising business, particularly when Dr. Ganji offered his help to establish a similar one in Reno. He invited me to go to Texas and see his establishment.

Nasser flew back to Reno from Kuwait and again asked me about a business. I told him all I could do was talk to my long-time friend Dr. Ganji and no one else because I was extremely busy with the *in vitro* clinic. Nasser reported my findings about the type of business, its expenses, etc. to his boss, Mr. Dehghani. He suggested we look at Dr. Ganji's bakery and offered to pay all of our expenses for a trip to Texas. We both went to Texas for a weekend. Dr. Ganji showed us his six franchise shops, explained everything to us in detail and took us to the warehouse at 11 pm to see the process of bread baking, which appeared to be very successful and well managed. The next day his daughter took us to three different bakeries and pastry shops. We returned to Reno on Sunday afternoon and while we were on the plane we reviewed our observations and findings about a promising business.

On Monday, Nasser reported the results of our trip to Mr. Dehghani. He agreed to send money to the States and also send me a full power of attorney to open a bank account for a business and arrange its development. The bank account was established with the First Interstate Bank of Reno, Nevada and, because of his status, I had to have my name on the account with either/or signature. The money was sent from Kuwait to the account. Later he came to Reno and leased three large spaces next to each other in a very modern and prestigious mall and asked me to order whatever equipment and furniture was required to setup a modern French-style bakery, pastry and coffee shop. It took almost a year to complete and get ready to open.

Mr. Dehghani asked me to invite Dr. Ganji to come to Reno at our expense to see the area and help me to buy the equipment. He agreed and spent a weekend in Reno with me. He visited the site and met with the building engineer. In the meantime, many Iranians contacted me to apply for a managerial position. Mr. Korosh, a civil engineer who had been out of a job for eight months because of economic problems in Reno, was chosen. He accepted the offer, but like me he didn't have any knowledge of bakeries or pastry shops. I told him we didn't need to know everything in this world; we would try to learn something every day. We would learn when we got a skilled chef. Dr. Ganji explained how to register the business under a similar name of a Kuwait firm and then add the fictitious name of "dba Café de Paris" to satisfy the purpose of Mr. Dehghani's permanent residency through investment. With plenty of his money in my hand, a good modern idea and the assistance of Dr. Ganji, we ordered all the baking equipment from a manufacturer named Gemoni in Texas and the furniture from a California-based store recommended by the building engineer. The Gemoni manager introduced Monsieur Gaston, a chef, to me in December 1983 just two months prior to the bakery grand opening. On December 10, 1983, he came to Reno to visit the town and the shop and to visit with the bakery's manager Korosh and me. The three of us had lunch and then I told them it was time for a real business talk.

I had to be at the clinic by 4 pm. Mr. Gaston gave me his resumé and told me he couldn't accept the gross salary because he was a Frenchman and didn't want to deal with the U.S. Government. I became suspicious of what was behind this. I asked him what he meant by net salary and what was his reason for it. He said it was a sad story that he wasn't sure I wanted to hear. I told him I felt for him and that I also was an immigrant and had to deal with the U.S. Government. I believed we were both in the same boat but that paying him net and accepting his responsibilities toward the government was not my job; he might be very smart but I didn't understand it. Once again he asked me if I really wanted him to tell me why; I said, "Yes, if you don't mind." He started the story and said in the city that he was born, raised and educated; jobs were scarce for a long, long time. All of his friends and relatives including his fiancée told him if he went to the United States he could get a job immediately. It was a very nice and attractive point so he decided to go to the American Embassy and get a permit to enter the US. He left his old parents and young fiancée behind, assuming he could get a job at least a week later. He entered the US in New York and they stamped his passport for six months. It was his first time to leave his country.

On the plane he talked to a young man sitting next to him. When the man understood that he was traveling "blind," he gave him his card and told him to give him a call if he needed anything. He also gave him a phone number for accommodations that was very helpful. When he left the airport he didn't know what he should do or where he should go, so he called the number for accommodations. Someone answered the phone and asked him his name, his character, his height, his weight, the color of his skin and the color and description of his clothes, and then told him to wait by the same phone and that it would be less than an hour for someone to come and fetch him. The man said his name was Mark and that he would be wearing a dark chocolate raincoat. He arrived with a long navy blue Chevrolet and took him to a Motel 6 where he was the manager. He wanted him to fill out an application and told him if he stayed long enough, he would give him a good discount. He signed up for two weeks assuming he would find a job in a few days.

Three days later after jet lag was over he started looking for a job. Mark tried to help him and found a bakery address, but wherever he went they refused to hire him because of his accent and his status. They asked him if he had a permit to work and he told them yes for six months; then they asked for his passport and told him he had a permit to stay in the US but not to work there. Mark was so kind to him and always tried to help him by giving him some dirty work at the motel to compensate for the rent. Every morning he went job hunting and early afternoon he went back to the motel to help Mark as much as he could. Therefore little by little he got used to the language; every other evening he went to an English class to learn more.

In a short while the six-month permit expired and immigration sent him one letter after another but he ignored them because he was still looking for a good job while satisfied with the work at the Motel 6. He assumed that the immigration officers would come to the motel in the middle of the day to find illegal people. And since he left the motel every day early in the morning, they wouldn't find him. However, one Monday morning, he woke up very early and although he tried to sleep a bit more he couldn't. While he was shaving, the immigration police knocked on the door; he thought it was Mark and opened the door. He saw the officer but in a different outfit. The man introduced himself as FBI and ordered Mr. Gaston out of the room. When he asked why, the man said, "You were deported two months ago; I will accept no excuse what-so-ever and I can only allow you five minutes to get your passport and your belongings." Mr. Gaston said he picked up his valet, his passport and his overnight bag. The immigration officer took Gaston to his car and went to the airport. At the airport he ordered Gaston to buy a ticket and Gaston said he had no money. The officer took him to a vacant room with a column in the middle of the room.

As Gaston was telling me the story his face became red and his eyes were full of tears. He said the policeman put handcuffs on both hands and then with a strap tied him to the column and left. He said he started talking to God. He had promised his fiancée that after he got a job he would apply for her to join him in the States, but whatever he had in his mind was gone with the wind. Gaston said he stood there for 3-4 hours; he didn't know exactly how long. He thought the officer left him in the room to die because he started to feel dizzy; he was thirsty, frustrated and scared. Meanwhile an airport worker opened the door. After a short time, two airport police officers entered the room, immediately released him from the column and removed the cuffs from his wrists. The airport worker brought him a drink and later a hot dog. The two police officers returned to the room and asked Gaston some questions and told him to leave the airport, change your home and if you can, stay with an American and try to marry an American.

Gaston left the airport and called Mark who understood the situation and picked him up by noon. Instead of taking him to the Motel 6, he took him to another part of town to live with an old American couple; he was to take care of them. Gaston stayed there for three months until their young granddaughter came to visit her grandparents and fell in love with Monsieur Gaston. They got married four months later and have a two-year old daughter. Gaston said after all he had faced there was a happy ending; he found a job but his main problem was that he didn't want to deal with the government. He said if I was willing to pay net he would be very happy to start working in this beautiful bakery. He asked for $120,000 per year, 12 hours a day for six days a week. He also asked for two weeks paid vacation but would not be using it until the end of the third year. I consulted Dr. Ganji who told me all French chefs have the same idea; our accountant would take care of his taxes. He also told me he heard that Gaston was honest, skilled and capable and that the salary he was asking for was normal. In the meantime, Gaston told me that Mr. Philip, his assistant, was willing to come with him to Reno if I could pay him $60,000 per year. He would take care of his own taxes, as he was a real American (I understood that he meant "American Indian"). I called Mr. Dehghani to consult with him about their salaries. He told me that the reason he gave me full power of attorney was so I could do whatever was required. I told him that he might lose the entire business if we spent more than we should. He said that although his objective was permanent residency, his main goal was to bring good people together and help them as much as possible by creating a permanent job for them.

Korosh was a young Iranian civil engineer from a high-ranking family, but due to the recession, particularly in engineering firms, he couldn't find a permanent job for almost a year after his graduation. At the present time he was working as a chief engineer for Cal-Trans. I asked Korosh to interview Gaston first then started negotiations about his salary and Philip's as well. Although I was very busy with the *in vitro* clinic, I had plenty of time, especially in the morning, to talk to people in the east and do many things by phone. I did this for the entire year. Everything was ordered and on the way to be installed in the shop. The full-time manager, the chef and his assistant were available; and Korosh started hiring about ten young Iranian women and men, all of them students at the University. He also hired eight American women and Mexican men. So the bakery had a total of 18 young men and women, all of them students, working part-time shifts.

The shop was well decorated with royal blue-covered white-framed chairs, white tables and pink tablecloths; everything was brand new and shiny. The women's uniforms were pink with white aprons. The logo of the bakery was nine feet tall and made of metal by a famous artist. It was the Eiffel Tower with tiny red, blue and white electric bulbs on the top of the roof shining at night; it could be seen all over the city of Reno. The shop was located in a strip mall with a blue and white awning

hung on top of a wide glass door. It had a beautiful and sophisticated view.

About the same time that Godiva chocolate was introduced to Reno from San Francisco and cappuccino and
espresso coffee machines became popular, we began selling
French pastries. The chef started a week prior to the formal
opening to test the equipment to make sure it was functioning
properly. He made a variety of breads, croissants, French-style
pastries and cookies for free sampling on six consecutive days
while he was testing the equipment.

The formal opening took place on March 1, 1984. The manager sent 100 invitations to high-ranking personnel from hotels,
casinos, the city mayor, university professors and staff, also
attorneys and physicians. Radio, television and newspaper
reporters were present. The business opened and did very well
for the first year with no trouble and the income of the shop
covered all the expenses.

During the second year the chef started nagging and criticizing management. He was very temperamental and so
proud of himself. He never understood the necessity of prof-
it in business. He constantly argued with the manager to
reduce his twelve hours work according to his contract to
eight hours. And contrary to the bakery industry norm that
work started at 10-11 **pm**, he started at 4:30 to 5 **am**.
Therefore everything that had to be ready early in the morning - to cool before delivery - was late resulting in the loss of
long-term customers. He made a variety of pastries and cakes
in the French style that were beautiful and tasty but he never
understood why we charged so much. He raised hell and
started arguing with the manager. Gaston called upon me to
advise him and convince him about the pricing. I tried to
explain that the price was based on the cost of raw ingredients
plus the employee salaries. Most of the time he believed me
and accepted my guidelines; but at other times he tried to
destroy whatever he had in his hand and would immediately
leave the store by the back door in a rage.

One day I went to see Korosh, but he was off. His assistant Kevin (who today is a well-known and very successful dentist in San Francisco) was very nervous and agitated, running back and forth into the walk-in freezer and refrigerator while two women were standing by the counter waiting for something to be picked up. Kevin's sister Mariam (also a successful dentist) came to me and told me Kevin couldn't find the birthday cake that had ordered the previous week for pick up that day. The cake was for the women's boss. The Mexican busboy told her Gaston made the cake, decorated it and then dumped it in the wastebasket; it was still there. I called Kevin into the manager's office and told him not to show his apprehension; go and tell them, "The chef made your cake but forgot to decorate it. I have called him and he is on his way to the shop. As his house is a bit far away, if you go on to your office, we will deliver the cake to you as soon as he finishes the decorations." Kevin followed my directions. The women left the shop and Kevin came to me and asked me what we should do. It was 2:30 pm and they told Kevin they needed to have the cake no later than 4 pm. Kevin told me it wasn't possible to bring Gaston to the shop. I told him not to worry, to go and bring the stock out of the freezer and he could help me make the cake. With great surprise he asked me if I could do it. I said, "Yes, if I can make a baby in a Petri dish, surely I can make a cake in the shop; you will see." He brought the cake stock and placed it on the kitchen table out of sight of customers. I used the cake-making instrument and sliced the cake stock. Instead of making a round cake, I made a four layer rectangular cake and added the cream mixed with some Grand Marnier and Kalua between the layers. With Kevin's help, I put on the topping and decorated it with white, red and yellow roses made of almond paste; then I asked Kevin to write what they ordered and leave it in the freezer for 15 minutes to harden. The cake was delivered on time and everybody gave a sigh of relief. Two days later the same two women came back to the shop and ordered exactly the same cake that they had never tasted before. Korosh and Kevin kept calling me. "The chef is in a good mood today; he apologizes for his bad attitude last week and he is asking for the exact ingredients of the cake." The problem was I couldn't remember what the ingredients were. Although Kevin was helping me that day, both of us were angry enough with the chef and his actions that neither of us remembered what I mixed!

This wasn't the first or the last incident for Mr. Gaston; he repeated the behavior at least once or twice a month. Although we had some knowledge of how to run a bakery, we didn't have enough skills about how to run such a large-scale business. Therefore we had to get along with him and try to hire another chef to give Gaston more rest. Unfortunately his wife filed for divorce, which caused him such sadness and disappointment that he resigned.

His replacement wasn't as good as a pastry chef as Gaston but he was more friendly and much more concerned about doing a good job. But I still had to go and solve the everyday problems at the bakery. After Korosh found an engineering job and resigned, Mariam was accepted in dental school and Kevin was preparing himself for his last year of college to enter dental school. All the original employees had been replaced by local people, most of whom had worked for the casinos, and the quality of our products had begun to decline. At the same time, we were wanting to move to San Diego, so we decided it was time to sell. Until a buyer was found, I had to go to the bakery every day to keep it in good shape. The man who bought the business had a small bakery and pastry shop before Café de Paris started and wanted to buy it to eliminate his competition. It was sold for next-to-nothing but later it was closed because of the high cost of rent.

Although the shop cost Mr. Dehghani a fortune, his purpose was served, as he wanted all his family to become American citizens, and he had helped a group of Iranian students start their careers while enjoying their youth activities. Despite the overall loss, Mr. Dehghani and his wife Manijeh have continued to maintain a family friendship with us. I later learned that many others such business relationships ended up in arguments and court cases. I believe ours to be one of the rare examples of a long-term congenial relationship among the Middle-Eastern immigrant business history.

Mr. Aliyar Dehghani and his wife Manijeh, founder of Café de Paris (the bakery) in Reno, 1983-88

Chapter 16

Minoo's Life in the U.S.

It was the summer of 1983 that Minoo and her husband Mohsen came to Reno to visit their children. They were very happy when they saw how the girls were living, their education standard in school, their piano lessons and life in general. They started to think about immigrating to the US themselves – something that he previously was strongly against. At the same time, they had a lot of valuables in Iran and it was not easy to ignore and leave those things behind. They knew what would happen to all of our belongings. If the revolutionaries found an unoccupied "silent" house, they would confiscate whatever they could find including the entire property even if it belonged to a close relative. Just as Nasser confiscated Adib's cottage even though Adib was the sole cousin his son Hessam.

After their visit, Minoo and her husband left Reno and returned to Tehran. During the flight, they talked it over and decided to sell all their belongings and their property and transfer the money to the US, then come to Reno to join their children. It was September or October of 1983. Minoo was still working at the Tehran clinic and her husband at an oil and gas company. Minoo telephoned and told me they sold their property by the Caspian Sea as well as their house in Tehran but they faced a big problem sending money to the US through the bank because the revolutionary government forbade the transfer of money. I am sure that this was the main cause of anxiety, disappointment and severe depression in Minoo. It is never an easy task to dispose of everything you worked for, collected or established during a long, long period of time – to dissolve it with your own hand overnight. It took a lot of courage, a lot of will power to give up and forget all these sentiments. For many families, especially where the woman is the focal point of the family, it would be impossible. It wasn't an easy process and I'm sure this had a lot to do with Minoo's problems. Any time she called and told me about it, I felt her exhaustion and anxiety and her loneliness in Iran. Finally Minoo and Mohsen returned to the US, but by separate routes and at separate times. Mohsen went to Boston and stayed with his brother until Minoo arrived. Minoo left Iran two weeks later by herself and entered the US in Detroit. Then Mohsen joined Minoo at Nikrou and Ali's house. They stayed there for two months and applied for their permanent status in the Detroit immigration office.

It was in the spring of 1985 when they came to Reno to join their two daughters. Minoo found out that the nursing educational system in the US had changed and she would have to sit for an RN license exam, so she had been preparing for the exam which was to be held in Reno. We all were very happy - I will never forget the joy of that period. Shayma was graduating from high school. Minoo arranged a big party for her and invited Mrs. Watts and her family from London, including her oldest son who was a resident of Washington State. (Mrs. Watts and her family were visiting her son at the time. Mrs. Watts was Minoo's landlady who had been very kind to her while Minoo was a student in London; Minoo really loved her and accepted her as a Godmother.) We all attended the graduation ceremony, followed by a dinner party at home.

The next day, after all the guests had left Reno, Minoo told me she had never felt so tired and exhausted. She told me the same thing had happened in Tehran at the airport when they opened her suitcase and took every single item out and didn't find anything they were looking for. Afterwards, the examiner told her to move and collect her stuff from the table. She felt so weak that she started crying so he himself moved her suitcase and all of her things to a corner of the airport and told her to sit down and arrange it the way she wanted. She said she was so weak, so tired and exhausted that she wasn't even able to move her hand. Fortunately one of her colleagues who came to see her off helped repack her suitcase. Minoo was so pale, her friend walked with her to the stairs of the airplane.

On June 3rd we were going to Café de Paris. I was driving the car and Minoo was talking about her husband's lungs and his coughing up pinkish phlegm both of which caused her to worry about lung cancer. I told her she had better think of other problems rather than his lungs; she had had the same complaints ever since she married him. I said, "You'd better think of yourself and plan to go for a physical to find out why you're always tired." The way she explained it, it appeared to be unusual to me. It was 1 or 2 pm that same day when she came to me in a rush and asked me if I had any nitroglycerin. I said, "No, what do you need it for?" She told me to call 911. When we arrived at St. Mary's Hospital, the diagnosis was a massive heart attack. The cardiologist proposed an immediate angioplasty, which was performed by an interventionist. There will always be doubts whether the surgeon was skilled enough; if the main artery was completely blocked, why they didn't perform a graft; or was it just my fate to lose Minoo and suffer for the rest of my life.

The third day after the episode, while Minoo was still in the hospital, she told me not to get mad at her but she was going on a trip to Texas. "I must go," she said, "and I'll go by air." She had been invited to a wedding where the groom's father was an old family friend in San Antonio, Texas. I asked her if she wanted me to make a reservation for her right then. She laughed and said, "Yes, just in case." Somehow Minoo recovered and came home. But she tried not to tell me about her spells of coughing or the swollen spots in the veins of her legs. Sometimes she had severe pain in her belly or her kidney area. Her sister, Nikou, lived next door and spent time with Minoo and talked with her secretly. We took Minoo back to St. Mary's Hospital and spent time there with her. Doctor tried so many ways or different medications to relieve her pain a bit. Despite her obvious pain and discomfort, Minoo always pretended to be happy and healthy.

Minoo's last photo at her friend's wedding reception in Texas,
August 1985

One day while I was driving, she told me she was so happy that this episode happened in the US. If it had occurred in Iran and I hadn't been around, she would be dead by now. I suggested and insisted on a second opinion. Nikou accompanied her to San Francisco to see a famous cardiologist. He told her nothing extra could be done. From June to the end of August she suffered from many episodes but she never cried out in pain or complained about her health. She was preparing herself and Shaparak to attend the wedding ceremony at the end of July. Nikou and her son Hessam accompanied them. I don't remember why Mohsen didn't go with them. When they came back to Reno, Minoo received a letter from the immigration office in Detroit about an interview set for Tuesday, August 26th. So Minoo and Mohsen left on Sunday the 24th and were to return the next Friday or Saturday. She told everyone she would be back no later than next Sunday and "See you on Monday." She took me to the MGM Hotel and from the shop bought a navy blue crystal bowl for Nikrou. She wanted to make sure the bowl would go with her side lamp. On Sunday morning, August 24th, 1985 I gave them a ride to the airport and they left for Detroit. She didn't tell anybody that she was suffering from nausea, shivering and had a fever the night before. As soon as they arrived at Nikrou's house she couldn't stand it any more and told her sister; she made her promise not to tell me. It was late Sunday afternoon when Minoo went to bed. Nikrou managed to arrange for her to see a friend of theirs who was a cardiologist on Monday morning. They went to the doctor and he recommended hospitalization. Minoo disagreed and told him that she had to go to the immigration office first; then she would do whatever he suggested. They returned home again. She was in pain and went to bed and reminded Nikrou about her promise.

About this time, the cardiologist in Reno called me himself and told me that from the results of her urinalysis her kidney was severely infected. She needed a high dose of antibiotics immediately. I told him she had left for Michigan the day before. He said Minoo should have antibiotics but under supervision of a cardiologist who would temper her other medications. As soon as I finished talking with him (about 6-7 pm), Nikrou called and reported on Minoo's status. I asked her why she hadn't accepted the doctor's suggestion and Nikrou told me "You know her better than I do." I called her physician and also Nikrou's husband Ali and asked for help to convince her to go to the hospital without any delay. When Minoo finally agreed to go to the hospital she called me and said, "You did your duty by remote control, didn't you? I am ready to go now." I realized it wasn't an easy case when her doctor told to me about her kidney infection so I decided to go to Detroit. I kept calling the airport ticket office. They told me there was only one flight, leaving Reno at 9 am and arriving in Detroit at 12 noon. I left Reno and upon arrival, Nikrou's friend took me to the Saratoga Hospital; I got there at 1:30 pm. Minoo was in the ICU laughing and joking, talking about her residency status.

Every morning Nikrou and I went to the hospital and spent time with her. Nikrou's friends came to visit her or sent her flowers. As her fever dropped, she was transferred from the ICU to a special ward on Friday, August 29th. That day while we were alone she told me about the sale of her property and sending the money through her nanny's son because the bank didn't sell currency any more. She said after he took the money he started to bring them a lot of excuses. She said she didn't believe she would ever see the money in her lifetime. I asked her if she had it now and she told me yes but she still had nightmares about it. While she was talking, I tried to comfort her, she said "Could you ever imagine that we sold two properties in Iran and endured so many problems sending the proceeds to the U.S. in the hopes of living at the same standard? And now I'm in the hospital." I told her "Minoo, trust me. Your health insurance will cover all of the expenses." Then she told me she wasn't worried at all. She wasn't worried for her girls; she knew I would take good care of them. Her only worry was her husband's health. He had a chronic lung disease and a stomach ulcer.

I tried to change the subject and ask her to relax, have lunch and we would talk about these matters later on. She said she had a lot to tell me because we had never had a quiet time to talk to each other since she arrived in the US. She asked me when I was going back to Reno. I asked her if she was worried about the girls and said that Nikou was there for them. She said, "No, I'm not worried; I know how you will train them - as you did me; I always tried not to do anything that you told me not to, even when I was a student in London. I recall your face with the word NO in your mouth. But right now I want to ask you to do two things for me without any discussion or question." I asked her what she wanted me to do. She said. "I will tell you after my lunch. You'd better to go to the cafeteria and have yours." I left her alone to eat her lunch.

When I came back she was napping. I quietly sat in the chair next to her bed. About a half an hour later, she woke up and once again started talking. She said, "First of all, tell me when you are going back to Reno." I told her I wasn't in a hurry; the girls knew their schedule and Nikou was there; I wanted to be there with her. Then she said, "Promise me that as soon as you arrive in Reno you will go to Macys; go to the right hand side of the store and you will see a lot of gray scarves. Please take one exactly like the one I bought you for my aunt; buy it on my account and then please send it to Iran by mail." I promised to do just as she told me but I told her that Firoozeh (my niece) was going home and I could give it to her. She said no because she wanted her aunt to have it much sooner, before Firoozeh returned to Iran. I promised her I would take care of it and asked her why she was so worried about it. She said, "If I don't insist, I'm afraid you might forget." I said, "Minoo, if I promise to do something, I will do it accordingly and you can be sure that I will never forget what you ask for." She told me it was time for me to go home and asked me where Nikrou was. I told her she was in the hallway.

Nikrou came in and they spoke to each other; Minoo asked Nikrou if she had talked to the physician about when she could go home. Again she told me she preferred to stay in Michigan longer because of the fall color changes. She asked me when I would return to Reno; I told her I wanted to rest and stay here with everyone. She told me I'd better leave the hospital and go home; visiting hours were over and she would talk to me tomorrow. So Nikrou and I returned home. I wasn't able to talk to Nikrou about anything and had no words to explain my feelings. I can't adequately describe how worried I was; how sad the entire subject was and that I could do nothing about it. It was a truly miserable time. Friday passed and I don't remember how many times I called the nurse's station and how I begged them to stay alert to her situation. That night if I slept it was only for a few hours or maybe not at all.

Early Saturday morning I asked Nikrou to take me to the hospital; I told her she didn't have to stay there and that one of us was enough to stay with Minoo. When we arrived Minoo was eating her breakfast. We greeted each other and then started talking. I told her that I slept well the night before and took my shower early. She laughed and told me that, "All the nurses are careless. They wake you up for vital signs very early, then breakfast comes and they come to change the bed; then they disappear. Thank God no one came to this room after that. I want to tell you something and I expect you to do what I want you to do." I asked her, "Minoo, what is it this time?" She told me this was another matter she was very concerned about. When she was in Iran and Firoozeh used to come to her house with Negar, Minoo promised to take Negar to Disneyland when she came to the States. She said, "I know it's hard for you but I want to ask you to please help me. When you return to Reno, take Negar to Disneyland." I told Minoo that Negar could wait until Minoo could take her herself. She replied, "Do you think I could walk around Disneyland? No, it would be hard for me, but I want to do what I promised her. I ask you to do it for me as soon as you return to Reno." Then I asked her what else she wanted to tell me and she said that was all; but please not to forget. My Saturday visit with Minoo ended when she said, "Today you must leave earlier because Nikrou invited a lady who is one of the Senator's assistants to have dinner with us. Since I can't go, I want you to go to the dinner for me and give her my best regards. Tell her that as soon as I get out of the hospital I will personally go to her office to meet with her. I heard a lot about her from my sister."

When I left Minoo and kissed her goodbye, she told me to bring something sweet like honey or rock candy with me the next day. She said sometimes she felt nauseated. It is impossible to describe the feelings that I had that night - the pain and sadness I suffered. I was not myself; I had to pretend that I was OK, while in my mind I was in the hospital watching Minoo or talking to her rather than sitting at the dinner table. Every second of time seemed to be more than an hour; I wanted to avoid all conversation. I wasn't alone at the table; those who didn't know about my feelings were talking and I had to attend (listen) but attend what?

As soon as I got home I called the nurse's station and begged them to let me come to the hospital; the answer was no. Then I begged them to please go to her room and tell me how she was doing. The attendee told me she had just checked on her before I called and she was feeling better tonight, much better than the previous night.

Early the next morning, about 5 am, Nikrou and I went to the hospital; it was about 6:10 am when we got to her room. Minoo told us she was so glad we both came early that day and that the antibiotics didn't hurt her too much yet. I told her we brought her some honey and rock candy and asked if she would like some. She said, "I'm waiting for the nurse to come and take my vital signs first, then I would like to take a shower." She also said, "Please pick something for my lunch from the menu." The nurse entered the room and tried to take her blood pressure. After a little while, she removed the cuff from her right arm and said she had no pressure at all and would like to try her left arm. All of a sudden, as the Chinese would say, "the volcano erupted." Her heartbeat surged to the sky; the nurse's station announced a code blue; they notified her cardiologist and the emergency physician came to her room and started asking her about her status last night. She said, "I had a strong pressure in my chest twice but I decided not to bother the nurse." She was rushed back to ICU. One of the nurses told me that I couldn't go with her. As I am writing this, her voice is still in my ears and her beautiful face is in my eyes. I could only say, "God help me." I had no idea how long it was before her husband and Ali came to the hospital. Nikrou called Reno and told Nikou to bring the girls with her to Detroit. At the last moment, one of the nurses came to me and told me, "Your daughter is so bright and has accepted God's order because while I was going with her to the

ICU she said, 'Surely God will help me; I'm not going to make it this time.'"

I don't remember anything else. It was and always will be the saddest story of my entire world. No one could understand the magnitude of losing a child; no one except the lady who was passing by the hospital lobby and told me, "I feel your misery; I went through this same situation last year." Surely there are millions and millions of mothers like that woman and me, but no one else can understand how strong the pain was; I am still and will be in that state forever. Minoo never left and never will leave my heart. To me, Minoo is as alive, as cheerful and as joyful as ever. Her soul is always in my mind and her spirit in my heart. Although her physical being is out of my sight and remains in the United Memorial Garden in Detroit, her spirit will live with me forever. Although her purified soul has gone to the Infinite Universe, she will never disappear from my eyes and my every day life. Today, whenever I see Shaparak and Shayma and while I am talking to them I feel Minoo is sitting by me watching them. When I talk to her grandchildren, my great-grandchildren, I feel sorry and ashamed. It should have been me that was taken, God - where is she? I must confess that any happiness for them somehow brings my thoughts back to this sad event although I try to act as normal as possible and not show my pain.

Nikou and the girls returned to Reno four days after that tragic and miserable event. I returned to Reno ten days afterward. I went back and stayed with the girls and my niece, Firoozeh, and her daughter Negar who had stayed in our two houses with Hessam and his cousin during that tragic period. I must express my appreciation to one of our neighbors, our friend, the late Raheleh Hashemi who spent time with Firoozeh during that period of true hardship. The day after I returned to Reno, according to Iranian custom, a service was arranged in the house and all of our Iranian friends living in Reno gathered to attend the service. The next day our American friends, including Dean John and Barbara Nellor, Dr. Pacita Manalo,

Dr. Sher and his wife Charlene who sent flowers, personally expressed their sorrow and offered their condolences to me. After nineteen years, my wounded heart still bleeds strongly, my eyes still shed tears and my mind still thinks of her every morning. I still wake up with her memories. It was about the twenty or twenty-fifth day after her death that I had to do all of her wishes. The first day, I went to Macy's, followed her directions, bought the scarf and mailed it to my sister as Minoo requested. The day after that, I took Negar and her mother Firoozeh to Disneyland to fulfill Minoo's wishes. We spent two nights and three days at the Disneyland Hotel.

No one but God and only God knows how I felt. I believe that Minoo's requests and her insistence that I promise to complete them was because she knew she had no more time. I was in such an emotional turmoil that I didn't understand what was happening. I believe all my senses were numb; I kept telling myself that there was absolutely nothing I could have done, so I had to surrender to my faith. I felt a great obligation to do exactly what she requested, step by step; but as I did so it almost broke my heart. It was such an unbearable and difficult time at Disneyland to make Negar happy and therefore to accomplish my mission; but to the eyes of those who didn't know why I was doing it so soon after such a great tragedy, it appeared very, very strange and unbelievable. A week after our return from Disneyland, Firoozeh and Negar went back to Iran. Today Negar is a graduate student at SDSU and works in a large biotech laboratory, living with Nikou and me; her parents visit us every six months.

Two weeks later I went back to Detroit, Mohsen was still with Nikrou and Ali. Nikrou had arranged for a memorial service on day 40 (a common arrangement among Iranian Muslims). I stayed there for 10 days and visited Minoo's grave several times, although everyone knows the one who flies away never comes back again. Then I returned to Reno to be with the girls. I hesitated to stay with Nikrou longer because I wanted her to return to her normal routine and continue her life with her son and her husband.

About two months later I received a formal invitation from the University regarding Shaparak's award. It was so hard and sad for me to take Minoo's place; I couldn't make up my mind and I finally asked Nikou and Shaparak's father Mohsen to attend instead. The Chancellor, Joe Crawly, and Dean Nellor were expecting me but I just couldn't do it.

Little by little I ended up with a severe sadness that took me to the border of deep depression. Every once in a while when I remember the last day of Minoo's life, the way she spoke to me about her two daughters, I tell myself not to let depression engulf me; the girls need me and Minoo told me repeatedly that she was not worried for her children because they would be under my supervision. So I have to keep myself out of depression.

Everybody knew and understood how frustrated I was. I kept recalling her saying, "Shaparak and Shayma are so young and need your supervision." Every minute I told myself to be strong and try to take good care of them. Anytime I saw any of Minoo's friends or when they wrote to me repeatedly, their first comment was that they wondered why Minoo would tell them repeatedly that she was not worried for her girls because they were living with me. It was like a clock - every few hours the ringing in my ears reminded me to watch for Shaparak and Shayma, this was Minoo's wish always. At the same time, I couldn't sit and do nothing. I tried to keep myself occupied as much as I could. I decided to go to a crowded area like Café de Paris. I was so depressed that I always cried loudly and talked loudly as well.

Most of the time, I would go to some secluded area and sit in the car and cry until my eyes were dry. One day the police came and knocked on the window and asked me why I was crying. As I explained to him, I found his eyes full of tears. He told me that he understood how I was feeling because he had just lost his sister a few days beforehand. He said that at first he thought I was drunk but when I opened my window he changed his mind. He advised me to stop crying and suggested that I get out of the car and go for a walk in a crowded area; that I shouldn't park in such a secluded area anymore because it wasn't safe for me. The incident shocked me, especially when he mentioned that the area was unsafe. From that day forward, I decided to go shopping in some good store instead; and the best appeared to me to be Macy's, Marshalls, Venstock and a few more places that had return policies. So, after that, anytime I felt exhausted and sad, I would go shopping. I still do so today.

Macy's was always first on my list; whenever I went in the store I recalled that the directions Minoo gave me were completely correct. Unconsciously I would go to the scarf area, just walking around. How many sales people came and asked me how they could help me! How tough it is when you don't have any desire to talk to anyone. I had been trying not to buy anything but finally I picked up some dresses without trying them on. I brought them home but never took then from my car. Two or three days later I went to return them.

One day the store manager came to me and started talking to me, then asked me why I bought so many dresses each time and returned them without touching them. She said she was a student in a psychology department and asked me to please help her to understand and to tell her the truth. I explained my sad situation - the day that the policeman found me, the advice he gave me and what I believed myself to prevent my depression and to hide my sadness from the girls. Today I must confess that I feel very sorry for Hessam who saw my tears and my sadness more that anyone, because I spent most of my sad time with Nikou at her house to prevent Shaparak and Shayma from seeing my sad moments.

My Life after Minoo

I must admit that I always attempted to live away from any of my sons-in-law's houses to keep my own independence and their freedom intact, but I didn't realize that my faith against all odds would force me to live with them. After the tragic death of Minoo I decided to keep the living standards of her two daughters

Shaparak and Shayma as consistent as it was beforehand. Therefore I accepted my faith and lived with her husband (my son-in-law) for more than three years. Although I never had any disagreement with him or was ever mistreated by him and we both were trying to keep a favorable atmosphere for the girls, it was very hard and sad for me to spend time with a person in the absence of our actual link. It may have been true for him, too. Anyway, I had to suffer the absence of Minoo no matter what.

Soon Shaparak was due to graduate from the University of Nevada-Reno. We all were waiting to see what her plans would be for further study - if it were medicine, in what state? Shayma was in the second year of college and their father was preparing to go forward and find his destiny. So it was time for all of us to decide what we were going to do about city and state of residency after Shaparak left Reno.

Since we had been sharing the house so we would have to sell it and each of us move forward. Their father decided to move to San Diego. Shaparak graduated from the university and applied to medical schools; Shayma was registered for summer courses. As a graduation gift to Shaparak I offered her a trip to London and Italy. We applied for a visa to London but the Italian embassy required six weeks advanced notice. My friend Dr. Bakhtiar told me I could get a visa in London in a matter of one day, as he had done for himself. So Shaparak and I left Reno to San Francisco and from there via British Airways to London, the city where we earlier lived for a year and a half. We went to the American Embassy Suites Hotel to spend a week then planned on going to Italy for the next two weeks. The day after our arrival we went to the Italian Embassy for our visa but they told us we should have waited for the six weeks because we were traveling with an Iranian passport not a British one. So our trip to Italy had to be abandoned. We kept trying other countries like France and Spain, but the answer to our application was the same - six weeks. I told Shaparak, "Let's try other countries which require no visas." Then we found Turkey, which needed no visa for Iranians.

After a week in London, we went to Turkey and Dr. Bakhtiar accompanied us for his own business. We visited Ankara, Istanbul, Izmir and a few other cities with so many famous areas in each town that might be missed if you visited by yourself rather than with a good guide who was familiar with the area. After the third week, we returned to San Francisco and from there Shaparak went to San Diego to spend some time with her father and I returned to Reno. Shayma was in the process of her summer final exams. I found her unhappy and upset because Shaparak and her father were both gone. I talked to her and asked her if she wanted to transfer to San Diego and continue her college there or stay in Reno and finish her first degree. She told me she wished to be with her father and close to Shaparak who could visit with her from time to time. Therefore she was prepared to move to San Diego and live with her father and transfer to one of the colleges in San Diego.

Meanwhile, Shaparak called for help and wanted me to go to San Diego and help her move to Los Angeles and find a place to live and register at USC. So I flew to San Diego and spent more than two weeks with Shaparak until she found an apartment to share with three other girls, all medical students, and until the process of her registration was completed. I then returned to Reno and waited for the final process of the sale of the house to go through. Shayma left Reno the last week of August while I was in Detroit for the third memorial service for Minoo. It was the third year since Minoo had left us forever. According to Iranian custom, every year we would visit the grave on the same day that the burial took place. This process would continue until one could not do it anymore, like myself at the present time. Her husband Mohsen also came to Detroit to attend the memorial service. He returned to San Diego after 3-4 days and I stayed at Nikrou and Ali's house for two weeks. When I returned to Reno, the sale of our house was finalized and we had to move out. Shayma and her father came to Reno by plane and rented a U-Haul truck to move the entire household. Shayma drove her car and Nasser and Mohsen and drove the U-Haul truck and shared the driving to San Diego.

I decided to stay with Nikou and her son until the sale of her house was completed. Nikou had to resign from her teaching and research faculty position at the University of Reno Medical School. During that three month period, I was in a car accident. I was trapped in my own car that had been hit from the front and the rear and ended up with a broken wrist.

Finally, in December of 1988 my entire family moved from Nevada to Southern California. Nasser was in Reno to help Nikou and Mohsen came from San Diego to return Nasser's help during his own move from Reno to San Diego. Because of my broken wrist I was unable to drive such a long distance so I asked Shaparak to fly to Reno on Friday night and drive my car back on Saturday morning. Nikou had to drive her own car with Hessam. At 10 pm the Weather Channel announced that a snowstorm would begin around midnight in the Sierra Mountains. At 6 am the news said that snow chains and snow tires both were required. We were prepared but didn't know what to do, whether we should start to move or wait for further news. Nasser and Mohsen made up their minds and decided to move out at 7 am. Fortunately the road service trucks were cleaning the roads, removing the snow in front of our vehicles. Nasser and Mohson were leading in the U-Haul and we were following them. After we passed the Sierra Mountains and entered California, the weather was beautiful and enjoyable but the Sierra Mountains remained closed for 25 days after we left.

We arrived in Los Angeles at 4 pm. Shaparak went to her house. Nikou, Nasser and Hessam decided to stay there over night. Mohsen and I went on to San Diego because Shayma was alone in their apartment. The next day, December 21, 1988, they went to the house Nasser had rented for 3 months in the Scripps Ranch area. That afternoon, Shayma and I followed Mohsen in my car to Nikou's house, which was half way furnished by that time. Nikou's family and I settled in the rented four bedroom home temporarily while looking for a house to buy.

Meanwhile I registered in the Anthony Real Estate School because I couldn't sit silent and inactive. I had to keep my brain occupied until I found a better way of life. I started going to school three days a week and on the other three days was I looking for property around the San Diego area. The real estate course took three months and at the end I had to sit for an exam. I passed the exam and received a real estate license, which I never used; but it is stored on top of all the other scientific degrees and is part of my history.

Nikrou, Ali and their son Adib had been planning a vacation trip to San Diego in December 1988 long before we moved. They planned to stay in the Embassy Suite Hotel close to La Jolla. We enjoyed their presence on New Year's Eve and especially on New Year's Day; it was very joyful. We wanted to have them for New Year's Day dinner at our (Nikou and Nasser's) house; but they didn't accept. So we all decided to have dinner in a restaurant, forgetting the need for a reservation on such a day. Everywhere we went, even in the fast food restaurants like McDonalds, either they were closed or there were no seats available. Nikou managed to find an Iranian restaurant that, since then, we all call Khaneh Omid or "Hope House." The manager made a very good chello kabob for us. As Persian-style thanks, Nikou told him his restaurant was our Hope House because we all were hopeless and foodless that day.

Ever since we moved to San Diego I have been living with Nikou, but not voluntarily. I have never wanted to live with any of my sons-in-law. But initially I had to stay with Nikou and Nasser until I could buy or lease my own property. But sometime in 1986, I developed a super ventricular tachycardia (SVT) that was very scary, especially at night. I had to live very close to one of my family members - preferably Nikou, who had lived within walking distance from me in Iran and was my next-door neighbor for six years in Reno. Therefore, I had to think twice about the distance between a single-family home and an apartment at that time.

During the three months we were in the leased house in Scripps Ranch, I looked at more than 150 properties from north to south and east to west with no success because the housing did not match with what I was looking for. I was unable to find an apartment for myself that was close to a house for Nikou's family. In addition, the price of property was unbelievably high when compared to Reno. Each of us sold our residences after six years occupancy including cost of landscaping and beautiful fixtures for the same price as we purchased them minus the 6% realtor fees. We had to buy, but how could we? Finally I found a house for Nikou and Nasser but not for myself. However, in the short period since I had been living with Nikou in Reno as well as in San Diego, I suffered heart problems more than seven times. Furthermore, Nikou's son Hessam (17) who always lived near me kept talking to me and trying to convince me not to move away from them. He told me I couldn't stay alone in a place far from their house; even if I found a property close to their house then someone would have to come and take care of me, especially at night. Instead of living in a private apartment, he told me I should live with them - take the benefits of being with my daughter, enjoy the presence of my youngest grandson and share the house with his parents as I did with Shaparak and Shayma. His proposal appealed to me, so I started thinking over and over and asking myself, "Does this teenage boy know what he thinks or should I be wise enough to refuse his idea and find my own property no matter where or what?"

I kept looking for a property and I couldn't find anything better or more reasonable than what I had already found; I saw it again with Hessam alone, then with Nikou and her husband. The beauty of the house attracted all of us but its price didn't agree with their budget. Nasser sent an indirect message via his son Hessam, that if I agreed to pay for 1/3 of the house in cash, they were willing to buy this property; otherwise it was out of his budget. At the same time I found that Shayma was planning to get married so I had to make up my mind; with no more doubt, I announced my agreement and paid 1/3 of the property's price in cash. I accepted Hessam's proposal because the back yard of this house reminded me of my childhood house in Iran, especially the landscaping, the gazebo, the big pond full of Koi fish, and the trees, shrubs and flowers. It was and still would be a copy of my childhood home except for the building structure, which was French style, common in those days in Iran versus the Mexican-American mix style of the present structure.

One of the best qualities of this house has been the many happy occasions held in the house since we purchased it. The first was Shayma's wedding ceremony on July 1, 1989. The second was Shaparak's wedding ceremony on September 30, 1995. The third occasion was the engagement garden party for my oldest grandson Adib on August 21, 1999. The most pleasant and enjoyable period in this house was during Shaparak's residency at UCSD while she lived with us from 1992-1995. The moments that I have enjoyed most in the back yard were the times that all my great-grandchildren from 2? to 12 years of age played together; I called it the "boys' party." At the present time my youngest grandson Hessam who advised me not to live by myself is living in his own apartment. Instead, my great-niece Negar, Nikou and I are living together in the same house, enjoying the presence of each other while waiting for Negar's Master's Degree graduation or a marriage party or both.

Nikou and her son Hessam, San Diego, 1999

My second generation (L to R):
Adib, Shaparak, Hessam and Shayma

My second generation as adults (L to R):
Adib, Shaparak, Hessam and Shayma

Chapter 17

Life in San Diego

And so we all settled in to a new life in a new state. Nikou transferred to UCSD and started her job as a research faculty member in the Medical School and Hessam registered at Mesa College.

Shayma kept us busy indirectly because she had planned to get married to a young Iranian engineer and PhD candidate at UCLA, Behrooz Mortazavi. All the members of my family were happy about her choice because he was one of the very well known and well educated, very decent Iranian gentlemen. His sister's family was close friends and neighbors of my daughter Nikrou in Birmingham, Michigan. Shayma became engaged on February 11, 1989 and her wedding date was set for the first day of July. The wedding ceremony took place at 4 pm and was followed by a beautiful and well-prepared reception at home (our present residence).

Shayma and Behrooz's wedding reception,
July 1, 1989, San Diego

On July 3rd, she had another wedding reception in the Irvine Hilton Hotel hosted by the groom's family; it was an unforgettable event.

Shayma and Behrooz's second reception, July 3, 1989, Irvine, CA

A week later, Shayma and Behrooz went to Paris for their honeymoon where his older brother Dr. Reza Mortazavi and his family had resided since 1979. They couldn't attend the wedding in San Diego because the US Consulate Office in Paris wouldn't issue an entry visa to them. Today Shayma and Behrooz have two sons, Cameron, 14, and Kevin, 12.

Shayma and Behrooz's sons, Cameron and Kevin Mortazavi

In the spring of 1992, I witnessed 4? graduate students in my family, 3? in California and one in Michigan. Behrooz Mortazavi, Shayma's husband, received his PhD degree from UCLA. His wife, Shayma, who was six months pregnant with their first child, Cameron, received her BSc degree from Fullerton University.

Behrooz Mortazavi, PhD, UCLA 1992

Shayma Mortazavi (Kamarei), Bsc, UCF, 1992
Cameron Mortazavi at 6 months (in Shayma's womb)

Shaparak Montakhab Kamarei received her Medical Degree from the University of Southern California (USC) and Adib M. Nasle received his BSc degree from Michigan State University where his father Ali Mousavi Nasle and his grandmother (me) received our degrees in 1964 and 1966, respectively.

Shaparak Montakhab Kamarei,
MD, USC, 1992

Adib Mousavi Nasle,
Bsc, MSU, 1992

The graduation celebration was held in the Irvine Chantel Restaurant, hosted by Nikou and Nikrou. Although I wanted very much to attend, I couldn't because I had to go back to Iran after being gone for 12 years to take care of an urgent matter. I left the US on April 10th and the celebration was held on May 29th. That year, in addition to all the good omens that I received from the graduations I learned that Shaparak had been accepted at UCSD (University of California, San Diego) for her residency program and she decided to join us at home. While there were so many controversies in Nikou's life and indirectly in mine at that time, her presence in San Diego, especially at home, during her four year residency, was a great gift from God.

In the spring of 1990, Nikou met a retired Iranian professor who came to San Diego from the east to attend the La Jolla Cancer Research Institute annual meeting. He had planned to move from the east as he called San Diego his dream place. He invited Nikou to be one of his active partners to set up a biotech laboratory when he moved to San Diego. At that time, it was only talking and planning, not real action; therefore, Nikou didn't really take his proposal seriously. The professor's wife, three sons and two daughters-in-law were all attorneys-at-law. The children came to San Diego to investigate their parents' plan and the residence that they had decided to purchase. Meanwhile, the professor visited with us again and repeated his proposal and his promises. Nikou was very reluctant at first because she was working as research faculty at UCSD and had her own grant for AIDS research. The professor tried very hard and kept calling day after day until they moved to San Diego and settled in. He invited all of us for Thanksgiving Day, including my daughter Nikrou, her husband Ali and their son Adib who had planned to spend their Thanksgiving Day with us. We celebrated that Thanksgiving Day in 1991 at the professor's house with all members of his family and mine as well.

After that, he started to look for a large space to lease and move his laboratory equipment from the university where he had retired. Since he had a claim against the University, it was very surprising to me how he could take the entire 30 years of laboratory equipment from the University to establish a private business, unless something had happened that was entirely unknown to us. The retired professor was so insistent in his proposal and strongly urged Nikou to resign from UCSD. She finally became convinced and resigned from her position. Although I advised her against it and tried to discourage her from resigning until she made sure on what spot she was standing, she didn't pay any attention to my concerns.

Perhaps it was my fault - that I didn't insist or I wasn't brave enough to insist upon my idea. I believe that after he became sure Nikou's resignation was approved and finalized he changed his mind and decided otherwise. He didn't lease the designated laboratory space. Instead he secretly leased a storage space and stored the contents of three trucks of equipment the list of which he had sent to Nikou to convince her to resign. He never mentioned where he stored the equipment, what the fate of the valuable laboratory equipment was and how and where he liquidated it. He didn't call Nikou again because he was ashamed of himself and his unprofessional, stupid actions.

Indeed, the year 1992 started with a series of bittersweet events. The first and the best were the graduations of my 4? grandchildren. The second was my successful trip to Iran to visit my motherland, my relatives and friends after twelve years of separation. The third and the most exciting event was the birth of my first great-grandson Cameron Mortazavi. So he was considered the half amongst the other four. The fourth was Shaparak's four year residency in San Diego.

The first bitter event was Nikou's resignation from UCSD for the professor's deceptive plan; my family and I have never understood his mysterious reason was for disturbing Nikou's job, although it turned out for the best in the long-run. The second bitter event was a serious flood in the house resulting from a broken hot water pipe that caused extensive damage to the property. The third bitter event and the most unpredictable and unexpected was the changes in Nasser's attitude after his return from Iran. The changes resulted in the termination of their marriage after 20 years.

The year 1992 ended with a very exclusive decision - the establishment of a biotechnology laboratory called Molecular Diagnostic Services, Inc. that was registered as a corporation on December 24, 1992.

Valentine's Day 1995 started with an early morning telephone call from Michigan. Nikrou called at 7 am and, according to Iranian tradition, told me that Mrs. Rabbani had called and asked for my phone number because her son Ramin planned to visit San Diego on April 5th to spend a week to get acquainted with Iranian girls in California. The Rabbani family had lived in Michigan since the sixties and had been friends and neighbors of Nikrou and Ali since 1980. It took almost a month before Ramin called to talk to me and asked for Shaparak's private phone number. She was on-call that night. The next night he called and talked to her and told her that he would like to come to our house on April 5th at 6 pm and take her to dinner; she accepted the invitation. The April 6th, Saturday, he went to LA, then San Francisco, and returned to San Diego the following Thursday. He had lunch with Shaparak again and left San Diego. Although Shaparak didn't believe in long distance relationships, they kept talking by telephone until they became so well acquainted with each other that on June 5th of the same year she became engaged to him - a young American-born Iranian cardiologist, Ramin Rabbani, who was an interventional cardiologist fellow at Cleveland Clinic.

Shaparak became engaged in June 1995 and her wedding date was set for September 30th. She was preparing for her boards in Internal Medicine in August 1995, exactly one month before her vows. The marriage ceremony of Shaparak and Ramin took place at 4 pm, Saturday, September 30th, 1995 at home followed by a glorious reception at the Hyatt Regency Hotel in downtown San Diego.

Shaparak and Ramin's wedding receptions
San Diego, CA,   *Detroit, MI,*
September 30, 1995   *October 30, 1995*

She moved to Detroit, Michigan on October 25th and the groom's parents held a wonderful and exceptional reception at the Hyatt Regency of Dearborn, Michigan on October 30th. Shaparak and Ramin went to Hawaii for their honeymoon and returned directly to Cleveland, Ohio where Shaparak started her teaching and medical practice at the Cleveland Clinic and Ramin his fellowship in Interventional Cardiology. Drs. Shaparak and Ramin had their first son, Keon, on October 25, 1996 and their second, Kayhan, on July 1, 1998. In August 1999 they moved to California where they started their practice at USC the next month. Their third son, Mateen was born on March 19, 2001. Shaparak started her own private practice in March 2002 in Orange County and her second clinic in June 2006 in Los Angles County. Since then, her husband, Dr. Ramin Rabbani, started his own group practice.

L to R: Keon, Mateen and Kayhan Rabbani

In September of 1996 Nikrou, her family and their private business moved from Birmingham, Michigan to San Diego, after 16 years in the east. Nikrou's son Adib became engaged in February 1999 to Dr. Mahsan Yazdi. Their beautiful garden party engagement was held at our home on August 25th and their marriage date was set for October 16th. Their marriage ceremony was held in the Hyatt Regency Hotel in downtown San Diego, followed by a fantastic reception. They went to Haiti and the Vera Cruz Islands on their honeymoon. During the course of five years of happy married life, they traveled to Italy, Spain and China. Their son, Alexander Ali Nasle, was born on February 5, 2002. Unfortunately, the young couple decided to split and change their directions in 2005. Alexander is my sixth great-grandson or better said, he is the sixth star in my blue sky.

Adib and Mahsan's engagement party, August 1999, San Diego

Mahsan and Adib's wedding reception, October 16, 1999

Alexander Ali Nasle

On October 23, 2005, Negar the last girl of my entire family married Dr. Kambiz Aghili, a young Iranian computer scientist and PhD graduate of Santa Barbara University in California. The marriage ceremony was held at 4 pm, followed by a great garden party reception at home. The bride's parents traveled from Iran to attend their beloved daughter's wedding. But the groom's parents were denied a visa from the US Embassy in Dubai and were unable to attend. Presently, the young couple is living in San Diego. Negar is a PhD candidate at UCSD and Dr. Aghili joined one of the most famous and prominent computer firms in San Diego.

Negar and Kambize's wedding reception, October 23, 2005, San Diego

Bride's parents, Firoozeh and Abdi Ghahramani

L-R Behrooz & Shayma-Kayhon, Mateen, Keven, Keon,
Camren-Shaparak & Ramin
Alexander's picture is posted because he was not present in Negars
Wedding 10-23-2005

CHAPTER 18

Miscellaneous Revolutionary Thoughts

The onset of the Revolution in 1979 was followed by group executions and imprisonment of innocent people every day, resulting in strong fears and frustration among the people. Nonsense accusations became common practice, especially among those of low rank against those of higher rank, regardless of education, experience, capabilities, etc. The personal lives of all the people, their relationships with other life styles and their reputations and integrity were under the Revolutionary microscope. The Revolutionaries tried as hard as possible to find a needle in every haystack to use against you, to disturb your emotions and your power until you were forced to surrender to their wishes. The majority of the people lost their human character and fairness no matter how kind and fair you were toward them. It appeared that they actually lost the ability to recognize the difference. They tried to grab on to whatever they could find to upset you, to be able to present you as being with dirty hands and an ugly face. People who had been living side-by-side with you for so many years and had the same privileges now turned away from you, joined the crowd and left for no reason. They were under the assumption that the Revolution could replace you with them.

I wasn't an actively aggressive woman, not a pro-revolutionary; I never had been and never would be. Not that I was religious, not that I criticized the budget that had been spent without any hesitation to satisfy the architectural desire of Shabanoo Farah in Shiraz's Art festival. For sure, none of them.

The first item that disappeared from my office at the Institute for Paramedical Sciences was my last photo taken with the Shah and his wife Farah at the last meeting in the Golestan Palace. I had a feeling that the housekeeper in charge of my office grabbed it. He was the only one that had enough time to search my desk at night because he and his family lived in an apartment fully furnished and free of charge inside the Institute. Yet I doubted it because he was the son-in-law of my grandson's babysitter who lived with my daughter for almost 8 years. He probably grabbed the photo to destroy my family and me during that dreadful period of anarchy when no one could recognize the innocent from the guilty.

The housekeeper and his stupid boss (the revolutionary dean) assumed that my photo with the Shah could destroy my reputation if for some reason the new government decided to keep me at the Institute. They believed they had enough evidence in their hands to have me ousted. That foolish dean was instructed by his superior to be very compassionate with me and treat me with great respect. He never realized that at my very first meeting with the Revolutionary Secretary of Health I mentioned that I met with the Shah four times a year and that this fact might create a problem for the Secretary if I started working with him. The Secretary told me that he was aware of everything about me and I shouldn't worry.

As I look back on that incident 27 years ago, I am sure that it was neither my imagination nor assumption because the photo that disappeared from my office later appeared in the hands of Dr. Saami, the late Revolutionary Secretary of Health. He told me that they sent him the photo. He couldn't give it back to me because a picture of the Shah was one of the most forbidden items and had to be destroyed by fire.

There were 11 women and 139 male students at the University that first year. According to the system of education at the time, there was a single exam for each of the subjects that we had studied during the previous nine months. The exam was in two separate sessions. The written took place at the same time for all students; the individual oral exams took place over several days, face to face with the professor. On the day of the oral exam, the students were called to enter the professor's office in alphabetical order. He would ask at least 10 questions for each student to answer. If a student failed either the written or oral exam they had to study further by themselves over the summer and go back for the fall exam on that subject. If the student failed a second time, he or she had to repeat the entire year of classes. We all were very worried and tried hard to pass every subject the first time so we could relax during the summer. For this reason every single student tried as hard as possible to finish all the requirements of that year on time.

Even after 50 years, I still vividly remember the time and date and the event of my oral exam. We all knew how religious the geology professor was compared with the others, so all the women students except me decided to wear a scarf during their oral exam. When my name was called and I started to go in, they begged me to wear a scarf but I ignored them and entered the professor's room with no scarf. I stood in front of him waiting for the first question. He started his questions and I tried to answer as well as I could. At the end, he said "This is a personal question, if you don't mind. All your classmates entered this room wearing a scarf. I noticed it was the same scarf that they passed to each other. Now I see you without it and I am curious why they didn't lend it to you." I told him, "Professor, they are still waiting outside. They tried to get me to wear it but I refused because I have been attending your class for 36 sessions without a scarf, so why should I wear one during the final exam? If God was watching me, how could I?" At that moment my heart was pounding and my hands became shaky while I stood and waited for his last words, which were never spoken but motioned. Finally I left his room with a red face and shaking hands. All my classmates tried to comfort me but criticized me about the scarf. I remember his face while he was questioning me and remember the entire situation. That was my last face-to-face conversation with him. It was June of 1955. Four years later I left Iran and became a busy student once again. This time the extensive effort was not due to my family or working and studying at the same time. It was due to the language problem - I had to spend 3-4 times longer than American students to understand a subject.

At the onset of the Revolution it became obvious that the geology professor and his son were the most influential and powerful keys to the underground revolutionary network but I don't believe they ever expected the bloody mess and chaotic situation that was created by Khomeini and his followers. The underground religious network had always existed at the University, primarily because the university was the place to manipulate young active enthusiastic students that could be brainwashed and trained to be prepare for revolution.

I had no news about anyone in the biology department at Tehran University for almost 9 years. When I returned from the US and transferred to the University Medical School I decided to go to the Biology Department and visit them. When I called to make an appointment the operator told me almost all the professors that I wanted to see were either retired or had been dismissed. I became suspicious and tried to ask more about them but I received no clear answer or explanation until Nikou got a research position in the School of Public Health at Tehran University. She became acquainted with the daughter of my geology professor and later found out that he had been dismissed from his professorship because of his political affiliations. He had left the University and started his own business. Her brother, an engineer, had been in prison for many years somewhere outside of Tehran. Because of this simple friendship, any time her mother or other family members had medical problems Nikou helped them unbeknownst to the rest of us.

About My Cousins

In spite of the religious fanaticism and old-fashioned ideas of my aunt (Marziyeh Khanoom) that always dominated my mother's mind and eventually her decisions, the unconditional love of my mother for her only sister made for a great relationship between the two sisters' families. My aunt had nine children, five boys and four girls. Including my sister Azam and me, that formed a total of eleven children of different ages. We all were friendly, kind and compassionate to each other.

Two of my male cousins, Mehdi and Muhammad, were almost the same age as my sister and me. They were our playmates and childhood friends. Unfortunately, Muhammad died at 21 during a typhoid epidemic. Mehdi remained my best friend up to his last day of life in 1981.

I had great respect for my oldest female cousin Malak; she a wonderful woman, understandable and kind. She married when I was in third grade and had her first child when I was in high school (ninth grade). Malak was a very wise and respected person; although she had only the basic education of her time she lived in a modern life style.

My second female cousin, Malihe, went to a private primary school until sixth grade but she didn't pass the state exam. It seems the last day of the exam was set for a sewing test that required half a yard of fabric plus the necessary additional sewing items to be provided by each student for their test. She asked her mother for it on the day of the exam but her mother (my aunt) was busy and had no time to go and buy it for her. Therefore, my cousin couldn't go to the exam, was considered absent and failed the class. Her mother said whatever she had learned up to that point would be more than enough for a girl like her daughter Malihe. It was not a matter of money. Her father had more than one could imagine. And it was not only my cousin either. Thousands and thousands of girls faced similar situations. In those days, parents didn't believe in female education.

Malihe was a happy person but extremist by nature. In spite of her modern lifestyle, she couldn't be melted in the pot of emancipated women as she desired; and she couldn't participate in modern society because she lost her confidence as a result of her lack of formal education. Malihe was a modern housewife and lived a very comfortable life but was always starving for some "different" things - unique - to be distinguished from the other members of the family. Therefore, she was attracted otherwise and secretly became a member of an underground religious and activist group for many years. None of her family, her husband, her brothers or any of her sisters, discovered her activities because she didn't change any of her habits. She kept her face so strong and indifferent that no one noticed any change in her lifestyle.

One day when Malihe was in a very good mood, she told her husband that she was going to the mechanic to get the car repaired. She disappeared and didn't return home for thirty-five days; no one knew what had happened to her. They looked everywhere, even in the morgue, but found no trace of her at all. Her oldest sister, Malak, who had a broken bone at the time, called their friends and business partners living in other cities of Iran and found her in Qum city, almost 240 miles from Tehran. Malak asked me to help her by going to Qum City instead of her since she couldn't travel at that time. So my sister Azam, their youngest sister Iran and I went to Qum city. Malihe had rented a very small house and had furnished it. We found her house, met with her and we all tried to persuade her to return to Tehran with us. She in turn gave us so many excuses why she couldn't, including her husband's unfair attitude. We all begged her to put those aside and come back to Tehran. Her last excuse was her car's mechanical problems; she tried hard to convince us that it would not be possible to drive the car. Fortunately, Hossain Shapoor, the institute driver drove us to Qum so I told Malihe he would drive her car and I would drive the Institute's Chevrolet; we would follow one after the other. It was 4 pm when we all left Qum City for Tehran. It turned out to be a 7-hour drive rather than the usual four hours driving time because of the slow speed of her car, my amateur driving (I wasn't used to such a crowded road) and the fear for everyone's safety. I drove bumper to bumper with Shapoor. When we arrived I invited Malihe to stay in my home until her husband came and apologized for his unfair act. We all accused him but never realized her secret activities. For almost twenty days her husband tried to prove his innocence; finally she forgave him and went to her house. A year passed and both of them appeared in good spirits with a perfect relationship, going back and fourth to London, planning to buy a house. (At that time, Iranians were free to enter England - no visa was required during the Shah's time.) Finally, they bought a rather large four-bedroom house in a London suburb. It was there that I spent a week with them when I was in London waiting for student visas to be issued to Shaparak and Shayma by the US Embassy in January 1980.

Early one morning in the spring of 1975, one of my youngest boy cousins called and said Malihe was lost again. She had gone to visit her daughter in Germany. After 15 days she decided to return to Tehran and her daughter Mahshid took her to the Frankfurt airport and left her there. It had been 25 days and they had had no news from her. They all were very worried and asked me to call their sister Malak. I decided to help them as much as I could so I called my cousin and offered my help. She was almost in tears and said Malihe might have left the airport, lost her way, been killed by a car, and been buried in an unknown cemetery; who knew where and when and what happened to her. I sympathized with her, her husband and the rest of my cousins and asked what I could do for them. She asked me to call my nephew Amir who was chief manager of the IranAir Office at the time to check all the passenger lists from Frankfurt to Tehran for the last 28 days. I promised her to do my best. I called Amir and explained the situation. In response he told me, "With all due respect to my dear aunt, it is not possible to do because every time an aircraft lands and all the passengers get off the plane, the list is shredded." (There were no sophisticated computer systems in those days.) I called my cousin and gave her the bad news, everything my nephew explained to me. My cousin Malak said her husband decided to bring their daughter back from Germany to Tehran to arrange Malihe's memorial service. We all were very sorry for her and waiting for Mahshid to arrive. Two or three days later, my youngest boy cousin called again and told me he had good news. His sister Malihe had arrived in Tehran from Syria late the night before. She went to her house by taxi. Two days later I went to visit her and find out where she had been. We spoke about everything and I criticized her actions because her entire family - husband, brothers and sisters, including myself - was disturbed and worried for her. I asked her, "Please tell me where you were during this period of time." She said while she was waiting in the Frankfurt airport for the flight to Tehran, a very kind gentleman was sitting next to her. He started talking to her for about an hour and invited her to Syria for a few days to visit and make a pilgrimage to the Shrine of Roghayeh, the great-granddaughter of Muhammad. Malihe was attracted to pilgrimage and decided to change her ticket from Frankfurt to Syria and then Tehran. So she went to Syria. With great surprise I asked her how she could trust this man and she replied that he was one of the great mullahs. Once again I asked her, "Honestly, tell me what the purpose of this was and why you spent such a long time. Didn't you think of your family? Didn't you realize how worried everyone would be?" She said, "You want me to answer in an honest way?" I replied, "Yes, please. Tell me what's the matter." She said, "I wish to be as free as a bird, to fly anywhere I decide and to live on any planet I prefer." I must confess that none of us under-stood why she acted this way; we all thought it might be related to silent brain damage while she was traveling by herself that remained unrecognized and ignored.

In 1977 as the stability of the government came under sur-veillance little by little, Malihe started preaching and kept advis-ing me that I should try hard to add two hours of Koran read-ing and also teaching guardianship of the Islamic Jurists "Velayateh Farhih" written by Imam Khomeini to the student curriculum. She didn't realize that any changes in curriculum required the approval of the Ministry of Science and Higher Education. She tried to invite me to their meetings of Koran reading and interpretation and to be familiar with the students' function and their movements outside of school. I was so exhausted about the students' movement that I always refused her entire suggestions. Once she said, "Are you aware that the Islamic guideline and Koran interpretation should be the prerequisite of university acceptance? As much as she informed me, I questioned more and became more and more confused. How could she know? From where did she collect this information? To be honest it was beyond my assumption and imagination; sometimes I tried to bring out her actual ideas and kept asking her how could I force the students to change their lifestyle and interpret the Koran? It is in Arabic - I wished it was in Farsi so we could read it well but I asked her to tell me how she understood its meaning in detail. She said it wouldn't be too long before everyone had to realize the future of Iran. Why did our young generation have to be kept in the dark? She said to come and see the mosque at night, how crowded and how many boys and girls gathered there. Every night countless numbers of Korans were given away free of charge in each mosque. They distributed the Koran as a gift to every single member of a family. I asked her who paid for them and she said the money came from bazaar business owners. Then she asked me, "Have you ever wondered what would happen if a mullah grabbed the power of the Shah? Change the system and put an end to the monarchy." Once again I thought she must be crazy. I never believed and ever dreamed of it; therefore I didn't pay any attention to whatever she said. We were very kind and friendly to each other but as the time progressed and 1978 arrived, the chaotic state coincided with banishment. The London BBC started propaganda for Imam Khomeini and protested abuses of human rights under the Shah. The Farsi voice of the BBC spread like a wind across the country, even in the small villages of Iran. The BBC reported Khomeini's idea of free land, free gas and free basic necessities of life like food, medication and housing, especially for underprivileged people. The Shah fled the country on January 16, 1979, Khomeini returned from Paris to

Tehran February 1st of the same year. During this two week period, the Farsi section of the BBC kept its broadcasting action to the max and used its evil power to brainwash the masses who were on general strike and had nothing to do except listen to the BBC news and attend discussions about it. The BBC tried to present Khomeini as supernatural and make a worshipful Imam out of an ordinary man by its strong propaganda about Imam Khomeini's miracle; it tried to prove it by demanding the people look at the "Sureh Baghareh" on page 22 (if I recall correctly) to see a hair which originated from the Imam's beard - it kept everyone busy enough to find the hair in the midline of the page. But no one realized or thought how a hair could travel to a book and sit in the middle of a certain page unless it was fabricated by man, especially when they found it in all newly-published Korans that were distributed in the mosque. My cousin Malak called to ask me if I saw the hair; I jumped to the bookshelf and grabbed the two Korans that I inherited from my parents. I opened them both as she guided me and found no hair, even with the help of a magnifying glass; I didn't see any hair at all. So I called her back and asked her, "Do you really mean it?" She replied, "100% positive." Again I asked her to make sure. She said, "Three Korans are on the dining table and in all of them I can see the hair easily." At that period, Malihe and her family had been moved to her London house. I asked my cousin Malak why the people lost their ability to think and differentiate the truth from a lie; I couldn't believe this "miracle." It would be a big lie in the middle of a holy book. I'm sure our grandmother advised her also. She told us, "If you lie, God never forgives you and in eternity day let you burn in the fires of Hell." When my friends and a few family members including my cousin Malak informed me to look at the moon to see the Imam's face, I went to the balcony of my apartment, sat in the chair and looked at the moon for almost 45 minutes. I really felt the moon I was looking at was entirely the same as the moon of half a century ago. At that moment, my mind had been traveling to a summer of my childhood period. I recalled the house, the fish pond, and the beautiful yard with pomegranate trees, roses and other fruit trees. The Persian carpet laid on the ground and sheer tent erected. My mother and/or grandmother would tell us stories about the creation of the universe, the sun, the moon, the stars and the earth. I could see and recall everything except the Imam's face on the moon. In the end, after so many years of completely secret activity with the underground religious activists, I feel cousin Malihe unfortunately hadn't had a quality life up to the end to realize clearly what happened to her country and the Iranian nation. She had been trapped in Alzheimer's net and didn't recognize the amount of bloodshed, the degree of peoples' suffering as a result of eight years of the Iran-Iraq war. She died in 2003. Cousin Malak, who was a moderate Muslim and remained the same, lived in a completely healthy mind but also died as a result of complications of a broken hip in 2002.

R-L My aunt Marzyeh, her two daughters Malak and Maliheh wearing chadoors

CHAPTER 19

My Family after the Revolution

Two of my daughters, Minoo and Nikrou, and their families lived very close to each other and owned beautiful homes located in the northern part of Tehran in a very exclusive area. Nikou and her family lived in a three-bedroom rental condo about 15 minutes walking distance from my two-bedroom rental unit in a three story apartment building where I lived after returning from the US in 1967 supposedly "for good." During the 12–13 year period when I lived there I had been so busy with my jobs that I never thought of moving. It was a quiet place located in the upper part of Tehran, in a newly developed area.

In 1974-75 the government agreed for the development of a high rise building in northwest Tehran. Nikou and I decided to move and applied for two units next to each other, 2 bedrooms for me and 3 bedrooms for her. The estimated time for completion was 3-4 years. The first 30 stories of the modern apartment building became ready for occupancy in February 1979, about 2-3 months following the onset of the revolution. While the rest of us left Iran, Nikou's husband remained in Tehran; he took care of everything and moved into the new apartment temporarily. I had completed all the paperwork but I didn't occupy my apartment because I planned to leave, so my unit was rented to our family friend, a physician, through my attorney who was also my son-in-law, Minoo's husband.

By the advent of the revolution, most of us faced danger because of our high ranking positions in the Shah's government, especially my youngest daughter Nikrou and her family. They had to leave their home and stay in hiding with me until they were ready to leave Iran. Nikou and her son Hessam and Nikrou and her son Adib left Tehran on August 1, 1979. Nikrou's husband Ali walked out of Iran in September or October of that same year. Then I decided to go to Mecca for a pilgrimage. My sister Azam and my daughter Minoo accompanied me.

When we returned from Mecca I found myself alone in the apartment building; the tenants from the first floor had moved out without a forwarding address. The owner who lived on the third floor disappeared because he was Christian/Armenian; but he left me the phone number of his Muslim friend in case of any problems in the building or if I decided to move out. I began to suffer severe anxiety, worry and depression; I couldn't stand the loneliness. I was not able to sleep at night because I was really worried for Nikrou's health. She was the most fragile of my three daughters and when she left Iran she was still in shock about what was happening to everyone. Every night, after hours of reading, if I fell asleep I would face horrible nightmares. I preferred not to sleep at night because I was also afraid of intruders or thieves who might come in assuming the building was vacant. My front door neighbor owned a famous flower shop and I was one of his permanent customers. I asked him to park his truck in front of my building next to my car to show that more than one person was living there and at least one (the truck owner) was probably a male. I tried to be strong and resolute but everyone who knew me realized how unhappy I was.

I had a lot of family in Tehran but I didn't know who was pro-Khomeini and who wasn't. Finally I decided to make a trip to the US to visit my children. I spent January 1980 with them. When I returned to Tehran, Minoo came to pick me up at the airport and told me it wasn't safe for me to go to my apartment. She said I must swallow my pride and come and stay with her. Although all of my family was aware of my feelings that I didn't want to live with any of my in-laws, at this time I had to accept my fate and I agreed to move in with them. So two days after I arrived I started to prepare many of the large household items for sale. First, my Persian carpet; then the big furniture imported from China that was fashionable in those days. I moved to Minoo's and stored the remainder of my belongings there.

In the meantime, Minoo received a job offer from a London clinic that she had applied for during her husband's surgery. She decided to go to accept the job and left for London on April 15, 1980. After she left it didn't take long until I had to leave Iran definitely - for good. Shaparak and Shayma accompanied me on May 13, 1980 to London. Although we all had entry visas to the U.S., President Carter decided to suspend all Iranian visas due to the hostage crisis.

Minoo's husband and her nanny remained in Tehran so her house was saved. Her two daughters and I were living with her in London. She was working at a London clinic and teaching at the Royal Free Hospital. I started working at the Westminster Medical School and Shaparak and Shayma attended the Quinton Kynaston School. We all were waiting for our future fate, which was dependant on the resolution of the hostage crisis and the presidential election in the U.S. Once that was over and the American Embassy again accepted the Iranian applications, we applied for Minoo and her two girls. They left London for the US in August of 1981 and I left in September of the same year.

After almost three years from August 2, 1979 to August 10, 1981 of separation they got together again and I joined them in September. Minoo was preparing herself for the American Nursing Board. Shaparak and Shayma went to high school and I got a job in the department of physiology and pharmacology in the medical school in Reno, Nevada. In the summer of 1981, Nikou arranged for her husband Nasser to receive a visa and come to visit their son, Hessam who was 9 years old. In addition, Nasser received his permanent residency at the same time.

After we left Iran, Nasser started working as an engineer for the newly formed revolutionary government so he had to return to Iran. The day he had planned to leave the U.S. the first bombs were exploded in the government assembly and more than one hundred high ranking revolutionary officials were killed instantly, including his boss. Therefore he changed his mind. He asked his family in Iran to move into his apartment temporarily and he applied for a job in Kuwait. In February 1982 Minoo decided to leave the U.S. and rejoin her husband who was the only one left behind in Iran. As soon as Minoo arrived in Tehran, she received a job offer from one of the most modern hospitals, the Tehran Clinic, as the chief hospital and nursing manager.

During the peak of the Iran-Iraq war, in the summer of 1983, Minoo and her husband Mohsen came to the U.S. to visit their two daughters and the rest of us. They spent their 30-day vacation with us and then returned to Iran. As Minoo told me later, while they were on the plane on the way back to Iran, her husband who had been strongly against leaving Iran in the past decided to sell all their property and other belongings and move to the U.S. - no matter what. When they arrived in Tehran, their decision became stronger because the revolutionary government demoted her husband's position for the third time. It was very hard for a man who worked in a high-ranking job with so many educated and expert people and refused those promotions that the revolutionary government offered at the beginning. The new revolutionary government decided to demote the incumbents to demoralize them as much as they could until they would leave their jobs voluntarily and ask for early retirement; they would be replaced them with people who had proven their loyalty to them. Therefore, Minoo and Mohsen decided to sell their house and their cottage by the Caspian Sea. Minoo called Nikou's husband Nasser and made an agreement to move into his apartment if they sold their house before they were ready to leave. Then they started selling their property and big furniture and moved to the apartment.

Thus, in that 3-bedroom apartment, one complete household and two sets of collected valuable belongings were stored.

In January of 1985 the last two members of my immediate family, Minoo and her husband Mohsen, came to the U.S. and joined us for good. Unfortunately, the enjoyment of this gathering did not last long and was terminated by the tragic death of Minoo on September 2, 1985.

Six or seven years after the tragic death of Minoo, her husband returned to Iran and moved from Nikou's and Nasser's apartment and into his own place. All my belongings and those of Nikou's remained in the apartment.

My trip to Iran (1992)

Everyone, especially my sister Azam and her husband, had advised me not to return to Iran after the revolution. Finally, about February 1992 Azam and her husband asked me to return to Iran to take care of some unfinished business. My sister repeatedly told me, "This is the time for you to come home; don't be afraid or don't worry; your name is clear. My husband used one of the revolutionary's computers through his closest friend and couldn't find your name." Therefore, I decided to go home despite the serious opposition of my family. Everyone tried to change my mind but I resisted. After 12 years, I dared to return to Tehran for three months. On April 10, 1992, with many good reasons and on the advice of my sister Azam, I left the US by British Airways to London and from there to Tehran. As soon as the plane entered the sky border of Iran, the pilot announced that all ladies were obligated to wear a scarf regardless of their nationality or religion. The plane landed safely at 1:30 am local time. The airport was extremely crowded because three airplanes landed at the same time. To me, the first surprising situation was that every airport worker who came close asked you where you were from. If the answer were "the US", they would not accept any money except dollars. Then they tried to convince you they were a group of only four; in other words, they asked you indirectly for $20 not $5. The inspectors were a group of young revolutionary women in Islamic black dress, covered from head to toe. Each one tried to find something brand new or questionable in your suitcase to ask for custom duties. Although they were relatively good looking they were very hard to deal with and had really bad tempers. With my Iranian passport, I entered the country with no problems.

My sister and a few nieces and nephews were in the airport to welcome me. It was really so enjoyable to see them after such a long time. We left for home and arrived at 5:00 am, a good 3? hours after the plane landed. Therefore, I went to bed immediately and rested after the 21-hour flight. It was noontime when my sister woke me for lunch. It was a very tasty meal and a most pleasant experience - after 12 years once again we all were together around the dinner table.

After lunch, my sister started telling me about my apartment. She said, "I understand your tenant plans to charge you twice or maybe three times as much as she paid in rent when you plan to sell. (In other words, I would have to **pay** her to move out.) She understands you want to sell and has met with the buyer; but none of us could take any action; every time I would try to say a word she would interrupt me and say, 'You are not the owner; I will only talk to that American, not you.' That was why I told Nikou to 'send your mother to Iran' and as I told you and promised, everything is safe." The brand new apartment complex where I owned one of the two-bedroom units was completed during the early days of the revolution. I had no chance to occupy it but I finished all of the paperwork in a rush before leaving Iran.

My attorney, who was one of my relatives, rented it to a prominent physician and one of our family friends for the most minimum price. I had to accept the deal; otherwise the revolutionaries would confiscate my vacant apartment without cause. The revolutionary guards had made the physician homeless overnight. They dismissed him from his job, held his salary and confiscated his travel documents so he couldn't leave the country and had no home or money. Their reason was that the former queen had delivered her last child in his hospital. He was living on income from his private practice that was really very low in those days because most of his patients were afraid to go to him for treatment because of the accusations. Fortunately, due to his background, the need for skilled physicians, and in the absence of so many others who were either executed, in jail or had left the country, he was called back and worked until the age of retirement. He lived in my apartment for eight years; then he bought his own apartment and moved out.

After the physician moved out, the apartment couldn't be kept vacant, so my sister rented it to someone else. When she heard about the tenant's plan, she called me and facilitated my trip to Iran. Before I bought my ticket I outlined a dated plan for myself not to miss anything during that short three-month period. The first plan was to get my 12-years of accumulated pension in order to have some money in hand. The second plan was to sell the rest of the household belongings that couldn't be taken out of the country. The third plan was to sell the apartment that had a qualified buyer. And the fourth was to officially transfer the deed to the cottage to my sister so that if we wanted to sell it there was no need for us to be present and she could do it by herself.

My Pension

Exactly one day after my arrival in Tehran in 1992, I started working on obtaining my pension. I was sure that I couldn't do anything without the help of people who were working for the government. So two of my nephews that were my colleagues at the Institute offered their help. My older nephew Abbas Farzinpoor who was retired offered me a ride to the downtown area every day where only cars with a special permit could enter. That was a really great help because I had forgotten the route and it saved time for me. I told them I could stay only three months because Shayma was pregnant and I was obligated to be with her at least for a few weeks before the end of her term. My great nephew Akbar Ladievardi was a chief accountant in the

Institute and had a high-ranking position at that time. He arranged every step for me so I would be able to get my 12 years accumulated pension in a lump sum instead of 3-4 installments over a period of a year.

My great nephew, Akbar Ladjevardi
whose great concern has been unforgettable

The day after I arrived, my nephew came to pick me up and go to the retirement department in the Ministry of Health. He told me I could go forward and be assured that he wouldn't be far from me. In other words, he kept watching me from a distance; at the same time my great-nephew was in his office in case someone caused me any problem. To be honest, if I had known why they were guarding me I never would have been brave enough to go forward. Everything was perfect. Those who were in charge of calculating my 12-year pension were very kind and courteous. They treated me with good care and great respect and admired my past achievements in higher education and the services that I provided to the country. The entire process took about two hours because my nephew had talked to their boss personally and he had had them prepare my file in advance. While I was waiting in the office, I could see and also feel that they were whispering about chickens. I didn't know what it meant; I thought chicken was a password and I tried to keep quiet and not to ask any questions until they finished their calculations and gave me the results. (For some unknown reason the revolutionary people kept their real names secret and referred to women as sisters and men as brothers. The older and most respected men were called Haji Agha and women were called Haji Khanoom.) Finally one gentleman or "brother," came to me and informed me that everything had been completed at his end and I should take my file to another office located in another part of town. I thanked them all and returned to my nephew with my file. He took me to the other office - a department for final investigation and approval. I had never worked in any office of health but had indirectly be placed in the Health Minister's group because I had been elected as the Academic Advisor to the Secretary of Health while I was founder and active Dean of the Institute of Paramedical Sciences and received my salary from the Institute budget. I entered a rather small office, well populated by a group of six ladies all in black, Islamic dresses that covered them from head to toe with no makeup. All of the rooms were very dark because the power was off. They were chatting and talking about chicken, the price and where it was being sold. No one paid any attention to me waiting. I wondered to whom I should speak and hand my file. After about 15 minutes or more an old man who was the record-keeper asked me what I needed. I told him I had brought my file from the main office and I didn't know to whom I should give it. He took my file and said that I must talk to sister Malihe; she was sick today but might be in the office tomorrow. All of a sudden the ladies left their desks and went downstairs in a rush. I was surprised and asked him what happened and why all the ladies suddenly vanished. He didn't tell me anything but asked me, "Don't you know today is chicken day? They went to get their chicken before it's finished." Then he said, "Would you believe how they could steal the brains of Iranians to make this revolution possible? You'd better go home today because there is no power and even if Sister Malihe was here, she couldn't help you in the dark. Besides, their children were in school for only half a day and will come here to have lunch with their mothers and make a lot of noise and I am sure you would get tired." Then he insisted that I go home and come back tomorrow. I returned home with my nephew who had been waiting for me.

On our way home I asked my nephew if we could go to the bank; my sister had given me my savings book so I could get some money and possibly my pension. I had heard that the government deposited everyone's pension into their savings account. He took me to the bank where I had been a customer for 13 years. Most of the bankers recognized me and came forward to greet me and talk to me. I gave my savings book to the teller and asked about my pension. He said I should talk to the bank manager, a middle-age revolutionary. He asked me for my letter of clearance. I didn't know what he meant. He told me "Haji Khanoom, you must go and get a letter from the Ministry of Health, approved by the secret service, and then come and talk to me." I decided not to say a word and return home. Meanwhile, the teller called me to receive my savings. He said it was 80 and I thought it would be 80,000 because they used to say one for every thousand unit. While my nephew was talking to his friend, I interrupted him and told him my handbag was small and couldn't carry that much today. He said, "Doctor, you can't carry 800 toomans? It isn't 80,000 toomans; please take it from the teller." Then everyone in the bank started laughing. When I went to the teller to get the money I noticed he had closed my account. I wondered why he did so without my request. I asked him and he said that I must use the bank nearer to my home, no matter how long I had been a customer of this bank. It is Islamic rule and everyone must obey despite the fact that all the brothers here recognized you.

It was almost 2 pm when I got home. On the way, my nephew told me that he would never let me go any place alone. He would pick me up at 8 the next morning with pleasure. I later realized that he had a doctor's appointment and I asked him if he would allow me to take a taxi because it would make me happier so I wouldn't have to bother him. My sister who usually took a nap every day after her lunch hadn't gone to bed. She was waiting for me to return and tell her the story of the day. I had my delicious lunch that she prepared herself. Late every afternoon a group of our relatives usually came to visit me; I became very busy and enjoyed seeing everyone again after 12 years. The next day, my nephew and I returned to the office where I had been the day before. Fortunately the power was on; the dark building appeared bright and well lit. I could see many "sisters" coming and going and talking to each other respectfully and very kindly.

When I was called, I went in but didn't know which desk to go to. My name was called again from the corner of the next room and I followed the voice and found the woman. She was Sister Malihe. After greeting her, I introduced myself as Massoum Montakhab. Sister Malihe repeated my name and asked me if I was the Dean of the Institute of Paramedical Sciences or if I was her sister. I told her I was the one she was looking for, Massoum Montakhab. She kept staring into my eyes and with great anger said, "Do you know what you did to me?" I replied that I had no idea; as she could see, I was too old to remember. She said, "Don't play with me and don't try to fool me. Everyone said you were so smart, how come you don't recognize me now?"

At that moment I really couldn't think of anything except being arrested and put in jail. My hands started trembling; I felt very cold and started shivering. I tried very hard to keep myself together. Then she said, "Do you remember your room and the chair next to you? Don't you remember the day the results of the entrance exams were announced and I came to your room very angry with an envelope in my hand? You asked me why I was so angry." At that very moment, I was so scared I honestly couldn't even remember the location of my desk but I had to lie to her. So I said, "Yes, I remember; please tell me what you have in your mind now and what you had that day?" She said, "My name was not posted and I lost my chance to be accepted in Medical Technology. Further, you didn't pay any attention to the letter that I had from Dr. Ahmad, who introduced me to you and recommended me. You told me if Dr. Ahmad came and took your position then it would be his decision to make; but since that was not the case, you were unable to give the place of someone who passed the exam to me just to satisfy my goal."

I honestly had no recollection of that incident. How would you have reacted if you were in my shoes? I was scared to death; I wasn't able to sit and continue her trial and judgment and endure her anger. I decided to keep my face strong and show her no fear or weakness; I tried to change the subject by asking what her status was at the present time and how I admired her strength and Islamic belief. I told her I went to Mecca for an actual Hajj with my late daughter and my sister in 1979 and I explained a few philosophical views about my life before and after I left Iran. When I finished, she said, "That day when I left your office, I told myself 'If she could offer her position to my boss Dr. Ahmad who recommended me, she must be a deeply religious person' so I decided not to report you to the revolutionary guard." After that conversation we became friends and little by little my anxiety and fear started to dissipate. She asked me to stay until the noontime prayer was over and then she would look at my file and prepare the required documents.

As soon as she left the office some of the other sisters who didn't have to leave start talking to me, asking for advice about their health, diet and birth control. I asked them why they didn't talk to their doctors. One young, good looking woman told me birth control was forbidden and her husband kept reminding her that by Imam's order she was to conceive as many Muslim children as possible; she already had four children. To me, for such a young person with no help and a full-time job it would be too much and sometimes even overwhelming. I myself had three children but I had a great deal of help. I asked her if she had tried to convince her husband to stop further pregnancies. She said, "Believe me, no man could be found like those of your time. Anytime I try to discuss the future of our children his response is 'If you don't want to have any more children, I have a chance to have three more wives according to Islamic law.'"

After prayer was over Sister Malihe came back to prepare the necessary documents and give them to me. She told me that I had to take one of the documents to the Ministry of Health offices of the secret service. It would take a minimum of 15 working days to be approved. "After this letter has been approved and signed you must bring it back to this office. Then with this second letter, you must go to the office next door and they will stamp it. That would complete everything from the retirement department. Then you would go to the Office of Credit and Budget to receive your pension."

I got a taxi to return home. My problem was that I didn't know the directions. Although I had the postal address, the driver still asked me for directions. I told him I was a stranger in town, had just arrived and that I could give him the postal address but not the directions. The driver was very kind and told me not to worry; he would take me home this time but I should make sure I have the directions with me anytime I wanted to take a taxi. It was 4:30 when I got home and a few of our relatives were there waiting for me.

After I had my lunch, I joined them and started talking about all that had happened that day and the letter I had to take to the Ministry of Health secret service office. My niece suggested that I go to the office of the Secretary of Health and give the letter to his secretary who had been one of my sister's employees for about ten years before the revolution. Also, his cousin was the telephone operator at the Institute for about six years. The next day I left the house and went to the Ministry of Health by taxi. The person at the front desk asked me where I wanted to go and with whom I would like to meet. I told him I wanted to see Haji

Agha Ali (my sister's former employee). They called his office and gave him my name, then immediately sent me to the elevator. As the elevator door opened on the 6th floor, Haji Agha Ali was standing by the door to receive me. He took me to his office and I handed him the letter that was supposed to go to the secret service office. He called the secret service office himself and said something in Turkish that I could not understand. Then he sent my letter to an office located on the same floor that was really the secret service office. He started talking to me and kept asking about all of my grandchildren and their status in the US. He knew all of them while he worked in my sister's home. I didn't really know him personally and he had never worked with me but he helped me in appreciation of my sister during the 10 years in her house. I received my letter that should have taken 15 days in a matter of 15 minutes. I returned to Sister Malihe's office with the letter in my hand. This time everybody knew me; I had become friends with them so there was no fear, no anxiety and no cold sweat. They directed me to the next room.

I opened the door and saw two brothers, each one behind a desk. I greeted them and said I had a letter to be approved by them. Both of them had long beards; I didn't recognize them. I handed my letter to one of them and he looked at me, then signed and stamped the letter and gave it back to me. I asked him if this letter was a permit to enter Heaven. The one farthest away said, "You don't need this letter to enter Heaven; your name is already written on the arch of Heaven's door." I was quite surprised. The other brother said, "Dr. Montakhab, if there was one man in the Ministry of Health that one was you." (This is a Persian slogan that is used when a women has just as much power as a man.) I asked them, "Who are you, I don't recognize you." They told me they had been my students in Industrial Health at the Institute and today everyone "feels for you and admires your efforts." Then they said, "Please don't linger here; we would like to talk to you more and ask you about your daughters but it is forbidden." I went back to the women's office to say goodbye and wish them well as they did for me. I returned home by taxi. When I went to pay I found I had no money. My 5,000 toomans was gone; I only had 50 toomans and I needed to pay 1500. I asked the driver to wait and rushed into the house and asked my sister for 1500 toomans to pay the taxi driver. It was 2:30 pm on April 14, 1992. After lunch once again, my sister brought me a stack of money and told me that I needed much more because Iranian money had lost its value.

Everyone in my family asked me why I was in a hurry and why I couldn't stop working and enjoy my time there. My response at that time was the limitations due to Shayma's pregnancy.

I called my grand-nephew Akbar Ladievardi who had arranged my official paperwork and told him I would be ready to receive my pension at 8 am the next day. He said, "This part will be easy because I recommended you to the wife of my closest friend. She works in accounting, credit and budget of the retirement department located across from Tehran University. She will be waiting for you at 8:30 am the day after tomorrow." That morning I left the house at 7:45 and arrived right on time. The officer at the front desk told me to go to the 4th floor. There I found three rooms, I didn't know the woman I was to meet and my nephew couldn't describe her to me as he hadn't met her either. The first room was an office of women. I entered and greeted them all and then asked for sister Afsar. They told me she was on leave. I said I didn't think so because she was to meet with me at 8:30 and it was now 8:40. From the other side of the room one of the ladies said, "Don't you know? She is in labor at this very moment." I was very surprised and told her that my appointment had been arranged the night before. She said that she had probably gone into labor after that. I believed her big lie and left the room.

I went back to the front desk and asked for the manager of the accounting department and was shown to his office. I knocked on the door and entered. After greeting each other I introduced myself. He was a modern, well-educated revolutionary officer. He told me very politely that although this money was mine, there was a rule that it was to be paid in three or four installments. But if I agreed he would pay me half today and the other half in one month. I had to accept the offer because the woman who was his assistant was in labor. He wrote me a check for half the amount. I thanked him and left his office. It was less than 15 feet from his office that I saw a very good-looking but a little chubby woman with at least four different scarves on top of each other and a black chadoor over everything standing in the hallway. As soon as she saw me she called my name. We greeted each other and she told me she had been waiting there since 8:30. I asked her if she was the same lady that was in the delivery room a while ago. With great surprise, she said, "What?" I told her what I had been told and explained about the two installment payments. She apologized for the action of her colleague and then said, "Can you believe what kind of people I have to deal with every day?" If I had responded, "Why do you?" her response would have been, "Why did you act as an anti-revolutionary?" So instead I told her to not criticize the girl who lied to me; let her be happy for what she did and what she believed in. I didn't mind coming back again for my second check. I appreciated her efforts. She promised to do her best for me and she did. She later called my nephew and informed him that I could go back to the same office and receive the check for the rest of my pension in a week instead of 4 weeks. Although she was one of the revolutionaries herself, she was broadminded enough to know the difference between an evil attitude and the act of an honest person no matter what their religious beliefs.

Selling my House

My next plan was to sell the remaining household goods and keep those that had sentimental value for me. Nikou was still in the United States and I decided to wait until she arrived before I sold anything. Therefore, I decided to prepare everything that was required for the sale of the apartment; I assumed that would be the easiest task of all. It was only a dream - as the usual story of my life, it didn't happen as I had planned. It was very complicated. I couldn't find the deed to the apartment; a crucial document for the sale of the unit because the tax clearance and city tax all depended on the deed. I looked everywhere but as much as I searched I couldn't find the deed. I had found Minoo's handwritten note in one of the chest-of-drawers in Nikou's apartment but the deed no longer existed in the world. I even went to the post office dead letter center in case it had gotten lost during the move. I had no success whatsoever.

Finally, I decided to apply for a copy of the deed but this appeared to be impossible. During the period of instability and violence a lot of counterfeit copies were smuggled in and absentees' properties were sold. This process was easy for the revolutionaries because no ID card was ever required. It was especially easy when a woman was involved in the transaction because no males were allowed to look at the woman's face closely. When I applied to buy the apartment originally, I had to write the name of the buyer and any heir's names to follow in order. Since my name, Minoo's name and Nikou's name were on the original application, we all had to be present in the city Office of Record to obtain a copy. How could I find Minoo? She had flown away from us and left this world almost seven years beforehand and Nikou was in the US. I had no choice so I told the city office manager that I had called my two daughters to come to Iran but they had prior obligations. He advised me that the best thing would be to hire an attorney. I returned to my sister's house where I was staying and remembered that one of my colleagues introduced me to a gentleman who was an expert in this area. The next day, I went to him and told him my story. He said the charge would be 60,000 toomans (about $6,000) in advance. He would research the situation and let me know within two days. I accepted the deal and two days later he called and said, "Doctor, it is a very difficult and unpredictable situation. Although Mr. Ghaffari introduced you to me, I must tell you I am not able to do it."

Fortunately I had plenty of time; I had no job assignment to be worried about. I kept looking for another person to help me but I had been out of the country for twelve years and I didn't know anyone. Those with whom I was acquainted had either been dismissed, had retired, had left Iran or were dead. It was imperative that I find some reliable person to accept help me. My great-nephew came to visit me and I asked him for help. He mentioned a gentleman, Brother Ahmad, who was working for a title company. He recommended him as a hard worker, honest and reliable person. Early the next morning, I went to the title company and introduced myself and told the man my story. He said not to worry, he could take care of it but it would cost me 100,000 toomans. I had no other choice so I accepted the deal. He then told me he needed one week. He took all my information and some related documents but didn't ask for any money in advance. I returned home and waited for him to call me.

A week passed and then a month with no word from Brother Ahmad. I went to the title company every morning for 30 days and kept asking for him and was told he would be in the office the next day for sure. One day I accidentally found him on the street close to his office. I started talking to him and he told me I'd better come to the office (it was against Islamic law to even talk with a known relative on the street). I went to his office and he apologized for the delay. He told me he had gone on a trip and forgotten about me completely. I asked him to please help me. If he could direct me to where and to whom I should go and ask for my copy of the deed; I was ready to do it myself as I was really pressed for time. I would be very happy to pay for whatever was necessary. He started thinking and then asked me if I had a car, I told him, "No - I came by bus." Brother Ahmad then told me if I could sit in the back of his car like a passenger, he would take me to the city center. I told him, "Brother, I would do it with great respect to the country's law."

We went to the city office of records and reprints and he asked the receptionist to call Sister Fatimeh to come down to the waiting room. After a short time a woman in modern Islamic dress, black in color, covered from head to toe came to the waiting room. I don't think they had met before, as they didn't seem to recognize each other. Although it was almost 13 years after the revolution they still hid their identities and their actual names and used the words Brother, Sister, Haji Agha and Haji Khanoom. Sister Fatimeh came to us and introduced herself to me. She had well-prepared eye make up, dark blue eye glasses and a very fine light face make up and light pink nail polish under black gloves (I saw the color because the tip of one glove finger was open). Brother Ahmad asked her to please take good care of "my cousin, Haji Khanoom." She left the waiting room in a rush, took me to her office and asked me why I was looking for the reprint. I tried to tell her the story of my recent life and the reason why I still lived in the US with my two granddaughters. She told me she would introduce me not only as her cousin but also as a very close family friend of her own mother. She never asked for any money and advised me not to pay anyone unless she told me to and how much to pay. In the meantime, she asked me whether my daughters could come to Iran because it would be necessary for them to be present when the reprint was ready to be picked up.

Fortunately Shaparak had graduated from medical school and I had offered her a round trip ticket to Iran as a gift. Nikou decided to accompany her for the last fifteen days of my trip to Iran and we would all return to the states together. (Nikou was worried about me and thought I might not receive an exit visa from the government. That is why they had agreed to come to Tehran for such a short period - to make sure there would be no problem for me.) So I promised her they would be in Tehran on time. She started to work facilitating whatever was necessary. She prepared and finished everything at her end in a matter of 10 days. Then she sent me to another office and introduced me to another woman. She was as active as Sister Fatimeh had been. At this office they had to advertise my request for the reprint in two famous nightly newspapers for two weeks in order for everyone who had a claim for this property to come forward.

Finally all the lawful steps were accomplished and the results transferred to Sister Fatimeh's office in the city records and reprints center. Meanwhile they found out that 8-9 years beforehand one of the title companies applied for a title insurance search. Although no transaction had been made, I had to obtain a confirmation letter from that particular title company. Thus Sister Fatimeh kindly asked me to follow up personally and bring the letter to her office. I was very lucky that this particular title company remained active. If it had been closed by the government as so many others had been, I wouldn't have been able to get my reprint whatsoever. A woman from Sister Fatimeh's office found me the correct address so I wouldn't wander around the area the whole day looking for the office. I took a taxi to the address but I couldn't find the office because there was no sign for the title company and no building number. The building was 5-6 stories with no elevator and the height of each step was 3-4 times the height of modern steps. You can imagine how hard it was to climb up to the third or fourth or fifth floor and see no sign and then return down to the street and start asking about it. Many shopkeepers said there was never any such title company in this area. Another said, "I saw such a title company but on another street far from here." I was so tired and confused and disappointed because on each floor I had observed no movement and all the doors were locked – I thought maybe they were all vacant. I told myself, "It is almost 11 am so I'd better try all over again" and decided to climb up all the way to the top floor. When I got to the 5th floor I saw a tall middle-aged gentleman standing in the middle of the hallway. I asked him to please show me where this title company was located. He smiled and said, "You are in its hallway." I said, "How come there is no sign?" He asked me if I had come from abroad since "it is very odd that someone doesn't know about her surroundings." I agreed with him but told him that my only request was to see the manager of the company. He told me to go inside the main office and talk to the man facing me. I entered and greeted everyone in the Iranian custom. Around the room shoulder to shoulder were men of all different ages sitting and waiting for something to be done for them. I went to the man in charge of the books and showed him the letter from the city records and reprints office, and then with much respect I asked him for a confirmation letter. He laughed at me in a very cold-blooded way and told me it would take at least one month to find this record and confirm its status. I tried to convince him that I had a time limit and he said, "I don't care, I'm busy; don't you see how many people are waiting here?" I asked him to let me explain my problem and he said," Lady, it's from 8 or 9 years ago; all of our books are in storage; I have no time for this kind of work. I told you no less than one month but it may take longer." Meanwhile the gentleman that I met in the hallway came in while I was begging him to learn the name of the manager. The tall gentleman came forward and started talking to me while I kept asking for the manager. As he mentioned his name, Tabatabai, I asked him if he knew Mohsen Kamari. He said, "Yes, he is my cousin, how do know him?" I said, "He is my former son-in-law." Then he asked me if I was Minoo's mother. I said, "Unfortunately, yes" and started crying hard. He cried with me and started talking about her with great respect while all the men around the room were standing and some of them had tears in their eyes. Mr. Tabatabai took my arm as special respect, directed me to his office and ordered cold water for me and tea for himself. He explained that they had removed the sign to remain unknown to the revolutionary guard. He wrote a guarantee letter of confirmation to the city records and reprints office in a matter of 45 minutes. It was 2 pm when I returned home, feeling exhausted and helpless.

That day was the middle of the second week that Shaparak and Nikou were in Iran. Nikou had spent four days in bed with a temperature of 103oF and now it was Shaparak's turn. She spent five days in bed with a severe headache and 103oF temperature. We were all supposed to leave Iran in a matter of 8 days. I took the letter to Sister Fatimeh the next day. She asked for my two daughters to be present to receive the reprint of authenticity and to sign the book in front of a notary public. But Shaparak couldn't make it - she was still in bed. Nikou and I were present in the office of the notary public but not Shaparak. Sister Fatimeh came and said that she thought that two out of three could make a majority. We could sign, then she would record it and give it to us. So after almost 75 days of the constant effort of Sister Fatimeh, her crew and myself I finally received the reprint. At the end we both hugged her and prayed for her success. I handed her an envelope that contained a good chunk of money and promised her that the money was not a bribe; it was a gift to show my appreciation of her efforts, honesty, help and kindness. I had had to do the same for everyone; otherwise I would not have achieved my goal.

To me Sister Fatimeh was one of the very rare women that proved her hard work, her friendship and most importantly, her real honesty. She worked with full power and pride. She was not afraid of anyone and made no mistakes in her decisions or her actions. I am very grateful to her. Although I never met her again, I always pray to God to bless her soul and her heart and give her health and happiness wherever she lives.

But this would not be the end of the amazing story about the sale of my property. Just about the time the title papers became ready I had to leave Tehran. I found out that one of the most potential buyers didn't wait and bought another apartment. The second buyer left for Europe for his own business and the third buyer postponed the deal due to a family emergency.

So I had a plan to sell the remainder of my household goods during Nikou's fifteen days in Tehran. As soon as she arrived I decided to find someone who was in the business and knew us from before. One day on the way to the city records and reprints office I happened upon a jewelry maker who used to deal with Nikrou and come to her office to present her with jewelry that she had ordered. He recognized me and he started asking about Nikrou, her husband and her son. In return I asked him what his status was at the present time. He said, "I am in the business of buying and selling household goods." I was elated, gave him my phone number and asked him to give me a call. Fortunately with no problems and with peace of mind, I sold whatever I couldn't keep. The rest of my own heritage I collected for my present and future trips to Iran to smuggle out and away from the revolutionary guard. On that trip I decided to take as much of the valuable silverware that we all had because it was allowed to be taken out of the country. We were three people, each with two suitcases and we left Tehran in a hurry with mixed feelings of real fear of, for no reason, my passport confiscation. We all forgot about whatever we could carry with ourselves other than the silver items and the saffron. We left Tehran on June 30th via British Airways at 1 am and arrived at LAX at 2 pm the same day.

Two months after we had returned from Tehran Shayma's son Cameron was born on September 2, 1992 in Corona, California. That day was and still is and I believe it will always remain one of the most bittersweet days of our lives. On that particular day, calculating the time difference between the moment that Minoo in Detroit and Mr. Mahmood Mortazavi (grandfather of Cameron) in Tehran stepped out of this world and the time that Cameron stepped in, you can imagine why this boy is so dear to all of us. We believed God sent us Cameron as a gift to exchange our sadness resulting from their absence for the happiness of Cameron's presence.

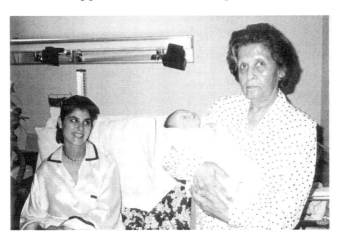

My granddaughter Shayma and my first great grandson Cameron

Cameron Mortazavi, now 15 yrs. old

Second Trip to Iran in 1992

In October of 1992 Nikou's husband decided to visit his mother in Iran after 10 years and to finalize the sale of their apartment. At the same time, a potential buyer applied for my apartment. So I returned to Iran on November 1st to take care of my own business of selling the apartment. In those days, none of the title companies was allowed to make any transactions for the value of more than one million toomans using a Power of Attorney. Therefore, the presence of the owner was compulsory. As soon as I arrived in Tehran, I started to collect all the required papers - property tax was delinquent for 2-3 years, city tax and a few other taxes were also due. I tried as hard as I could to finish the process of selling and presenting every required letter to the title company. Meanwhile I received a message that the buyer had to leave the country and go to Tokyo to attend a special business meeting. I was so disappointed and frustrated, I told my sister to let the apartment remain vacant because I had to return to the US. Nikou and I had planned to establish a diagnostic service laboratory and I could not leave her alone to take care of everything for the lab or to take care of all the repairs at home resulting from a broken hot water pipe. My brother-in-law to (Azam's husband) whom I owed more than anyone could believe advised me not to leave my property vacant because someone would occupy it and no one could do anything to eject him or her except me. If I rented it, it would be next to impossible to vacate the apartment in less than 2–3 years after their occupancy.

I was not brave enough to ask him to help because he strongly refused any involvement due to his previous sad stories in jail. At the onset of the revolution, no one differentiated the innocent from the criminal. He refused because he didn't want to see anyone who worked with the revolutionary government. Therefore, he spent all his time at home or with those who were working at his orchard outside of Tehran. I became very upset that after all the hard work to solve a lot of problems and spending so much effort and lots of money I was going to return to the US empty handed, without the apartment sold. At lunch as we sat together at the dining table, I was not able to eat or to talk; I was thinking, "How can I afford to come back again?" Meanwhile my brother-in-law asked me why I wasn't happy and what was going on in my mind. I told him, "Two things are bothering me. First of all Nasser offered me a price that was half the actual price today and then for only two thirds of it because originally Nikou's name was on the title. As you all know she never lived with me and never paid any money for it. The second reason is the hardship of the trip itself, which took 28–30 hours, and the cost of the airfare. And the third is that I need the money." Then he told me to enjoy my lunch and "Be happy you don't know your fate. Although it is against my wishes, if you are so concerned you'd better go on and get everything ready and in order and acceptable for the title company. Then sell it to me on paper (no money involved) and I will try to sell it as soon as a potential buyer comes forward. Then I'll send the proceeds to you via a bank." I immediately accepted the deal with great appreciation and started to prepare everything for the title company. Fortunately, since everything was in order, the sales transaction was completed the next day. As required, when I handed the deed and the other necessary papers to the title company, the computer manager searched the "forbidden list" to make sure my name was not there; then I was free to complete my business transaction and I did.

On that trip which took 45 days, I worked day and night and tried to manage and finish everything that I didn't have time for before. I thought of everything except the cottage that, according to an agreement written in February 1980, I had to transfer the formal title to my sister's name.

I returned to the US from that strange trip with my 13-year-old great-niece, Negar, who was my third adopted daughter (the first two were Shaparak and Shayma). I took advantage of her company and placed too many valuable items in our four suitcases. I placed my two antique Faberge lamps in a hardback case and carried two delicate crystal shades in our large handbag. One bag was for Negar to carry and one for me. With all four suitcases, two carry-on and one big handbag each, we left Tehran on December 10, 1992. One week earlier, Nasser had returned to the US but he did not carry anything of theirs in his suitcase because he was afraid of the revolutionary inspectors. Everything I placed in my suitcases had high sentimental value for me because the pieces were all inherited from my parents and my grandmother. Fortunately, none of the revolutionary guard bothered to look inside of our suitcases but they were very hard on some of the other old women who were going to visit their children in England. We passed all the security very easily in Iran and arrived in the US at 3 pm on the same day. We passed US customs and immigration with no problems. Nikou and Nikrou drove to LAX to pick us up. When I received my own two suitcases, I found the hardback case was broken badly. The two lamps, which I smuggled, my own inheritance from Mullah, were in that case. The other bag was intact. On the way, home Nikou tried to comfort me about the probable broken lamps. Nevertheless, we were greatly surprised to find both lamps intact although the suitcase was completely broken in pieces.

The Forbidden List

On February 12, 1993 my sister called me to warn me not to travel to Iran anymore. She told me that my name had been added to the "Forbidden List" and had appeared on the government's computerized list. I thought she was just kidding with me, but it didn't take long until my paternal niece Maheen wrote me that my name was on "the list" for sure. She went to the same title company for her own business. The computer manager checked her identity on the computer and on the screen my niece saw my name because she carried the same last names as I did. The manager was very surprised and asked her if she knew why this happened. She responded that she had never been informed of this before. Although it was very easy for my family to say "so what," it was not easy to believe how much this bothered my sister Azam and how much I suffered later on.

My paternal niece and closest friend,
Maheen Montekhabi, Irvine, CA, 2001

The story of my name on the forbidden list that appeared on the computer screen of the title company was not an unimportant matter to be neglected or dismissed. Because it had been

transferred from the central computer of the revolutionary government, that meant there was a great deal of accusation, resulting in me being prohibited from many activities, dismissed from
any position and also strongly prevented from exiting the country unless the charges could be disproved. I never understood
how or why such a strong falsified report reached the central
computer. Who tried to make my hands dirty and my face ugly
and accused me of whatever they wished to see? I had no idea. I
could only assume that it was my former son-in-law Nasser,
under the influence of some revolutionary woman who he had
to marry in an honest way, to prove that he would be one of the
revolutionaries until he could get a high ranking job. Later it
was proven to me that he succeeded in confiscating my grandson Adib's cottage and prevented my sister from finalizing the
transfer of the deal under her name according to the agreement
letter that we all (including him) signed in 1980 when all the
title companies were closed by the order of the revolutionary
government. The agreement was valid and she could transfer
the title under her name; otherwise the gardener's family
wouldn't let her in as it was common in those days to ask for the
original owner. I believe someone sent a written report to the
government that I was very close to the Shah and Queen Farah
and always spent time with them. That resulted in a massive
investigation for the revolutionary government and a great deal
of trouble and fear for my sister and me so that I couldn't return
to Iran for eight years again.

It is true that I had the Shah's support for all the progress
that I had made in the establishment of the Institute of
Paramedical Sciences. The original document of my proposal
for the formation of such an institution of higher education and
the reform in the system of allied medical professions was sent
to his office first and then to the Ministry of Science and Higher
Education. If I didn't know the route to his office my project
would never have been approved by that ministry no matter
how many supporters I had among the approval community. I
will never forget the final day of the committee meeting when

the late Secretary of Higher Education came in and told the committee members that they were two and he was the third member, so in the absence of the two other members that didn't attend in order to show they were against the project, a majority (three out of five members) was met. He said, "Before she reports to our boss's main office that her project is still pending, please give her final approval." They all congratulated me and wished me a successful future.

It took eight years and the help of my sister to disprove this accusation against me to the satisfaction of the government so my name could be removed from the forbidden list and I could return to Iran without any problems. It would be an untold story of why my family and I should suffer and face that many problems. There were so many whys that lay in between multiple difficulties. They reported me to the government so that they could include my name on the forbidden list to prevent my entry into the country because Nasser believed my power of telling the truth and convincing everyone that (1) the cottage he had confiscated had belonged to a 3-year-old boy Adib who was now twenty; and (2) Nasser had lived in the United States himself for 10 years and had become a US citizen. It was very unfortunate that this foolish corrupted person pulled off such a shameful crime when he had a developed garden of the same size under his own son's name right next to the one he confiscated. And when someone criticized him about it he replied, "I tried to keep it for them until they returned to Iran" while he reported that Ali, the innocent father of my grandson, was the right hand of the Shah. Furthermore he caused a lot of anxiety and frustration for my sister and her husband so she couldn't sell the cottage for eleven years. I will never forget the night that my sister called and told me the Superior Court of the revolutionaries called for her and me. She said, "I decided to go there to finalize the situation but my husband didn't want to allow me to go." I started talking to my brother-in-law and understood why he hesitated to go to the court. I told him to please try to understand what I was trying to tell him; "Please let my sister go to the court, give my name, address and telephone number to the judge and tell him that she would be willing to bring her sister Massoum Montakhab to the court If they gave her 24 hours so she could get from San Diego and to Tehran then to the court. I know that it wasn't easy for them because the revolutionaries could slap you in jail for no reason with no set time for release and no visitors. In those days everyone was scared to get close to the court to defend me. I got all my 12 years of accumulated retirement money in two installments one week apart; I got the copy of the deed for my apartment and sold it; and most importantly I took all my own belongings out of the country. Don't you think those things were enough for my name to be on the forbidden list of the government rather than to be accused of a friendship with the Shah of Iran and Queen Farah? If I had such a chance at friendship, I would have been very proud of it.

Despite all the problems along the way, life goes on. But it would be even better if it continued with an honest reputation and with pride.

Chapter 20

History of Molecular Diagnostic Services, Inc. and Its Subsidiary, Rabbit and Rodent Diagnostic Associates

Molecular Diagnostics Services, Inc. (MDS) was established in 600 square feet at 11545 Sorrento Valley Rd, Suite # 305B. It was located on the second floor with such a narrow and winding stairway that we could hardly move our two small office desks in. It took almost three months to prepare everything and make it a usable lab. All the furniture and equipment had been bought from UCSD surplus or other second-hand equipment shops. The incubator and laminar flow hood had to be brought up through the glass window by an electric lifting machine. An inverted microscope that we still use for cell cultures was brought by a sales person for us to try; the person never returned to pick it up or sell it to us.

It reminded me of an event in January of 1993 while we were busy organizing MDS. We happened to visit a friend who was a successful South African entrepreneur. We talked about life in San Diego and I mentioned the establishment of MDS. He told me the story of his successful business that started in the smallest place possible; when his wife, Anna, a professional seamstress decided to open her own shop. She transformed her inherited multifunctional sewing machine into a shop. She used her perfect taste in decorating the shelves with rather large white boxes that had been labeled with different color ribbons for each group of children. She bought a few yard of related fabric and made a complete set of dresses for young boys, girls and infants. She hung them up in the shop. On the widow she wrote, "Clothes for Girls, Boys and Newborn" and she used multicolor glittering ink. It attracted many people passing by the shop. They would stop by to talk to Anna and would leave rather quickly. One day, the first customer entered the shop at 5:30 pm and asked for a pair of bibs, one in pink and another in blue, but Anna only had one in white. She promised to make and deliver the colored bibs to the woman's residence no later than 8 am the next day. If the customer would pay for them then, they would have a deal. Anna made the bibs and placed each one in a proper sized box and decorated it with many colored ribbons. She delivered right on time. From that day on, the number of customers increased so they had no time to rest. People placed their orders and received their items the next day in a very presentable and neat way. It didn't take long before the two owners and the one sewing machine changed to 40 sewing machines and 50 workers. They named their shop the Children's Clothier Factory.

First week of MDS set-up, February 1993
Visiting friend Firoozeh, Nikou and me

That was the thing that attracted our attention - to keep all of the boxed kits and related items on the MDS visible shelves. Today they have all been replaced with the copies of complete experiment reports to our customers. During the period of establishment Nikou kept gathering, developing and writing laboratory procedures, molecular standard operating procedures, radioactive guidelines, etc. to submit to the Health Department to be eligible for permits and to receive a license for use of radioactive materials. In other words she prepared all the baseline information that was required to establish a biotech service laboratory for any kind of job related to biotechnology in general.

In the mean time, one of her former students and technicians who had been on vacation in Vietnam when Nikou resigned from UCSD came to our house to thank her for the training he received in DNA analysis. Nikou explained to him her future plans and her decisions. A few days later he called and politely asked for advice and guidelines in purchasing a computer retail shop. Nikou said retail shops didn't appeal to her. She advised him that it would be better if he worked in his area of study to receive good training and become skilled at it. A few weeks later he came to our future laboratory with a box of Sees candy and told us that he had changed his mind in purchasing a computer retail shop and asked us if he could join us and become a partner. He also wanted to work in the lab as a technician. Due to our situation at that period of time (both of us were out of jobs and Nikou's bank account became inactive because of her marital status) we decided to accept his partnership for a maximum of 10%. Nikou suggested that he keep his job and come to the lab after work every day and stay late until the business grew enough and became fruitful to pay him for a full time job.

It was a great idea for him so he kept coming to the lab every afternoon or early evening and asking about the laboratory facilities, equipment and other requirements. He started evaluating whatever we bought and criticized the purchase of the incubator and laminar flow hood. He believed they were useless. On the other hand he was "planning to reduce the number of heads" and at that time I wondered what he was talking about. We were only two and he himself would be the third. Who would be the extra person to get rid of?

One Friday afternoon he came in with an Apple computer on his shoulder. He said it was bought at an auction for $500 and he wanted to keep it for himself and install it on one of the lab desks. A few days later he asked for an extra key because he planned to stay and finish a job no matter how late it would be at night. At that time he never pretended to be interested in partnership. Instead he kept asking for all the equipment lists to see where and when we purchased them, what the price was, and he copied the sales slips. At the same time, he was busy collecting all the information that Nikou prepared and left on her own computer hard disk drive. When he achieved his goal in copying whatever he needed to establish his own business, he asked Nikou whether he could have 50% rather than 10% of the shares. That was entirely unacceptable to us and also to our business attorney. He quit coming for a few days and he finally came at night, picked up his computer and left without saying goodbye or handing in the key. So we had to change all the locks. Later we found that he bought an automatic DNA analyzer, leased a place and started working and breaking down the market value of DNA analysis to 30%. However, those who believed in manual DNA analysis kept their relationship with us in good faith. But we lost all the companies whose leaders were Far East born.

Meanwhile, a lot of time and effort was required to prepare a pamphlet to advertise the formation of our biotech service lab and make it acceptable to large companies, our colleagues and peers. That wasn't an easy task, with Nikou's knowledge and constant effort, a very simple pamphlet was completed and mailed to the drug companies as well as biotechnology laboratories and their scientists in the area. We purchased as many name and address labels as we could and mailed out pamphlets; we performed no radio or television ads because of our budget limitations.

One of the surprising responses to our advertisement had to do with the pricing of blood CBC analysis that was only $4. We had written that MDS offered free sample pick up and free delivery of the results without clarification of a minimum number of samples. As soon as the pamphlet was distributed, we received a lot of local telephone calls for pick up. One of them was from a University for pick up of a single CBC blood sample. This pick up had to be by FedEx overnight, which cost us $15. Looking back, it was really a funny business situation - $4 gross income versus $15 expense. Nikou thought it would be better to ignore it, but I said it would be bad for our business ethics. It was written in our advertisement and we had to stand by it and respect our word and the honesty of our business no matter the loss for this test today. For sure we could get it later on. We called FedEx to pick up the sample overnight and paid $15 COD and started testing the blood. We found it was everything except blood so Nikou decided to return the sample to the University with no $4 charge for it. She called the scientist who sent it and informed her that during 25 years of working experience in a diagnostic laboratory, this was the first time she had seen this kind of so-called blood sample. The scientist told her that her diagnosis was very much accepted and valued. It was a fake blood sample they sent to evaluate the accuracy of MDS' work. The first "real" batch of blood samples that we received from that University was worth $4,000 and since then, they have remained one of our customers for many different tests. Indeed, we made up for that $15 COD expense!

It didn't take long for us to receive the first cell culture sample to grow in very large scale that brought more than $120,000 worth of work in less than two months. MDS had been recommended to that biotech firm by an Iranian scientist, Dr. Vafa Kamali, upon his belief of our honest and accurate performance.

In May of 1993 my grandson Adib M. Nasle from Detroit sent me a paper that announced many different grants and contracts from NIH. Among them was a microbiology project contract of half a million dollars worth for a period of five years duration specified for "a small business owned by women." So we were eligible to apply for a perfect and suitable grant for MDS. To follow the requirement and complete its formulation we needed to invite a group of scientists to make a team which at that point of time we didn't have because MDS had just started in March 1993. We received the project information at the end of May with a deadline in September of the same year. We invited a group of scientists including a board-certified veterinarian, a toxicologist, a microbiologist, an immunologist, etc., each one with great experience and expertise. They accepted our invitation and introduced other scientists and consultants that are still working with MDS today. Among them an invited toxicologist called and told us he had no time except Sunday and was very interested to work with MDS. So he came to our house Sunday morning, got every single bit of information about the project, then he recommended a woman veterinarian to us and left. Although that veterinarian was unable to join us because of her fulltime job commitment, she introduced us to another woman veterinarian, Dr. Alexandra C. Bakarich, who lived in Ramona, northeast of San Diego. When Nikou called her, she invited us to her residence as she wanted to meet us before she joined MDS.

It was Saturday morning of the next week when we visited her. During that short meeting we really enjoyed talking to her and admired her knowledge and expertise in general. Dr. Bakarich and other scientists gathered and reviewed every item of the contract and prepared the related text. The budget analysis had been done by an expert according to the instructions provided. Nikou even added the name of the suppliers and the materials that had been planned to be used in that project. None of the scientists charged us except the budget analyst and that wasn't much but it was a relatively great expense in those days. The completed project was sent to NIH before the deadline. We were expecting the results later on, but we found out that the toxicologist who came to our house on that Sunday reported the project to another company and they applied for the grant as well. They won the bid by $2000 difference in price despite our being a small business owned by women. For sure, we were eligible but NIH believed that our team had not worked together long enough. Despite our first time experience in this regard, we made an offer that was so perfect and the pricing was so accurate that the difference was less than $2000. That brought us a lot of courage, confidence, knowledge, experience, friendship, and above all we were grateful to God that instead of such disappointment, we found wonderful colleagues who have joined us since 1993 without any expectation of partnership and any demand of fee for service or salary for two or more years.

Dr. Bakarich had lived in Iran from age 11-15 during the period that her father Mr. Creel worked as an expert petroleum engineer in Abadan in the southern part of Iran. She attended an Iranian school and learned Farsi and she still sings a perfect rendition of the old Iranian National Anthem. She has become a very close personal friend of our family. Not only is she a great scientist and board-certified veterinarian, one of her favorite hobbies is photography. She made a wonderful photo album from Negar's wedding that is beautifully hand-crafted and very eye-catching. Dr. Bakarich, Nikou and I worked seriously and earned no income for almost two years, but we were able to pay for routine expenses, equipment, supplies and so on. It was 1994 that one of the very famous Canadian Biotech companies approached MDS to negotiate a large-scale contract for cell culture. Every item proposed by the client company was reviewed by MDS consultants and agreed upon. Even the confidentiality letters were signed and a woman scientist who was the project manager called and made an appointment to come to the US and visit our facility. We had every single item she required except the large space. MDS had only 600 square feet of space and we were sure it would not be appealing to a big company. We were lucky that a large space (more than 2000 square feet) underneath the MDS building became vacant about that time and we leased it immediately and were able to buy more equipment. We equipped the new space for other tests and allocated the upper level to a cell culture facility, which was set from the first day we started. So, with no exaggeration or fabrication it was a perfect and rather modern laboratory. The Canadian scientist arrived at MDS on April 10th and visited both the upper and lower level laboratories and admired the well functional facilities. She returned to Canada to send us her purchase order including the signed contract. As soon as she arrived at her office she found that the entire business had been sold out confidentially. She sent us a letter with great regret and apology for what had happened. We all felt for her but at the same time we were worried about how we were going to pay the rent as we now had a two-year lease.

At 5 am on April 5th, 1995 I received an unexpected phone call from Japan. It was Professor Takeo Wada, our family friend. He said that one of his former students, Dr. Satoko Ishida, had lost her husband to cancer and had decided to contribute a lump some of money to a laboratory that Professor Wada believed to be in the hands of expert scientists. So, he recommended MDS. Two days later, we received the first grant money from Sapporo Medical School of Japan.

Professor Takeo and Mrs. Yuriko Wada

Dr. Ishida and her husband Professor Ishida

A few weeks later, someone was trying to reach a company who made robots and was located next door to MDS. Nikou happened to answer the phone and the caller asked for the phone number of the company they wanted. Nikou didn't have the company's phone number but promised to have them return his call. So she went to the company that was located next door to MDS. That company had quit making robots, but he asked Nikou how MDS was running. Nikou told him the story of the Canadian company and the expense that MDS had incurred for rent for two years. He advised Nikou to sublease the space or at least part of the MDS lab. By afternoon of that lucky day, a group of very famous and successful scientists came to MDS to see the space and the facility and the chief scientist said that there was not any item that they needed that MDS didn't have. He suggested we make a very simple lease contract for two years and sign it right then. They leased the entire second floor and part of the first floor. They also made a contract with MDS to make the solutions they needed; that created a lot of work and generated a good income for MDS. This was very beneficial to us, because it brought in a lot of support for us.

Dr. Alexandra C. Bakarich, our colleague, diplomate in Laboratory Animal Medicine, and the editor of this manuscript

Shortly thereafter Nikou discussed with Dr. Bakarich the possibility of establishing a division for research animals, perhaps eventually establishing a vivarium to function as a contract research organization. Thus, Rabbit and Rodent Diagnostic Associates (RRDA) was established as a subsidiary of MDS.

A few months later Nikou and Dr. Bakarich went to Las Angeles to attend a national AALAS meeting (American Association for Laboratory Animal Science) and they were introduced to a scientist who was in charge of expansion and development of an in vivo laboratory for his own company.

After they returned, the scientist contacted Nikou and started negotiations that ended up with a year contract between that company and MDS. The services that MDS preformed for them were perfect but the technician in charge was not happy with the rules and regulations that had to be applied to the in vivo lab by Nikou and Dr. Bakarich. She constantly ignored the regulations and made daily complaints to the scientist in charge, until the contract was completed; at the end of that year, upon the technician's recommendation another company replaced MDS. But it didn't take long before she was laid off and started to work for MDS as a consultant for 2-3 years. Shortly after termination of the contract with that company, another company approached MDS and asked for in vivo laboratory space to use and insisted a large area. The establishment of an in vivo lab required a large area to lease, a lot of equipment and supplies to buy, countless rules and regulations to write, a few more consultants to invite to work with us, and more skilled technicians to hire and teach on-the-job. The demand for in vivo lab space was so great that the MDS decided to do it. The RRDA vivarium opened for business in the new 4,188 square foot facility that MDS leased, located at 4202 Sorrento Valley Blvd., about 10 minutes away. The building had four complete suites, one main laboratory and one large washroom.

At the beginning of 2001 a project was announced by the Environmental Protection Agency (EPA) and Nikou and her assistant spent a lot of time and effort to make a very well prepared grant to present to EPA. The bid was accepted and the winner was MDS. We all were happy because this kind of grant continued at least for five years, but MDS lost its chance because of the September 11th incident. The person in charge was replaced and the new person, without any concern about his predecessor's signature or promise, offered the grant to another laboratory whose bid was either next to ours or probably he had favoritisms towards them. Since that time, the RRDA vivarium has become accredited by the Association for the Assessment and

Accreditation of Laboratory Animal Care International and continues to serve the surrounding laboratory animal community.

On September 18, 2001 MDS relocated its entire laboratory to 4204 Sorrento Valley Blvd., Suite G in 6000 square feet of space next to the RRDA vivarium.

Some of the scientists, staff and technicians the day MDS moved to its present location, 2001

I can say today, on July 16, 2006, MDS is 14 and RRDA is 11 years old, and now has more than 11,000 square feet rather then 600 at its inception on December 24, 1992. Instead of two permanent scientists, "a mother and her daughter" (Nikou and I), it now consists of 25 permanent scientists, board-certified veterinarians, physicians, and technicians, in addition to a group of consultants who work with MDS and RRDA upon appointment. The customers of both MDS and RRDA come from the local community, other states and also from Europe, Asia and the Far East. Their knowledge of MDS is through word of mouth and upon the recommendation of those who tested MDS and received complete accuracy in presenting the results of their experiments. The provide services in compliance with GLP regulations for both in vivo and in vitro toxicology, angiogenesis, transfection, and expression complimented by cellular and molecular biology, protein analysis, PK studies and many more advanced testing projects.

I no longer perform necropsies or other lab work but I maintain office hours at MDS, assist with office administration and remain on the Board of Directors. Dr. Bakarich has retired for a second time and has moved to North Carolina but she is in constant contact with us and still continues to actively work with MDS and RRDA as a consultant.

*Mr. and Mrs. Creel, parents of Dr. Bakarich,
talking with Prince Gholam, Abadan, Iran*

Dr. Bakarich at Negar's wedding

Final Thoughts

Despite everything that has occurred, my continuous work has helped keep me in high spirits and prevent me from breaking down during the sad times that I have faced. I have always had a great desire to create something that could be considered unique if I could grab the opportunity to do it. As long as I can walk, talk, and think in a proper way I will keep trying anything and everything possible because my mind and my curiosity are still alive. So I feel lucky that work is still on the horizon. My goal is to stay healthy and functional. I still wish to challenge myself and climb upward, no matter how rough and tough it may be.

My life has meaning with success, friendship and the importance of my children, grandchildren and great-grandchildren: My three daughters, Minoo, Nikou, Nikrou, that I loved unconditionally with great respect. My beloved daughter Minoo left us for the infinite world twenty-two years ago; her loss insidiously worked its way into my brain. However, her two daughters Shaparak and Shayma kept my focus. They helped my interests and were the reason why I laughed instead of cried. My two grandsons Adib and Hessam have always kept my spirits high and my self-confidence active. My six great-grandsons Cameron, Kevin, Keon, Kayhan, Mateen, and Alexander have made my blue sky so bright and shiny that it reminds me of those summer nights in the backyard of my childhood home. While I was watching the sky my grandmother tried to show me four stars in the four corners of a rectangle and three stars one after the other that made a tail; she called them the seven brothers (The big dipper), well visible in the absence of the full moon. But my six "brothers" (my great-grandsons) shine no matter how the full moon shines.

When I look back at the calendar of my life, I realize that I have worked for a very long period (60 years); almost twice as long as a normal working life. Even so, it isn't enough to suit me, not enough to stop challenging and quit working now. Not all of my life goals have been completed yet, but I have decided to slow down a little bit. I moved from the laboratory to the library to bring my past back to the present in order to write this memoir. It took me three years to think and to search the inventory of my memory center in order to bring to focus my unforgettable observations and experiences dating back to my very early years and even farther back through memories of my mother and grandmother. In completing this memoir, I hope it is as enjoyable to read as it was to write.

Epilogue

To those who read this memoir I offer the following life tips:

1. Always be happy; your brain is more active and functions better during happy times.

2. Always try to be supportive; you will taste the sweetness of it very soon or in a blink of an eye.

3. Be creative and follow what you desire.

4. Be consistent; don't give up until you have reached your goal.

5. Be resourceful, flexible, brave, honest and positive.

6. Be flexible in business but tough in experiments

7. Don't be fearful of new adventures. Accept a challenge; be persistent no matter how difficult it may be.

8. Don't think anything is impossible; try to make everything possible no matter how old and how active you may be.

9. Don't ever lose hope; there are so many ways to grab success.

10. Don't be disappointed and discouraged; you can grab an opportunity somehow, someday, somewhere.

11. Don't dwell over the past; instead work toward achieving your future

12. Don't be frustrated over a rough or rocky road; it will become smoother with tolerance and some patience.

13. Forgiveness has two keys; one key opens the gate to the prison of anger and the other opens the gate of paradise and will guide you in.

14. Work hard, it keeps your brain active and your body functional so you can feel the difference between a dark and a shiny life.